Joseph H. (Joseph Hankinson) Reading

The Ogowe Band

A Narrative of African Travel

Joseph H. (Joseph Hankinson) Reading

The Ogowe Band
A Narrative of African Travel

ISBN/EAN: 9783744751070

Printed in Europe, USA, Canada, Australia, Japan

Cover: Foto ©Andreas Hilbeck / pixelio.de

More available books at **www.hansebooks.com**

THE
OGOWE BAND

A NARRATIVE OF AFRICAN TRAVEL

By
JOSEPH H. READING

Late Secretary and Treasurer of The Gaboon and Corisco
Mission and Acting Commercial Agent for
the U. S. of America.

SECOND EDITION

Philadelphia
Reading & Company, Publishers
1019 Cherry Street
1890

Entered according to Act of Congress, in the year 1890, by
JOSEPH H. READING
In the Office of the Librarian of Congress, at Washington, D. C.

All rights reserved

American Printing House
Printers and Engravers

TO THE MEMORY OF MY BELOVED

ASSOCIATE

REV. C. DeHEER

THIS BOOK IS LOVINGLY DEDICATED

THE OGOWE BAND
By Joseph H. Reading

INTRODUCTORY

A BOOK to be heartily recommended this. I know the writer. His pen has painted and painted well his own experiences in Africa. One of the persons whose death in that land is mentioned, Miss Dewsnap, was a very dear early companion of mine.

The book abounds with charming pen pictures as well as deeply interesting literal ones. There is "ever-so-much" information about ocean travel, steamers, sailors, whales, sharks, "sea-serpents," etc. There is a burial at sea.

The vessel touches at Madeira and the Canary Islands. There are thrilling descriptions of rides down the mountain sides, two thousand feet!

Sierra Leone is described. Here's the way to keep cool when the "hot wind" of that land blows; sit in an earthen jar five feet high! Need'nt look about for telegraphs there; the public opinion of monkeys has not yet been educated up to this bit of civilization. They pull the poles down as soon as set up, and dance upon them!

Our party stop at Bonny, at Bishop Crowther's, the man whose history is quite as wonderful as fiction in some respects.

The drunkenness of the natives, or, as we would say, the African saloon, the curse of curses, the cancer of all lands; the horrors of it—read and see and wonder how Christian America can help on this horror by sending rum to that land!

But there is a brighter side. We must visit Mr. Reading's home and after a season of rest, he will show us about the mission stations and let us see what Jesus is doing, through His servants, among this degraded people, to make them better and happier and prepared for "His glorious appearing."

This book gives you the visit; it puts you among them. Now you look at their dress and wonder; you taste their food, notice their strange ways and get bits of strangest history.

But it is Christmas now. There is a dinner at Mr. Reading's missionary station. It is worth your journey there to see the provisions and sit at this African-American Christmas table. Having read this remarkable book, you will want to read the second volume, which is almost promised, about adventures among cannibals, pigmies, etc., etc., etc.

Reading about this "Ogowe Band," and my thousand Pansies who are in Missionary Societies will not want for something to say or do in the meetings; and who knows but some of my "Blossoms" will some bright day sail away to Afric's shore to fill some Miss Dewsnap's place, to lead those dark people into the light of God! May this book lead to so blessed an end!

MRS. G. R. ALDEN.

PREFACE

ALL the characters in this book are real, true people, and were living in the early part of this year when the book was written; but while it was going through the press news came of the death of Mr. Brier, at Batanga, and of Mr. Gilles and Mrs. Ross, at Old Calabar, together with many others well known to the writer.

All the scenes and incidents portrayed in this book are true, the only fiction consisting in making these the experiences of the Ogowe Band instead of the author. All the descriptions of scenery were copied from diaries written upon the spot, and are as accurate as it is possible to make them.

The illustrations were made expressly for this work from photographs, many of which were taken by native artists.

The plan of the book has been to give a realistic picture of West Africa, so that the reader may form a correct idea of just how it looks to-day.

Many of my friends who know the Coast well will be surprised at the omission of many things. It seemed to me best to pass by in silence, at least as far as possible, the deep shadow of moral evil which rests like a pall over African life, foreign as well as native. Let us hope that the Sun of Righteousness which is now rising over that dark land, may soon fill the whole vast continent with the light of heaven—with purity and love!

J. H. R.

Philadelphia, October, 1890.

CONTENTS

		Page
CHAPTER	I—Voyage to Liverpool,	1
"	II—Liverpool,	15
"	III—Madeira,	33
"	IV—Canary Islands,	50
"	V—Tropical Voyaging,	67
"	VI—Sierra Leone and Liberia,	85
"	VII—Ivory Coast and Gold Coast,	101
"	VIII—Bonny and Fernando Po,	116
"	IX—Old Calabar,	132
"	X—Kamerun and Eloby,	148
"	XI—Arrival at Gaboon,	164
"	XII—Baraka and Gaboon,	179
"	XIII—Church Work at Gaboon,	194
"	XIV—Nomba and Ovendo Point,	208
"	XV—Picnic Excursion to Sandy Point,	223
"	XVI—Benita,	238
"	XVII—Bata, Evuni, Batanga,	253
"	XVIII—Return to Gaboon,	268
"	XIX—Political Divisions on the West Coast,	277

LIST OF FULL PAGE ILLUSTRATIONS

FRONTISPIECE
    A Tropic Home

CHAPTER I
    Atlantic-Liner, "Lord Gough"
    Landing Stage, Liverpool
    Northwestern Hotel, Liverpool

CHAPTER II
    South Castle Street, Liverpool
    Outer Line of Docks, Liverpool
    Inner Line of Docks, Liverpool
    Princess Park, Liverpool

CHAPTER III
    City of Funchal, Madeira
    Landing Place at Funchal
    Madeira Carriage
    A Street in Funchal, Madeira

CHAPTER IV
    Funchal from the Mountain Side
    Las Palmas, Grand Canary
    Date Palm, Grand Canary

CHAPTER V
    Lou Rock, Madeira
    Native Women, Gold Coast
    Lady of High Rank, Old Calabar

CHAPTER VI
> Regent Street, Sierra Leone
> Native Village near Axim
> Mission House, Axim

CHAPTER VII
> Elmina, Gold Coast
> Cemetery at Elmina
> Cape Coast Castle, Gold Coast
> Accra, Gold Coast

CHAPTER VIII
> Canoe on the Bonny River
> Trading Hulk, Bonny
> "My Name he be Pea Soup"

CHAPTER IX
> Foreign Settlement, Old Calabar
> Interior of Palm Oil Factory
> Native Town, Old Calabar River
> Mission House, Old Calabar

CHAPTER X
> Government House, Kamerun
> A bit of Kamerun Beach, Low Tide
> A bit of Kamerun Beach, High Tide
> The Nubia at anchor in the Kamerun River

CHAPTER XI
> Eloby, Corisco Bay
> Baraka Mission Station, Gaboon
> Mrs. Joseph H. Reading

CHAPTER XII
> Little Lizzie
> Miss Susie Dewsnap
> Road-making in Gaboon
> Mr. Reading's Little Carriage

CHAPTER XIII
    "Good Old Uncle" Adaude
    Mpongwe Women, Gaboon
    Catholic Mission, Gaboon
    African Paper Money

CHAPTER XIV
    Gaboon River Village
    An African Belle
    An African King

CHAPTER XV
    French Trading Factory, Gaboon
    Gardener's House, Gaboon
    Palm Oil ready for shipment
    Native Women, Accra

CHAPTER XVI
    Church and School-house, Corisco
    Mbade Station, Benita River
    Mr. DeHeer's Church, Bolondo
    Scene on the Benita River

CHAPTER XVII
    Rev. B. B. Brier
    Mrs. B. B. Brier
    Waterfall at Batanga
    Native Trader, Old Calabar

CHAPTER XVIII
    Church built by Mr. Reading
    Interior of new Church, Gaboon
    Scotch Mission Church, Old Calaba

ATLANTIC LINER, "LORD GOUGH"

The Ogowe Band.

CHAPTER I.

VOYAGE TO LIVERPOOL.

THERE was bustle and excitement on the Pennsylvania railroad pier at the foot of Catharine street, Philadelphia. Quite a crowd had gathered; some in groups with serious faces, others rushing around looking for stray pieces of baggage, while carriages constantly arriving brought their occupants to swell the throng.

Just outside the shed was the four-masted Atlantic-liner "Lord Gough," the smoke curling upward from her great funnel and the steam blowing off as if to say "I am ready for a struggle with the storms." Mountains of luggage, and drays laden with sacks of mail, drove up to the forward gang-plank and were soon transferred to the steamer.

Near the outer end of the shed, in the midst of a large circle of friends, were the Ogowe Mission Band, the subjects of this story. They were a lively set of young people, six young masters and six misses; and they hardly knew whether to laugh or cry, as they looked out at the great steamer with all the strange adventures before them, and then at the dear ones gathered to say "good-bye," whom they could hardly hope to see for a year at least.

Just then a tall, middle-aged, kindly-faced gentleman alighted from a carriage, and walked quickly up the pier. This was Judge McGee, the gentleman who was to take charge of the gay little voyagers and guide them through the strange lands beyond the sea. He was warmly greeted by Miss Laura B. Cadmus, the leader of the band, and introduced to the fathers, mothers and other friends; he needed no introduction to the little travelers themselves, for he had several times addressed the band, and they both knew and loved him.

Kathleen, Miss Cadmus' maid, looked at the Judge askance, and exclaimed: "Sure and is this the gintleman that is after taking the darlints to Afriky?"

On being assured it was, she expressed the hope that the white bears and gorillas would not carry the dear children away, nor the Pagans roast them and serve them up for supper. The fog-horn of the steamer now blew a blast and an officer called in a loud voice: "All ashore who are not going."

"Come," said the Judge, "it is time for us to go on board."

In a few minutes the whistle sounded again, the gangplank was drawn ashore, the lines were loosened, and the great ship turned slowly away from the pier.

The warm-hearted Kathleen was much affected; she wiped her eyes with a corner of her shawl and flung an old shoe after the "darlints." "Sure," said she, "and I hope the horrid haythens won't eat them for supper at all, at all."

A large tug now made fast to the stern of the steamer, and two more to the bow. They pulled and puffed with all their might, and presently the great ship was fairly out

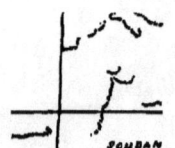

in the channel with her bow pointing down stream; the engines began to turn slowly, the tugs cast off their lines, the small cannon on the forecastle fired a salute, and the momentous voyage was begun.

Our little travelers stood on the promenade deck, which on the Lord Gough was in the middle of the ship, and waved their handkerchiefs at the dear ones on the pier until a turn in the river hid them from sight. Waving was not the only use to which their handkerchiefs were put; but after all, a good cry does one good, as the Ogowe Band found to be true in their case.

Judge McGee left them to their tears a little while, and then, after a few words of comfort, called their attention to the scenes about them, and it was not long before they had recovered their usual spirits.

It was a glorious September day, and as the start had been an early one in order to get the benefit of the tide, it was now not more than nine o'clock. They were just passing Chester where vessels in various stages of construction were seen near the river bank. By and by the river began to widen, and by noon they were abreast of the Delaware Breakwater. Here the steamer came to a standstill, a small boat came along-side and the pilot climbed over the side and down into it, the gangway passage was closed, the engines began to throb, the Lord Gough turned her prow to the eastward, and the sandy shores of Delaware and New Jersey gradually sank beneath the water.

The bell now rang for one o'clock lunch and the Ogowe Band lost no time in finding their way to the dining-room.

There were but few other passengers and there was abundant room and plenty of food for everybody. The

Captain sat at the head of the table and the purser at the foot, while the passengers occupied those places that had been reserved for them by the steward. The Judge and his young companions were seated next to the Captain, whom they found to be as jolly and good-natured as a captain could well be.

After lunch, at the Captain's suggestion, the little travelers arranged their state rooms; opening their portmanteaus and placing those articles they were likely to use where they would be handy. When this was done they took light wraps and soft caps and went up on deck. Here comfortable chairs had been placed in a cosy spot sheltered from the wind, and they sat down to spend the afternoon. Overhead was the immense blue dome of the sky filled with ten thousand joyous, fleecy clouds; beneath and around were the waters of the ocean; the sun shone brightly, and the fresh clear air was delightful.

Very soon the Captain joined them, and the little folks fired questions at him almost faster than he could answer them. He told them that usually the water for a hundred miles or so from shore was not rough enough to affect a large steamer like the Lord Gough, "for," said he, "the prevailing winds are from the west and they do not stir the water to its depths much short of a hundred miles out." This explained why the steamer was as steady as it had been in the river.

The conversation then turned upon life on shipboard. "Life on a steamship at sea," said the Captain, "has many peculiarities. The ship is a world in itself, and the bounds are narrow. You see the same faces day after day, and on a great ocean like the Atlantic there is little to attract the attention outside of the vessel that carries you."

"Yes," said the Judge, "one falls into a monotonous way of life, and the days run on one after another, till you find it difficult to distinguish them."

"I have heard, Captain," said Willie Richman, "that sailors are very superstitious, is that so?"

"Yes," said Captain Hughes, "they are a queer lot. I remember some years ago I commanded a large sailing ship in the California trade. We were about three weeks out from Liverpool when the mate reported that one of the men was sick. I went to see him and found the poor fellow was likely to die. I knew little about diseases or how to cure them, but the sailors were watching to see what the 'old man' would do, and I saw that, to save my reputation, I must do my best. So I opened the medicine chest and took out all the bottles. These I divided into two parts, the dry medicines and the liquid ones. I then took some of each of the dry medicines and mixed them all together, and from this mixture I made some powders. In like manner I poured out into a bottle some of each of the liquid medicines and when I had well shaken the bottle, to thoroughly mix the ingredients, I ordered a teaspoonful given the sick man every two hours, and at the alternate hours one of the powders.

"I reasoned in this way: in that lot of medicine there must be something suited to this case and although I do not know which one it is, in this way he will surely get it. My logic must have been correct, for the man got well. After that whenever a man was sick he would take nothing but the drops and powders, and I never lost a patient, which is more than any doctor can say."

The conversation flowed on in a steady stream and the afternoon passed almost before they knew it. At half-past five the steward rang a bell which the Captain told them was a signal to get ready for dinner, so they picked up their wraps and went to their rooms to arrange their toilets.

On all English steamers a cup of coffee or tea, with a little toast, is brought to your room at six in the morning. At half-past eight there is breakfast in the saloon, which most American travelers think is the best meal of the day; partly, perhaps, because the cooking for that meal is more like the American style. Lunch comes at one P. M., and dinner at six, while tea—toast and jam—is served at nine o'clock to those who call for it.

Dinner is the great meal of the day; there are several courses and every person who has a right to eat in the saloon is expected to be present and to be dressed in their best. Not all who are on board can eat in the saloon; this privilege is exclusively reserved for the officers of the ship and the saloon passengers. The sailors eat in the forecastle; the engineers in a mess room of their own, and the stewards in the pantry.

There is a feeling on board ship that the stewards live on the best the ship affords. An old captain once said, "Whenever I want something specially good, I tell my boys to hang around and watch to see what the stewards are going to have, and then bring me some." Whether or no this might be true, our little travelers could not tell, but they came to the conclusion that the stewards were a good-natured, hard-working set of people who never appeared to have time to sleep or rest, and they were sorry to notice that sometimes passengers spoke roughly to them.

The next morning the Ogowe Band were on deck in good season, and a lovely morning it was. The sun was about an hour high, and its bright rays were beginning to warm the cool, fresh air. They romped about the deck and had a real jolly time. The Judge took a hand in the fun and for the time was apparently as young as any of them.

Suddenly Robbie Campbell cried out, "O, look at that!" Everybody turned their eyes in the direction indicated and saw at some distance from the ship a small column of water rise to the height of seven or eight feet.

"Why," said Lulu Wright, "it looks just like pictures I have seen of whales."

"Yes," said Captain Hughes, who at that moment joined the party, "it is a whale." As he spoke the whale raised himself partly out of the water, gave his tail a flirt, and disappeared in the depths of the ocean.

Frank Harris asked why it was that the whale spouted up this column of water.

Captain Hughes explained, "The whale is not a fish, but a warm-blooded animal like a cow or horse, and must breathe the air just as we do. He takes a certain amount of water into his lungs along with the air, and when he throws it out it makes the spray you have seen, which sailors call a spout."

After breakfast whaling stories were in order. Grace Thompson asked if this was the kind of whale that swallowed Jonah.

The Judge told them that so far as known there were no whales in the Mediterranean; that the word in the original, translated "whale," means a "sea monster," and that no one knew certainly just what kind of a sea-monster it was that swallowed the prophet.

"Well," exclaimed Jessie Williams, "I don't understand it anyway. How did Jonah get his breath for those three days and nights; a whale don't breathe into his stomach?"

The Judge replied that it was easy to ask questions that no one could answer. "This event," said he, "was a miracle, and cannot be explained by the operation of natural law."

"What is a miracle?" asked Hattie Clark.

"A miracle," replied the Judge, "is a wonderful effect, superior or contrary to the laws of nature, and performed alone by the power of God."

He then went on to explain to them that God works in a uniform manner to produce the events he designs shall come to pass, and these uniform modes of the divine operation are called "natural laws," or the "laws of nature;" that sometimes, in order to attract the special attention of his creatures to some revelation he is about to make, he departs from his usual mode and produces an effect in some other way. This is called a miracle. It is no more wonderful than the events which occur every day about us, but it is unusual, and so causes remark.

In the afternoon the wind freshened, and the rolling motion of the ship was not altogether agreeable to the inexperienced voyagers. They were about to have a little taste of sea sickness, and from the appearance of their faces it was evident that it did not taste good. They lay about the deck in warm places where they were sheltered from the wind, and neither cared to talk or be talked to. But their malady did not last long, and by the next morning they were as merry as ever.

They asked the Judge to explain the cause of their trouble, but he shook his head and said it was a great puzzle. "The more I study it, said he, " the less I seem to understand it. As nearly as I can tell, it is a disease of the brain ; or, to be more correct, a disturbance of the

cerebral action, brought about by an unusual motion of the body."

"Is there no cure for it?" asked Grant Hillman.

"None that I know of," replied the Judge, "except to keep away from the water."

"To lessen its effects two opposite lines of treatment have been suggested ; one to stimulate the brain, and the other to depress its action. As the brain is a very delicate organ, both these plans are dangerous. It is best to lie quiet and take nothing unless the attack is very severe, and then call a physician."

The ship's Doctor confirmed the Judge's opinion, and stated that he gave but little medicine in cases of seasickness, and what little he gave was of a mild character.

Ten days after leaving Philadelphia some dark specks appeared on the Eastern horizon. They grew larger and larger until it was plain to be seen they were great brown rocks. The young voyagers were much excited at beholding the first land of the Old World. Captain Hughes explained that the rock on the extreme right was Fastnet, and the others Cape Clear and the headlands about Bantry Bay. The band gave three cheers for Ireland, and could scarcely be prevailed upon to go into the saloon for breakfast.

About eleven o'clock the Lord Gough passed between Fastnet Rock and the main-land, and from that time the coast of Ireland was in full view throughout the day. Having heard so much of the "Emerald Isle," they expected to see it "as green as grass," as Jessie Williams expressed it. What they did see was great brown, rocky headlands, with little bays between them. The ground was high and appeared barren. The surf beat upon the beach, and especially upon the rocky cliffs, with great force, sending the spray high up in the air. The Captain called it an iron-bound coast, and said that many a gallant ship had been driven ashore and broken upon these rocks. Now and then a few stone buildings or a lighthouse were seen, and at Crook Haven signals were hoisted on the foremast and mainmast to let the people on shore know that the Lord Gough was passing and would call that evening at Queenstown. The news would then be sent ahead by telegraph and a tender would be in waiting when they arrived off the entrance to Cork Harbor.

At four o'clock they passed the Old Head of Kinsale, one of the sternest and most picturesque headlands on the coast, and in less than an hour the engines stopped their throbbing and the vessel came to a standstill opposite the narrow entrance to Cork Harbor. Our young tourists were deeply interested in all they saw, and their tongues rattled away at a lively rate. Lighthouses crowned the hills on either side the entrance; just beyond them, where the ground was higher, were forts, while at the farther end of the bay, Queenstown could be plainly seen nestled closely by the water-side.

An open-deck, paddle-wheel steamer came cautiously alongside the Lord Gough and was made fast with ropes. A wide gangway was run across to the steamer's deck, and some of the passengers and all the mails were transferred to the tender, as the paddle-wheel steamer was called.

"Why are the mails put off here?" inquired Lulu Wright, "I thought they were for England."

"So they are," replied the Judge, "they will be in London by the time we get to Liverpool."

"How is that?" exclaimed several voices at once.

The Judge explained that railway trains could go much faster than steamers. "A fast train," said he, "is waiting for these mails there at Queenstown. It will take them on to Kingston, where a boat that makes twenty-one miles an hour will take them over to Holyhead in Wales; from Holyhead they will go to London on the "Wild Irishman," a train that runs at the rate of a mile a minute.

The thought of such speed fairly took the young people's breath away, and they were quite content to go by a slower route.

The men who carried the mail sacks worked with a with a will, and in half an hour they were transferred to the tender. The lines that held her to the Lord Gough were cast off, and she turned away towards Queenstown, while the Atlantic-liner moved on her way up the Channel.

Our young voyagers were thoroughly stirred by all they had seen, and the conversation during the evening was both animated and prolonged. About ten o'clock they went out on deck for a few minutes. They were not often allowed to sit up so late, for their kind friend, the Judge, believed in early hours for both young people and old; but this was no ordinary occasion, and the usual rule was suspended.

The stars were shining brightly overhead, and the light on Tuskar Rock could plainly be seen on the port bow. Captain Hughes told them that when they reached that light they would cross the Channel over to the Welsh coast and they would see no more of Ireland. He also told them that he would be up all night, for when they were near land it was the Captain's duty to be always on the bridge.

The Ogowe Band slept little that night, at least so they thought, but it is probable their dreams and waking thoughts were so mingled in their consciousness they did not distinguish clearly between them. At any rate they were up early and the first thing they saw on looking out of their port-holes was land. This time, however, it was on the right, or starboard side of the ship, and not on the port side as it had been yesterday. The chief steward told them that was just the difference between the English and the Irish; the Irish always got "left." "At any rate," said he, "most of them have left Ireland, for there are more Irish in England and America than in Ireland, and more Irish in London than in Dublin."

When the bright little voyagers reached the deck they found the steamer was just passing Holyhead and they were surprised to see what a rocky place it was. The shores of the Old World, so far as they had yet seen them, were quite in contrast with the low sandy coasts of Long Island and New Jersey. Many vessels were in sight both going up and down the Channel. It surprised them that sailing ships could go in opposite directions at the same time.

"I thought," said Willie Richman, "that a ship could only sail the same way the wind blows."

Judge McGee tried to explain to them how it was, but they did not come to a very clear understanding of it. That it could be done was evident, and so far as the young people could see, the sailing vessels got along as well as the steamers, only not so rapidly.

Large numbers of sea-gulls flew about the steamer, often so near as to be almost within reach. Whenever refuse was thrown from the ship, they settled down upon the water seeking for such scraps of food as they might find, and in this way got their breakfast.

They arrived at the bar off the mouth of the Mersey at lunch time, and were obliged to anchor. Captain

NORTHWESTERN HOTEL, LIVERPOOL

Hughes explained to them that the rise and fall of the tide here was from twenty-three to twenty-seven feet, and that large steamers could not go in and out of the river at low tide. "The tide," said he, "is rising now, and we will not have to wait very long." Sure enough, by three o'clock the anchor was up and they were steaming slowly into the greatest sea-port of the world.

As they drew near the city the sight that greeted their eyes was one never to be forgotten. The river was full of steamers and vessels of all kinds, and on both sides, as far as the eye could reach, was a forest of masts shut in by the lofty walls of the docks.

Presently a tender, like the one they had seen at Queenstown, came alongside and the health and customs officials scrambled on board. It was not long before a gang-plank was run out and the trunks and other baggage carried to the tender; then our friends said "good-bye" to Captain Hughes and his kind officers, and with sincere regret they left their floating home that had borne them safely over the broad Atlantic, and turned their faces toward the city in which they were to spend the next few days.

While at anchor outside of the bar, Captain Hughes had told them that vessels could only go in and out of dock at the very top of high water, and that the gates were open only about an hour every day and every night. The great Atlantic-liners go into dock near the North End, some three or four miles from the centre of the city. The officers must stay with their ship until she has made fast to the pier. Sometimes the captain leaves the vessel in charge of the mate, and goes ashore with the passengers; in this instance Captain Hughes preferred to remain on board.

A run of a few minutes brought the tender to the Prince's Landing Stage, an immense floating structure anchored close to the outer wall of one of the docks, and connected with this wall by four covered bridges. This stage rises and falls with the tide, so that the bridges are sometimes level and sometimes steeply inclined, according as the tide is high or low. Upon the stage are waiting-rooms, a restaurant, and houses where baggage is examined by the customs officers. This examination is not a very rigid one, and if travelers will only keep their tempers and be good-natured they will have no trouble. As the Judge was always good-natured he was soon through, and the sturdy porters carried everything up to the pier-head where a cart was engaged to take it to the hotel.

There are no baggage express companies in the Old World, and the care of one's "impedimenta" is greater than it is in America. Cabs were standing in a line waiting for customers; three of these were engaged and they were soon rattling up Water and Dale streets to the Northwestern Hotel, where they were to make their home while in Liverpool.

Chapter II.

LIVERPOOL

THE cabs drew up in front of the main entrance of the hotel, and a porter in livery came out to assist them in alighting and to carry in their wraps. The Ogowe Band knew little of hotel life, so that all they saw was a new experience to them. Judge McGee stepped to the office to register their names, while the young people warmed themselves at the open grate in the rotunda and gazed about them.

The elevator could not accommodate so large a party, so the Judge and the young ladies went in it, while the boys and two of the porters climbed the broad staircase. The party took rooms on the third floor. This they found was not the third floor *from* the ground, but the third floor *above* the ground. The ground floor is not counted, as with us. The rooms they occupied have curved-top windows, as seen in the picture.

After bathing their hands and faces and arranging their toilets, they came down to supper, or as the English call it, "tea." With the English, "supper" is a meal taken late in the night, as for instance, after the close of the theatre or opera.

The dining-room is on the ground floor, on the right of the illustration, and the cart that brought our young travelers' baggage is seen near the front entrance of the hotel. It has four wheels, and with us would be called a "truck."

After tea, the young folks wanted to go out on the streets and see some of the sights of the town, but Judge McGee would not consent. He thought they had seen enough for one day, and advised a quiet evening and a good night's rest. So they adjourned to the drawing-room, seen on the left in the illustration—and gathered in a cozy group by the front windows.

Before them was Great George's Hall, an imposing pile of architecture, in which the city courts are held; there is also a large organ and a concert room. In the paved court in front were equestrian statues of Queen Victoria, and her husband, Prince Albert. Two stone lions guarded the entrance. As all the places of amusement are near the hotel, the street was full of people. Grant Hillman said he could not see that the people looked like foreigners; he thought they looked more like Americans than the people one sometimes sees in our own cities.

"Well," said Frank Harris, "so they ought, for Americans are English, while our cities are full of emigrants from all parts of the earth."

"O!" exclaimed Johnny Ashton, "look at that street car, it's a double-decker!"

Sure enough it was. A circular stairway led from the rear platform to the top, where two seats were arranged lengthwise in the middle. The passengers sat back to

SOUTH CASTLE STREET, LIVERPOOL

LIVERPOOL

back facing the walk on either side of the street. Grace Thompson thought it would be splendid to ride that way, and the Judge promised them that they should on the morrow, if the weather was fair.

"Now," said he, "this may be a good time to learn that English people call many things by different names from what we do."

"Yes," said Robbie Campbell, "I noticed on the landing stage the porters said 'luggage' instead of baggage."

"Do they call a passenger elevator a 'lift?'" asked Mamie Belville.

"Yes," replied Judge McGee, "and a street car here is called a 'tram,' while the track it runs on is a tramway."

"Hereafter, while abroad, we will adopt English terms so we may be understood."

"Did you notice," said Frank Harris, "that the clerks in the hotel office were ladies?"

"Yes," added the Judge, "and the manager is a woman; you might almost be sure of it by the neatness and order in everything about the house."

"And the quietness too," said Jessie Williams.

"I thought," said Willie Richman, "that the man who met us when we first came in was the owner; he was dressed so fine and had such a grand air, just as I would expect a man to have who owned and lived in a grand building like this."

Judge McGee smiled. "That man," he replied, "was the head porter, but I do not wonder you thought him a great man; he is, in his way, and as things go in this country, he is both useful and necessary." He then went on to explain to the Band that this hotel belonged to the London & Northwestern Railway, a great corporation like our own Pennsylvania R. R., and that the railway station for London and all parts of England and Scotland was back of the hotel. Indeed, the hotel might be called the front of the station.

"Can we go and see the station?" asked Johnny Ashton.

"I should like so much to see it," exclaimed Lulu Wright.

This desire was echoed by the entire Band, so the good-natured Judge took them out to the platform where trains were awaiting the time to start for London, Manchester, Edinburgh and other places.

The young people were not long in finding out the difference between an English and American railway station. They found the cars divided into three compartments, with the doors in the sides of the cars. Each compartment had two seats as in a street-car at home, and on the outside it said, "First class," "Second class" and "Third class."

The Judge told them they were now in a land of class distinctions, and this classification extended even to railway carriages; "for," said he, "these are not 'cars' but 'carriages.' The engine is called a 'horse,' the engineer a 'driver,' the fireman a 'stoker,' and the conductor a 'guard.' These names have come down from the old stage-coach days and are now applied to railroading."

The boys noticed there was no cab to the engine, so that both driver and stoker stood right out doors in the sun and rain. After looking around awhile they returned to the drawing-room, and after the Judge had called a waiter and given orders for breakfast, they went up stairs to their rooms, and it was not long before they were in the land of dreams.

LIVERPOOL.

The next morning the Ogowe Band were not long in making a discovery, viz: that the English people did not get up very early in the morning. Here on this bright September day no one scarcely was to be seen in the street at eight o'clock, and the few persons to be seen about the hotel appeared to be half asleep. The eagerness of our young friends to see the city, doubtless made them a little impatient, and yet it is true that the English are not very early risers.

Breakfast had been ordered for half-past eight. While they were eating, Judge McGee told them he had letters of introduction to Messrs. Alexander & Christie, at 64 South Castle street, and proposed they should walk there after breakfast; "for," said he, "it is not much over half a mile, and this is just the kind of morning for walking."

At half-past nine they sallied forth, and a merry party they were. They went down Lime street, and turning to the right found themselves in front of St. John's Market, the principal market-house in Liverpool. Most of the girls had gone marketing with their mothers in Philadelphia and they were curious to know what an English market was like, so they all went in.

They found it much larger than any in their own city, but in its main features it was much the same. There was a fine display of flowers and a small one of fruit. What fruit there was for sale was of fine appearance, but high priced. Three large pine-apples attracted the boys' attention; Grant Hillman pointed to the largest and asked how much it was. The market-man said something about its being a pound, and Grant asked how much it was a pound. The dealer looked at him in astonishment and then replied, somewhat testily, "a pound; twenty shillings." Grant was somewhat taken aback by the man's manner, but he found out afterward that these pine-apples had been grown in a hot-house, and that they were indeed five dollars each.

The display of game was really wonderful. The boys in particular were carried away and wanted to go hunting that very day. Judge McGee explained to them that these deer, hares, and partridges were not wild ones, such as those we see in the American markets, but were raised for market the same as sheep and chickens. The girls greatly admired the beautiful pheasants and thought they would like some of the feathers for their hats.

On their way out of the market they met an old woman, crying "Hot snails! hot snails!" She had a great tray full of smoking hot snails. "What does she do with these?" asked Mamie Belville.

"Sells them for people to eat," replied Jessie Williams.

"No she don't either," said Mamie, "does she Mr. McGee?"

The Judge told them this was just what she was doing. Jessie was quite as much surprised as any of them, for she had only made her remark in fun. He then went on to say that there were few oysters in England, and these snails in some measure took their place.

"She reminds me," said Johnny Ashton, "of the old women who sell hot peanuts."

"I wish I had some peanuts," said Hattie Clark.

"So do I," chimed in the other five girls.

"Well," said Mr. McGee, "I am afraid you must wait until we get to Africa, for here peanuts are not eaten any more than snails are in America."

Grant Hillman thought he had read somewhere that peanuts were exported from the Congo region to England.

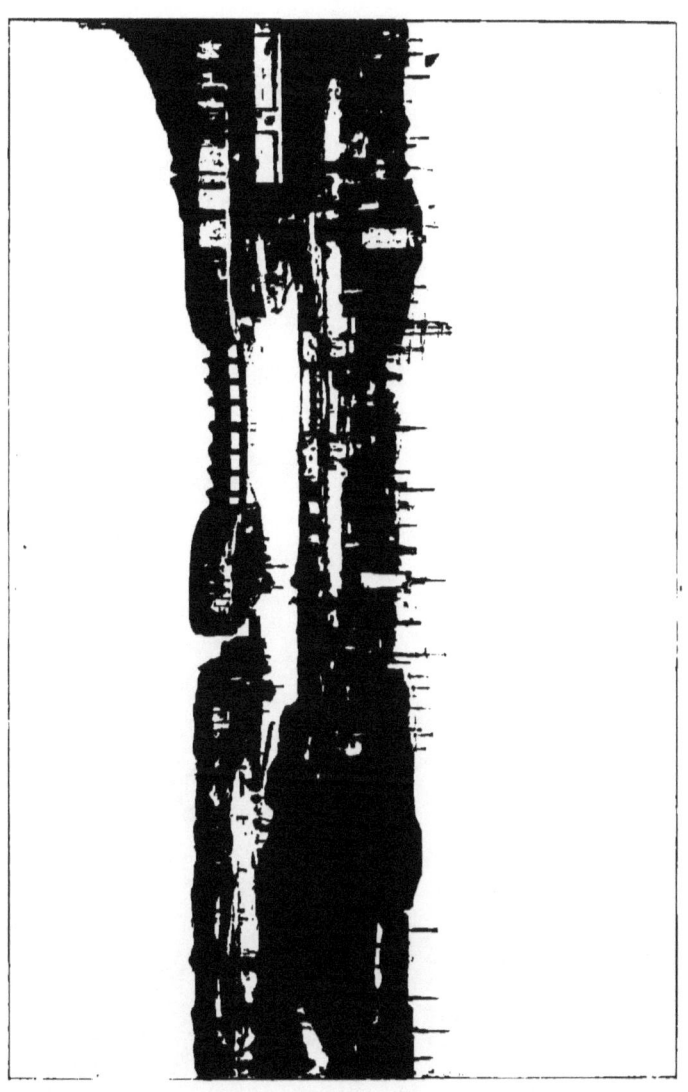

OUTER LINE OF DOCKS, LIVERPOOL

"So they are," the Judge replied, "but they are used for making table oil, and not for eating out of hand as with us."

The party now passed down Church street and Lord street into the Crescent, and turned into South Castle street. Elegant shops, with show-windows filled with the richest goods, lined both sides of the way. At the foot of South Castle street the great dome of the custom-house rose high above the surrounding buildings. Number 64 was near the lower end of the street, and on reaching it they found they must pass through a narrow passage and up a flight of steps in order to reach the offices of Alexander & Christie.

Mr. Alexander greeted them with quiet dignity, and after reading the letters Judge McGee had brought with him, inquired if their passage across the Atlantic had been a pleasant one, and what their present plans were. On hearing they wished to sail for Gaboon he told them they were quite fortunate, as the royal mail steamer "Nubia," in charge of the Commodore Captain of the fleet, was to sail on Saturday. He advised them to secure their berths at once, "for," said he, "these steamers do not have large passenger accommodation, and not unfrequently every berth is taken. The office of the company is in James street, but a few minutes' walk from here, and if you wish I will go with you."

Of course they were glad enough to have the pleasure of his company, so they all went to the steamship office. Mr. Sinclair, the agent, invited them into his private room, and while the gentlemen completed the business arrangements, the young folks looked at the pictures of steamers hanging on the walls.

While they were talking Captain Davis came in. He looked like a regular "old salt," and his merry eyes twinkled when he heard they were going out with him. "So you youngsters are going out to Africa, are you?" said he; "Well, you will wish yourselves back again long before you get there, now mind I tell you. Africa is no place for the likes of you."

Laura Reed replied that they expected to rough it; and Captain Davis allowed they would not be disappointed. "But," said he, "if you are bound to go, I will take the best care of you I can, and there is one thing you must do, you must come out to my house to-night and take tea with me."

They thanked the Captain for his kind invitation, and said they would accept it with pleasure, if Mr. McGee thought best. The Judge and the Captain were old friends, and it took no pressure to induce Mr. McGee to promise that they would be at Edge Lane at five o'clock.

On their way back to South Castle street they called at a shop in the Crescent to make some purchases. Judge McGee thought it best for them to get pith hats and yellow sun-umbrellas with green lining, such as foreigners usually carry in the tropics. Mr. Alexander introduced the party to Mr. Simpson, the proprietor of the shop, and he took especial pains to please them. There was some discussion as to which style of hat was best suited to a hot sun; the helmet, or the flat shaped. While the helmet is the more common style, it was agreed that the flat shaped crown permitted a better circulation of air over the head, and also shaded the face more than the helmet.

Mr. Alexander inquired if they had seen the docks, and when told they had not, he proposed they should go and offered to accompany them. "I promised the young people," said Judge McGee, "that they should have a ride to-day, on the top of a tram; if they are willing to wait another day, we will be glad to accept your kind invitation to visit the docks, for they are one of the wonders of the world, and no one who is in England should miss seeing them."

The young folks were anxious to see the docks, and so it was arranged that they should go forthwith. Mr. Alexander remarked the "docks were hungry places" and suggested it might be well to have something to eat first, at the same time inviting them to lunch with him. It was not quite noon yet but the suggestion commended itself to our young travelers, and the invitation was accepted with thanks.

Mr. Alexander took them to a neat restaurant nearly opposite his office where, he said, he had for years taken his dinner. The place was kept by a lady, and a sweet-faced girl, named Annie, waited on them. Mr. Alexander told his new friends that English people were not much hands to change about. "When we are suited," said he, "we generally stick to a place. There are men who have been taking their dinner here regularly for the last twenty years."

After lunch they walked down South Castle street, to the custom-house, and, turning to the right, one short square brought them to the Salt-house docks. To our young adventurers the docks appeared a labyrinth of ships, draw-bridges, warehouses and streets, and there were abundance of sights for the young eyes. After the first shock of surprise, the twelve young tongues began to rattle and the exclamations of wonder were frequent.

While the young people were busy looking about, Mr. Alexander explained the plan upon which the docks were built. "The Mersey," said he, "is not a wide river and the banks are shallow, but the rise and fall of the tide is great. This latter circumstance made the docks not only necessary, but a success. An outer, or sea-wall, was built in the river parallel with the bank, and the transverse walls were run to the shore. The space thus enclosed was excavated as deep as the bottom of the river; a wall on the land side completed the first dock. Others were then built, until now the total length is about nine miles. There is no advantage in having the docks too wide, for vessels must lie alongside the wall, in order to discharge and load; so there is a double line of docks, one inside or nearer the city than the other. All the docks communicate with one another and vessels may pass at any time, but they cannot go through the outer gates into the river except at the top of high water."

"How many weeks does it take to load a vessel?" asked Hattie Clark.

"When there is need for haste," replied Mr. Alexander, "a large steamer can unload, and take on a new cargo, coal and provisions, all ready for sea again, in four days."

It did not seem possible, but Mr. Alexander thought the work might be accomplished in even less time.

The party now crossed the draw-bridge and proceeded to the outer line of the docks. The accompanying illustration was taken at high tide. The closed gate is the one through which the steamers pass. The open one with the foot bridge over it, is for canal boats and lighters. The second line of docks is quite distinctly seen.

After walking about some time amid a maze of walls, sheds and bridges, they came to a narrow dock without any water in it. A steamer was in this dock and it was

INNER LINE OF DOCKS, LIVERPOOL

braced in every direction with heavy timbers to keep it from falling over. The dock narrowed toward the bottom and a large force of men were scraping the sides of the vessel, and some were putting on red paint.

This was called a graving-dock.

Mr. Alexander explained that every two or three months a ship, especially if she sails in Southern waters, must be scraped and painted; that not only will grass grow on the bottom, but oysters and other shell-fish will stick fast and greatly impede the progress of the vessel.

"A grass-field on the bottom of a ship!" exclaimed Johnny Ashton.

"Yes," replied Mr. Alexander, "I have seen grass on a ship's side several inches long."

"I had no idea," remarked Mamie Belville, "that so large a portion of a ship is under water."

"Nor had I," echoed Jessie Williams, "and I do not think they are nearly so pretty when you see the whole of them, as they are when floating proudly on the ocean."

"That," said Judge McGee, "is because they are in their natural element, while here in the graving-dock they are like people who are placed in a false position; they are helpless and appear to a disadvantage."

"What is that wheel sticking out behind for?" asked Grace Thompson.

"That," replied Mr. Alexander, "is the propeller; when it turns around it pushes the ship forward."

"I don't see how it can," said Grace.

"I admit," answered Mr. Alexander, "that it is not easy to see how such a small wheel can develop so much power."

"How does it get its power anyway?" asked Robbie Campbell.

"On the principle of the screw," explained Mr. Alexander; when you turn a screw it must go forward. The water is like a solid plank of wood; when this wheel turns in the water, it bores its way ahead like an auger or screw." The young people were still unable to see how so small a wheel could push so large a vessel, but they wisely let the matter rest and said no more about it.

It was now three o'clock and they were getting tired; they made their way presently to the street, and calling cabs, were driven to the hotel. Here they had a light lunch and rested awhile, and then repaired to their rooms to prepare their toilets for the evening. At half-past four they were on the station platform at the rear of the hotel.

"How convenient;" exclaimed Mamie Belville, "it is no more trouble to take a train here, than it is to go into the dining-room for breakfast."

As one compartment in the railway carriage would not hold them all, the boys took one to themselves, while Judge McGee and the girls occupied the other.

Ten minutes later they were on the platform of Edge Lane station, where Captain Davis was waiting to meet them. His home was but a few minutes' walk from the station, and was charmingly situated amid shrubbery and trees. The Band were delighted to be in a real English home, and Mrs. Davis was so kind and motherly they quite forgot they were in a foreign land. There were several young people, too, in the family, and that made it still more agreeable; besides, an older daughter was married and lived near by; she came in, and altogether it made a houseful.

Captain Davis was just in his element; it was hard to tell which he liked best, a party of young folks, or a good stiff breeze at sea. His house was filled with African curiosities; these possessed an added interest to the young visitors, as they were so soon to tread the shores of that wonderful land. They had an elegant "tea," to which the guests did ample justice. It was the first time they had dined at home since leaving Philadelphia.

Mrs. Davis was a Devonshire lady, and one of the dishes of the evening was "Devonshire cream," something entirely new to the young Americans. They all agreed it was delicious. The hours passed rapidly and before they knew it, it was after ten o'clock. Reluctantly they put on their wraps and bade their kind entertainers "good-bye," and when they alighted on the hotel platform it wanted but five minutes of eleven.

Next morning they were not up quite so early as they had been the morning before. After breakfast Judge McGee proposed they should take the promised ride on the top of a "tram." The party were soon ready, and a few minutes later they were climbing the circular stairway that led to the top.

Frank Harris called it the hurricane deck, "because," said he, "here is where you get all the wind."

The motion was much easier than that of the street cars in America. This, the Judge told them, was because the track was much more solidly laid. "The English," said he, "are not so inventive as the Americans, but what they do, they do well; in this respect they surpass us."

Their route took them around Great George hall, past St. John's Church and into Scotland Road, one of the great thoroughfares of the city. They were greatly interested by all they saw, and the girls thought it was "just too jolly for anything." An hour's ride brought them to the village of West Derby, adjoining the estate of the Earl of Derby. Not far from the terminus of the tramway was the great iron gate by which admittance is gained to the grounds. Our young tourists remained on the top of the tram, and in a few minutes it started on its return trip to the city.

On arrival at the hotel they found a letter from Mr. Alexander awaiting them, inviting them to tea at his mother's home in Birkenhead on Friday evening. After the Judge had replied, cordially accepting the invitation, they all started out for a walk up London Road, the great shopping street of the city, especially for medium priced goods. They learned that a dry-goods store was called a "draper's shop," and notions were known as "haberdashery." Goods in the windows were priced in "shillings" or "guineas."

"How much is a guinea?" asked Lulu Wright.

"A guinea," replied the Judge, "is twenty-one shillings, and a pound is twenty shillings; a shilling is nearly twenty-five cents of our money."

"What is a sovereign?" asked Willie Richman.

"A sovereign," said Judge McGee, "is the name of a gold piece which represents a pound, and is the unit of value in English money as the dollar is of American money."

After lunch the party took carriages and drove to Prince's Park, and afterward to Sefton Park. These parks are exceedingly beautiful, and differ from most parks in American cities in that many residences are scattered about in them. "It must be just too nice for anything," exclaimed Mamie Belville, "to live in such a beautiful park as this."

"O! it must be just lovely," chimed in the rest of the girls.

PRINCES PARK, LIVERPOOL

LIVERPOOL.

The Judge quite agreed with them, but at the same time reminded his young friends that those who seem to have the most of the world to enjoy, are not always the happiest. The Band were willing to admit all this, and yet that Prince's Park was a wondrously pleasant place to live in, could not be denied. It was still early in the afternoon, and as they thought they would like to see a little of the country, they drove out to the village of Wavertree.

"Why do the English build such high walls around the grounds of their country places?" asked Hattie Clark.

"Why," added Lulu Wright, "I noticed one wall that must have been ten feet high, and a hedge growing on top of that."

The Judge explained that it was the nature of the English people to be exclusive, but that when one gained their confidence they were the kindest hearted of all people. But if the country residences were partly hidden from view, the fields were not. September is one of the most delightful months of the year, and our little friends may be pardoned if, as they drove along, they thought England must be the most beautiful country in the world.

Friday morning was spent in Brown Museum and the Art Gallery, both of which are near the hotel. After lunch they took a good rest, and at three o'clock they left the hotel to spend the evening with Mr. and Mrs. Alexander. On the Landing Stage they were met by Mr. Alexander, and as soon as the ferry-boat had discharged her passengers, they went on board. The tide is so strong in the Mersey that ferry-boats do not run "end on" in a slip, but come alongside of the pier and the passengers go on and off from the side of the boat, as on a Delaware river steam-boat.

Mrs. Alexander lived on the outskirts of Birkenhead, in one of those lovely homes for which England is famous. After tea Mr. Alexander took Mr. McGee and the boys up to his workshop, and while he and the Judge enjoyed a quiet cigar, the boys were busy examining the specimens of his handiwork. Among other things was a steamer, about three feet long, complete in every detail. Although so small, it was a real, true steamer for sure. A small lamp generated steam which ran a real engine, and the little vessel had made more than one voyage across the lake in Birkenhead Park. Of course it was so small that no one could ride on it.

Down in the parlor Mrs. Alexander was entertaining the girls with stories of English life; she also informed them that her son was a confirmed bachelor—a state of affairs the girls had already suspected. She thought her James was the best son in the world, and indeed two happier people it would be hard to find. By and by the gentlemen came down stairs and the conversation became both general and animated. It was a late hour when they left. Mr. Alexander accompanied them to the railway station, for they did not return by the ferry, but by the tunnel under the river.

Saturday morning was spent in making a few additional purchases and other preparations for their voyage. They were about to exchange civilization for an unknown and savage land—one that was popularly known as the "white man's grave"—and they naturally felt pretty serious about it.

At half-past two they were upon the Landing Stage, where they found Mr. Alexander and his partner, Mr. Robertson, awaiting them. Their luggage was carefully placed upon the tender, and they then paced up and down awaiting the hour of departure.

It was a busy and animated scene.

Porters with great trunks and cases on their shoulders, were hurrying down the bridges from the pier-head. Mail sacks and parcels of all kinds were brought from various directions and quickly transferred to the tender. Little family groups were gathered here and there to say "good-bye" to a husband, or a son—may be never to see the loved face again.

Our little travelers were much affected, for their own parting from dear ones was still fresh in their memories. At length the hour came, and they went on board the tender, which was soon speeding its way up the river.

"Why do we go *up* the river?" asked Grant Hillman.

"Because our vessel is there loading powder," replied Captain Davis.

"Powder!" exclaimed the girls in chorus, "is there powder on the ship, Captain?"

"Yes," said Captain Davis, "there is eighty tons of it."

The Ogowe Band were filled with dismay. The boys tried to look brave, but did not succeed very well. Judge McGee asked if it was customary to carry so much powder, and why it was done.

Captain Davis explained that this powder is used in trade with the natives and that every steamer going to Africa carries a large quantity of it. "I have known," said he, "a ship to take out as much as eight hundred tons on a single voyage. We have a magazine built expressly for it and will this time take no more than it will hold; but sometimes we take it between decks with the other cargo."

It was not a pleasing prospect, but our young friends had set their faces toward the Dark Continent, and were not to be turned back by the prospect of an accident; so they said no more about the powder. By this time they were alongside the Nubia, and in less than an hour the anchor was up, and they were on their way down the river.

CITY OF FUNCHAL, MADEIRA

Chapter III.

MADEIRA.

OUR little travelers found the Nubia a very different steamer from the Lord Gough. The latter vessel was built for the cold and stormy Atlantic; the Nubia was designed for warmer climes and smoother seas. She had accommodations for only about twenty saloon passengers, but her rooms were large, and there was abundance of air and light. Like the Lord Gough the saloon and staterooms were amidships, a rare thing on an African steamer, for usually these apartments are at the stern of the ship, where the motion is greatest. Some of the old hands prefer this arrangement still, for they think it removes them farther from the noise and confusion of working the cargo. Be that as it may, our friends were glad they were on the Nubia where they were likely to be far less seasick than they would be in the old style of vessel.

The ship took the same course they had followed when coming into Liverpool, until Holyhead was passed, when, instead of crossing over to the Irish coast, they kept right down the middle of the Channel. Their course was a little west of south, and for six days they steamed along without any unusual incident occurring. Occasionally a steamer was seen homeward bound from the Brazils or the Mediterranean, a long trail of black smoke streaming behind her; and sometimes they passed a sailing vessel making her way to some distant portion of the earth. But most of the time there was nothing in sight but sea and sky, and as it was not always fit to be on deck, they had a dull time.

At noon, on the sixth day, some brown rocks were seen on the horizon on the starboard bow; these, the Captain informed them, were the Desertes, rocky islands belonging to the Madeira group. They are small and uninhabited, but sometimes people go there to catch fish. As the afternoon wore away Madeira was seen rising grandly from the ocean, and in the early evening they were steaming past it.

The night was bright and clear, and the Ogowe Band were on deck until a late hour enjoying the novelty of the scene. Before them rose the island in majestic grandeur to a height of six thousand feet, its summit draped in light, fleecy clouds. The waves dashed against the face of the rocky cliffs, while above, on the mountain side, little clusters of lights here and there showed the positions of the villages. By and by the steamer rounded the Point, and in about an hour the great mass of lights ashore indicated they were abreast of Funchal. These lights shone so brightly in the clear night air that it almost seemed as if a part of the starry host had fallen upon the mountain side.

It was a lovely night, and from the steamer's deck the scene was novel and enchanting. All around was the wide sea, now lying as calm and peaceful as a babe asleep.

MADEIRA

Above, in the black vault of heaven, the stars shone like celestial lamps along the highways of the spirit world. To the right was the strange volcanic island, so little known in the Western world. In the quiet night the steamer appeared like a great live creature, its iron heart throbbing with a ceaseless purpose to bear them away to still more distant lands. Conversation was hushed; every soul was communing with the inspiration of the night; laying up in the treasure-house of memory a store of impressions as food for thought in the years to come. Nor did they find it easy to leave this fairy land and go down stairs to engage in the prosy occupation of undressing and going to bed. The steamer could not enter the roadstead until sunrise and so lay outside under "dead slow" steam the rest of the night.

Notwithstanding the late hours of the previous night, our little voyagers were up betimes in the morning. The Nubia was at anchor close in to the shore and was surrounded by a small fleet of row-boats, whose swarthy crews hoped to make a few shillings by taking passengers ashore. They crowded especially about the gangway and with loud cries sought to call attention to themselves and their boats. Some clambered over the side and brought with them basket work, feather ornaments, shells, needle-work, pictures, willow chairs and a variety of other goods for sale.

In two of the boats were small boys who seemed to be anxious to obtain some favor, but what it was our young people did not know. The ship's Doctor explained that they wanted to dive for sixpences; and then, drawing one from his pocket, he threw it into the water. It was so clear that the sixpence could be seen turning over and over as it slowly descended. When a few feet beneath

MADEIRA

the surface two of the boys dived, and presently one appeared with the coin in his teeth; after shaking the water from his face, he held it up in his hands so the Doctor could see that he had it. The Ogowe Band were highly interested and they threw a number of coins in the water, every one of which the boys brought out again. The water was so clear that every motion was plainly seen, and the Judge was as much interested in the performance as the young folks.

Our happy young voyagers now turned their attention from the boys to the shipping in the roadstead, and the sights and scenes ashore. They were surprised to see so many steamers, and so they inquired why it was, for they had thought Madeira was seldom visited.

Captain Davis replied that the island is just in the track of all vessels going to the South Atlantic. "All those steamers," said he, "that go to the West coast of Africa, all that go to the Cape of Good Hope, as well as those that go to the Brazils, and every part of South America, pass Madeira, and call in, like ourselves, for coal, water and fresh provisions." "This steamer coming in," said he, "is the Moor from Cape Town. The one just over there is the Corisco from the West coast of Africa, where we are going. Those two are the Carl Woermann from Hamburg, and the Angola from Lisbon; the one bound for the German and the other for the Portuguese possessions in Africa. That large one is the Hipparchus from Hamburg for the Brazils, and the small one which has just anchored, has come from the Azores, or, as we Britishers call them, the Western Islands."

Saxe Deemey asked if coal was found on the island.

"No," said Captain Davis, "it is all brought out from England."

LANDING PLACE, FUNCHAL, MADEIRA

"What is this large rock?" asked Laura Reed; "it looks like a castle."

"That," answered the Captain, "is Lou Rock; it is a fortress and prison all in one; it is also a signal station, and is a rendezvous for the health and customs officers. They were off here to see me this morning before you were out on deck."

"That old fort is no good anyhow," said Johnny Ashton, "one of our big rifled cannon would make a stone quarry of it in a couple of shots."

With this sentiment the Band were quite agreed. They indulged the conceit, so common among their countrymen, that America could beat the world, and was prepared to do it. The Judge well knew that a wider acquaintance among the nations would partly dispel this illusion; so he said nothing; and his young companions soon turned their attention to the sights ashore.

Just before them the city of Funchal lay, built in solid squares near the waterside, and then climbed the mountain in several directions. Along the beach, boats laden with merchandise were arriving and departing, oxen were drawing heavy loads in various directions, and numbers of people were hurrying to and fro. Above, the clouds were just rising from the mountain tops; among the peaks yawned great canyons as though the mountain had been forcibly rent asunder. The lower slopes of the mountain were terraced and planted with grapes and sugar-cane, which were now being ripened by the autumn sun. Above the town were many country-seats, almost hidden from view by the orange and lemon orchards that surrounded them. Near the sea, in sheltered situations, were small fields of bananas, their broad leaves waving gently in the slight breeze.

Captain Davis invited our young travelers to spend the day on shore with him, and ordered breakfast half an hour earlier than usual so they might have a good start. This invitation, it is needless to say, was accepted with pleasure. The Captain thought best not to go in his gig, as the native boats were better adapted to the rocky beach; so two were chosen, the Captain and the young ladies going in one, and Judge McGee and the boys in the other. These boats had a deep, thick keel, and the moment one touched bottom, the crew jumped out in the water, and, with the aid of their comrades who stood near, drew it upon the shingly beach out of reach of the waves.

They landed at the foot of a street that might be called the main entrance to the town. A double row of trees cast a grateful shade, for on shore the sun was warm. No guide was needed, for Captain Davis knew the way as well as he did in his own home city of Liverpool; but the beggars were so numerous and troublesome that old Antonio was hired, more to keep them off than anything else.

The Ogowe Band walked up the street in open-mouthed wonder; here they were, sure enough, in this remote island of the sea, with everything about them so new and strange. Perhaps it is hardly proper to say "new," for the island and its people are more like a portion of the middle ages preserved for our inspection, than they are like the nineteenth century.

Just then a sled with a carriage-top on it and drawn by two oxen, came around the corner. It came slipping and sliding along, the men who were managing it uttering loud cries, apparently to the oxen.

"What in the world is that?" exclaimed Lulu Wright.

As she spoke, one of the men threw a dirty rag in front of one of the runners of the sled, and when the runner had passed over it he picked it up again and took it with him.

"That sled," said Captain Davis, "is a Madeira carriage."

"A carriage, indeed," chimed in two of the girls at once, "where are the wheels?"

The Captain told them there was not a wheeled vehicle on the island, and that these sleds were the usual means for getting about unless one went afoot.

"What did that man throw the rag under the sled for?" asked Grace Thompson.

Captain Davis called their attention to the fact that the street was paved with small, smooth boulders set on edge, and that they were quite slippery. "Now," said he "when the sled does not seem to go ahead as easily as it should, that greasy rag is thrown in front of one of the runners and that oils the machine and makes it go more smoothly."

"Well, I think it's a stupid mode of getting around, anyway," remarked Jessie Williams.

"It may seem stupid to us," replied the Captain, "but it is well adapted to these mountain roads, and the conditions of life here. These oxen may be slow but they are sure-footed; they will subsist on much coarser fare than horses; and when their days of usefulness are nearly spent, they are sold to the steamers in the shape of fresh beef; thus bringing a fair profit to the frugal islanders."

Willie Richman thought the meat would be tough; but Robbie Campbell allowed that would make it go farther, so that it might be an advantage.

After passing along the public square, they entered a side street and went into the office of the steamship agents. Here the Captain sent a cablegram to Liverpool announcing the ship's arrival; ordered coal and some other supplies; and after a little chat with the agents, he said his business was finished and placed himself at the disposal of the party.

After a short conference with Judge McGee, it was decided to go about the city, make some purchases, take lunch at Miles' Hotel, and then go up the mountain. As they passed out into the street, a yoke of oxen went by, dragging a plank some eight feet long and fifteen inches wide.

"Is that another Madeira carriage?" inquired Saxe Deemey.

"That," explained Captain Davis, "is a truck; it is used for transporting all kinds of freight."

The boys thought they had come, sure enough, to the outer verge of civilization, but there was such an abundance of sights for the young eyes, that, for the present, the oxen and plank passed out of mind.

Just then they came to a shop where willow baskets and chairs were for sale. The Judge suggested the propriety of purchasing a chair and basket for each of his party; so they went in. It did not take the Ogowe Band long to make up their minds that they wanted pretty much everything in the shop. This was not so surprising, for the goods were mostly curiosities made for sale to tourists to carry home with them as mementos of their visit. Judge McGee called attention to the fact that they were outward-bound and it was best to defer the purchase of souvenirs until their return. "But," said he, "you might get a few pictures to send back by Captain Davis."

MADEIRA CARRIAGE

"They can go to-day by the Corisco," said the Captain; so the ones that appear in this volume were chosen, and sent, duly addressed, to the steamship office.

They had not gone far from the shop when Antonio led them through an open doorway into what proved to be the open court of a house. It was a house where feather-work and paper flowers were made for sale. At these places guides are paid a commission on all sales made to tourists whom they bring in. Our friends did not wish to purchase any of these commodities, but they spent a little time in examining the natural flowers growing in and about the court.

Such floral wealth they had never seen. A single heliotrope was fastened to one side of the house; it spread out to a height and breadth of over ten feet, and was covered with bloom. A fuchsia growing against the wall was even larger, and must have had at least a bushel of blossoms on it. A scarlet geranium was quite as large. The girls were more astonished by the flowers than anything they had yet seen, and could scarcely believe their eyes, and the Judge felt they were well worth coming so far to see.

The houses are mostly built on three sides of an interior court; the fourth side being closed by a wall covered upon the top with broken bottles. Toward the street the first story presents little more than a blank wall. The doors are heavy and often covered with iron; the few windows are heavily barred like a prison, and have no glass. The ground floor is mostly a lumber room, or is used as a workshop. Machinery is not esteemed in Madeira; nearly every kind of manufacture is carried on by hand. As our friends walked along they saw men plying their various trades and handicrafts, each at the entrance to his house.

After a while they turned up the street seen in the engraving, and met a pleasant-faced English gentleman, who, seeing they were Americans, invited them to step in his house and sit down a few minutes to rest. He introduced himself as Rev. Mr. Smart, agent for the British and Foreign Bible Society of London. His house is on the left hand side of the street shown in the engraving, about half way up. He took his guests across the street where Mrs. Smart was teaching an infant school. The little olive-skinned children eyed our young friends, and when introductions were over, sang "Safe in the arms of Jesus," in the Portuguese tongue. It was the first time our young travelers had heard singing in a foreign language and they were much affected.

From this interesting little school, Antonio led them through many streets, some of them crooked and narrow, until he brought them to a large building which proved to be a sugar-mill. The young folks were delighted and the Judge too was pleased; not one of the party had ever been in a sugar-mill before.

The cane stripped of its leaves, and looking like great bare cornstalks, was brought in on sleds by oxen, and run between heavy rollers to crush out the juice. After passing through several large tanks to allow it to settle and purify, it was run into long shallow pans and boiled. It was a hot, dirty, sticky place, but the Ogowe Band were glad they had seen it, for they felt they understood the manufacture of sugar as they never could have done from simply reading books.

It was nearly noon and they were hot and tired, so they were quite content, for the time, to give up sightseeing and go to Miles' Hotel to rest and have some lunch. When they reached the hotel, they passed through the hall out to the covered portico which surrounds the court, and, throwing themselves into the cool willow chairs, declared they were "just too tired for anything." In the centre of the court a fountain was playing and gold-fish were darting about in the water. Beautiful flowers lined the walks, while still others clambered up the walls. These sights caused the spirits of the young tourists quickly to revive; it was not many minutes before they were in the garden examining the strange plants and flowers, and their tongues rattling away at a lively rate.

Judge McGee and Captain Davis were content to enjoy themselves in comfortable repose on the cool veranda. While the young folks chattered away in the garden, they engaged in a quiet talk about the industrial condition of the island. The Captain informed Mr. McGee that Madeira was not as prosperous as in former years. Then wine was the principal article of export and it brought high prices; but a mysterious disease killed most of the vines and no branch of agriculture has since been found so profitable. "The island now lives," said the Captain, "almost entirely upon its trade with passing steamers. A few English tourists come out to spend the winter, but not so many as formerly. Every year there are new places of attraction opened on the continent, and besides, it is getting to be pretty well understood that Madeira is not especially healthy."

Judge McGee remarked that he had heard Madeira spoken of as a sanitarium.

The Captain replied that the climate was mild and agreeable, and for a strong, healthy man, in many ways attractive; but for consumptives and other weak persons it was too debilitating. Besides, the long ocean voyage required to reach it, must ever be an objection. "It was once thought," continued the Captain, "that it might be a good place for those who were suffering from the African malaria to recruit their wasted energies; but that idea too has been given up."

"I had been thinking of that myself," observed Mr. McGee.

"Well," responded the Captain, "I used to think so too, but I have changed my mind. When a man comes here from the African coast all broken down, he not infrequently gains for the first few days; but the improvement is soon lost, and too often a funeral ends the voyage for the poor fellow."

Lunch was now announced, and the call was responded to with alacrity. The food was good, but not very abundant. The salads and fruits were especially grateful to the little voyagers after the days they had spent at sea. The apples, grapes and bananas were not better than they had eaten at home, but the fresh figs were a new thing to them. They were the size of a small pear, and of a dark purple color; most of the Band liked them, but two or three thought they were "sickish." They were disappointed in not getting oranges, but were told it was not the season.

When lunch was over our young friends were so much rested that they were eager for new scenes and adventures, so it was decided to start at once for the mountain. Four sleds were engaged by Antonio; three were for the Band, while Judge McGee and the Captain reserved one to themselves; hand sleds were also provided to bring the party down.

It was an imposing cavalcade, and caused some remark as they passed through the streets. Each sled was in charge of two men who were very noisy, shouting with

A STREET IN FUNCHAL, MADEIRA

discordant voices both at the oxen and at one another; presently the way became narrow and crooked, and in some places steep; so steep, in fact, that some of the girls screamed and tried to get out. The drivers pushed them back and tried to tell them there was no danger, but it was all an unknown tongue to them; however, they understood they must remain where they were, so they tremblingly resigned themselves to their fate.

It was not much wonder they felt nervous, for the oxen struggled at times to keep their footing, and in the steepest places it looked to the girls as if the poor beasts would fall back on them. Nor must it be supposed that the boys were any the less alarmed; it is nonsense to think that boys are naturally braver than girls; in times of great danger they are often less so.

When part way up, the sleds halted in an open place to rest, and there was a lively time comparing experiences. They were now up among the gardens and low stone huts of the peasant people, but they were so occupied in describing the recent situation that they did not take time to look about them. The rest of the way was toilsome work, and when they had mounted another thousand feet, they were glad enough to turn off into the pleasant grounds in the midst of which was the mountain home of Mr. Reid, a Scotch merchant. Mr. Reid gave them a hearty welcome, and so did his daughter, who was just home from school in England.

The view from the piazza was grandly beautiful. In front upon the terraced mountain-side were gardens, vineyards, and patches of sugar-cane. At their feet was the city of Funchal, its white buildings seeming wondrously near, so clear was the air. Beyond the harbor with its shipping, the great ocean stretched away into infinity—

that ocean whose pathless wastes they were to traverse in quest of unknown lands and adventures—all this rich scene lay before them shimmering in the warm light of the autumn sun.

A solemn hush for the moment fell upon the light-hearted youngsters, as memory brought up before the mind the dear ones far away over that deep blue sea. By its power it stirred the imagination in an instant to leap the vast expanse of waters, and set before them the sights and scenes of the home land. The city, the streets, the homes, the dear ones, and all the loved scenes in which they had so lately moved passed in seeming reality before them, and, as the sense of the isolation of their position was filling their young eyes with tears, Mr. Reid arose and invited them to take a walk about the grounds. This broke the spell, and in a moment the Ogowe Band were their own bright happy selves once more.

Madeira, by its equable climate, is able to grow the products of both the torrid and temperate zones. Here upon Mr. Reid's grounds the young travelers saw growing oranges and apples, strawberries and pine-apples, pears and lemons, potatoes and breadfruit, cherries and bananas. Yet after all, these plants do not flourish, but they grow and bear fruit. However, if fruits do not flourish, flowers certainly do, and such roses our young friends had never seen.

While the gentlemen were talking about the state of trade and the various industries of the island, Miss Reid took the girls with her into the vineyard. The main crop had already been gathered, but some bunches had been left here and there, and it was a new pleasure to the girls to be in a real, sure enough vineyard, one that was, very likely, like those they had read of in the Bible, in the land of Palestine. The grapes were good, and grateful to the taste, more especially after one has been several days at sea, but they could scarcely be called luscious. Many kinds sold in the Philadelphia markets are as good, if not better.

While they were enjoying the grapes Miss Reid entertained them with a description of the kind of life young people live in Madeira, and of her own school-days in London. She was not half done when Captain Davis's voice was heard calling them, for the time was rapidly passing and they needed to be on their way. After a cup of coffee, they bade good-bye to their kind entertainers and went a little further up the mountain to visit a convent. There was nothing of special interest to see here, except the wealth of flowers growing in profusion everywhere about the grounds. Old Antonio told them that they were at liberty to pick as many as they chose; a liberty they all took full advantage of, and soon each one had as many as could comfortably be carried.

The time had now come for the trip down the mountain, and the men with the hand sleds were in waiting. These sleds have a body like a very small sleigh, with low runners, so that the weight is near the ground, and are capable of holding two passengers. Each sled is managed by two men, and behind is a handle for them to hold on by and guide the sled.

The perpendicular descent from the convent is full two thousand feet. Part of the way is narrow, everywhere crooked, and in places as steep as a house-roof. The road is paved with the narrow boulders set on edge, and are slippery, so that the ride down is not unlike a runaway train on the Switchback at Mauch Chunk.

It took some time to get the party seated and everything ready for the start. The girls owned up they were afraid, and the boys held back with a unanimity that was refreshing; even the Judge considered the chances very soberly. One thing was certain, they must get down some way, and this was the approved method; accidents were of rare occurrence and they must take their chances. And so it happened, that after a goodly number of "O my's!" "O dear's!" and "O, I am so afraid's!" they at length got started.

But if they were slow in getting started, they wasted no time afterwards. Captain Davis and Laura Reed led the procession; then came the boys; then four of the girls; while Judge McGee and Mamie Belville brought up the rear and were able to see what happened to the rest.

At first the grade was easy and just rapid enough to be exhilarating; the girls declared it was "too jolly for anything," and the boys fairly shouted. The pace quickened and the exclamations ceased; it was getting to be serious. The road now gave two or three quick turns and then seemed to just fall away from before them; houses, walls, rocks, flashed past in a confused maze, and they felt they had left the earth as they flew through the air. The speed was such it took their breath away, and their hearts stood still, as with open mouths, and bulging eyes, they awaited instant destruction. In ten minutes they were in the public plaza, nearly scared to death, while their sled men, reeking with perspiration, threw themselves panting upon the pavement.

The Ogowe Band could scarcely believe their senses when they found the journey was over and no one was hurt. It was indeed an experience never to be forgotten, and the Judge readily admitted it was both novel and startling.

The sun was now low in the West, and Captain Davis thought it was time to be getting on board, so they paid their men and walked down to the landing. The boats that brought them ashore in the morning were waiting for them, and it was not long before they were once more on board their floating home.

Chapter IV.

CANARY ISLANDS.

THINGS were in confusion on the main-deck of the Nubia when our friends came on board from their day of sight seeing in Funchal. The coal-bunkers had been filled, and there was a large heap of coal on deck besides. Several quarters of fresh beef hung near the galley, and two bullocks were standing on the forward deck with a pile of hay near them. There were bunches of chickens tied by the legs, and baskets filled with cabbage, lettuce, tomatoes, apples, grapes, walnuts and bananas; there was a prospect for something to eat at any rate.

On the saloon deck were the willow chairs Judge McGee had bought; the baskets had been stowed in an empty state-room. The agent came off to the ship just after our friends arrived, and brought the ship's papers. When he had arranged his business matters with the Captain, he bade them good-bye and wished them a pleasant voyage. Captain Davis went on the "bridge," the bell rang in the engine-room to "stand by," the steam-windlass on the forecastle-head drew the anchor chain slowly

FUNCHAL FROM THE MOUNTAIN-SIDE, MADEIRA

in, the engines began to "head slow," and with the company's flag fluttering at the main-truck, and the Union Jack astern, the Nubia turned slowly toward the south and the voyage was resumed.

After dinner the Ogowe Band settled themselves comfortably on deck in their new willow chairs, and now that they were somewhat rested, they began to talk over the events of the day. Nothing they had met with escaped their notice, but what had most impressed them was the ride down the mountain. To use their own expression, "It was just too much for anything," and how they got down without accident was still to them a mystery.

While they were talking, Captain Davis came from the bridge and took a seat with them. Judge McGee asked him why he had such a heap of coal on deck.

The Captain explained that it was customary for the African boats in starting to take on nearly enough coal for the round trip; at Madeira as much is taken on board as has been burned up to that time, and if the supply does not seem ample, some is carried on deck as in the present instance.

"Won't there be danger of the bullocks being washed away?" asked Saxe.

"No," replied the Captain, "we will have no more rough weather; we have now entered the region of balmy breezes and smooth seas."

"How do you manage about fresh water?" inquired Judge McGee.

"We have water tanks near the bottom of the ship," continued the Captain, "that are filled in Liverpool and are usually sufficient for drinking and cooking; for washing we use condensed water."

"I suppose that is why it does not smell good," remarked Jessie.

"And it makes my hands rough," added Mamie.

"Well, it's not nice anyway," chimed in Hattie.

The Captain admitted that condensed water was in many ways unpleasant to use. "But then," said he, "if there were no hardships at sea, there would be no glory in being a sailor."

The young folks had no thought of becoming sailors, so they did not reply, and for a while the whole party sat quietly enjoying the beauties of the night.

And a lovely night it was. The stars shone brightly, and the new moon declining in the west, shed a path of light across the trackless waste, as its pale beams were reflected from the quiet waters. By and by one or two of the boys began to nod and Judge McGee, rising from his chair, expressed the opinion that it was time to go to bed.

When they came on deck next morning they found the sailors at work putting up an awning; it was stretched from side to side across the ship, and was of two thicknesses of canvas. This kept off the sun which was now beginning to make his power felt, and made the deck a delightful place to spend the day.

In the far distance ahead, a dark hazy bank on the horizon was pointed out to them. From the upper bridge, with the aid of a glass, a dull, dark object could be seen in the cloud; this the chief officer told them was the Peak of Teneriffe. They watched it all the morning as it slowly rose from the water. The sun's heat gradually dispelled the vapors, and by noon its form could be distinctly seen.

"What is the height of the Peak?" inquired Jessie.

"A little over two miles," replied Captain Davis.

"Has any one ever climbed to the top of it?" asked Frank.

"Yes," continued the Captain, "but it is seldom done, for it is very hard work. For several hundred feet below the summit the cone is covered with a thick layer of fine ashes."

"Has there been any eruption of late years?" inquired Laura.

"Yes," was the reply, "but nothing was thrown up except ashes."

Hattie desired to know how the Peak of Teneriffe compared in height with other mountains.

Judge McGee answered that it was higher than the Alleghanies, Pyrenees, or Mt. Etna; but not so high as Mt. Blanc.

About three o'clock the steamer anchored in the roadstead of Santa Cruz which is on the northeast end of the island, about ten miles south of the point. Two steamers were in ahead of them; the Leipsic from Bremen; and Dom Pedro from Brazil.

Santa Cruz is not over one-third the size of Funchal. As the Nubia was only calling to land the mails and a few cases of goods, our friends decided not to go on shore, more especially as the surf was beating rather heavily against the stone pier where they must land. As the steamer was anchored close in, with the aid of glasses they were able to get a fair idea of the place.

The hills back of the town are not so steep as at Madeira, and appear to be rather barren, although they are cultivated. The Peak is to the left and is on the opposite side of the island; by this time in the afternoon it was again veiled in clouds, and could not be seen. To the right were ranges of steep rocky hills coming down end on to the sea; they were cultivated near their bases, and covered to the summits with some kind of low, coarse vegetation, much of it of a dull, gray color. The place is by no means so attractive as Funchal.

The Judge thought one might spend two or three days ashore comfortably, as long as every sight was new, but that it would soon become tiresome enough.

"I wonder if they have a daily paper here," queried Grant.

"No indeed," responded Captain Davis, "I doubt if many of the people can read, or would care to do so if they could. This little island is their world, and what may happen elsewhere is nothing to them."

"I should think they would want at least one paper," observed Grace, "so they could get the local news."

"Never fear," responded the Captain, "their tongues are quite equal to that, and do not cost anything either."

"Are the islanders poor?" asked Lulu.

"Yes," continued the Captain, "they have enough to eat and drink, but they are poor in income; there is not much that can profitably be exported, so that money is a scarce article among them."

"Well," observed Mamie, "these people are welcome to their island home, and I hope they are satisfied with it." The rest of the Band quite agreed that the life on Teneriffe was too solitary to be desirable.

"Where is Oratava?" asked the Judge.

"It is on the west side of the island," answered the Captain. "It is the place to start from if you wish to ascend the Peak; it has no commerce and steamers do not call there."

Just before they started away, several drip-stones were brought on board consigned to various ports on the

African coast. These drip-stones are shaped like a deep bowl, with square tops, and hold two or three pails of water each. They are chiseled from blocks of lava, and are used everywhere on the African coast to filter water. For this purpose they are admirably adapted. The sides of this huge bowl are three or four inches in thickness, and the water slowly percolates through it, leaving every particle of sediment behind. Once a week they need to be rubbed well on the inside with a scrubbing brush and washed out; by this means it is possible to have perfectly pure water.

Next morning, just as the sun was touching the tops of the mountains, the Nubia anchored in the harbor of Las Palmas, on the eastern side of the island of Grand Canary.

The rattle of the anchor-chain aroused the young voyagers from their slumbers, and they clambered out of their berths in a hurry. It did not take them long to dress and get on deck, for when there was something new to be seen, they were as nimble as only young people can be. They found the steamer in a small bay, completely sheltered from the waves by a long breakwater that had been built out from the shore. Near by three or four steamers and some small sailing vessels were at anchor, while ashore were coal wharves and a good many stone buildings. Upon looking around they saw, across the bay, a city larger than Santa Cruz, but not so large as Funchal. Behind the city were mountains, and the sun was clothing their brown summits with a glorious light of crimson and gold. In some places palms lined the beach, and a good many were growing in the town and in the valleys among the hills; indeed, the very name of the town, Las Palmas, means "The Palms."

Boats had already left the shore for the Nubia and were soon alongside. Captain Davis came out of the chart room and bade them a hearty "good morning, young ladies and gents." It was not long before Judge McGee joined them. He too had been awakened by the splash of the anchor, but he was not in so much of a hurry as the youngsters were; no doubt realizing more fully than they, that there is always sufficient time for all we have to do. He asked Captain Davis how long he would remain and was told that they would not sail before five o'clock.

"Now," said the Judge, "we were your guests at Madeira and I propose that you be our guest to-day. How soon will it suit you to go ashore?"

Captain Davis replied that he would be ready shortly after seven o'clock.

Boats came off to the steamer as at Madeira, bringing various articles for sale, much of which was merely trash; and guides and runners for various places solicited patronage. Judge McGee inquired of the steamship agent for the best hotel in town and the runner for that house was introduced to him.

Having made the necessary arrangements with him, all hands went below to get a cup of coffee and get ready for the day's excursion. At half-past seven they were going down the ladder, and a couple of boats soon carried them over to the pier. Here carriages were waiting and they drove through the port, past the coal-yards, and then along the beautiful road that skirts the bay until they entered the city of Las Palmas.

As it was still early they drove about the town before going to the hotel for breakfast. Las Palmas they found to be a more modern city than Funchal, and on that account, less picturesque. There were no bullock-sleds,

LAS PALMAS, GRAND CANARY

and some horses were seen, mostly attached to carriages; merchandise, so far as our young travelers were able to discover, was carried about on the heads of men and women. Stores and shops were abundant and displayed a good assortment of wares. Ladies were out marketing, with shawls thrown over the head and shoulders so as to conceal the face, excepting a little patch about one eye. The women in humble life moved about freely with uncovered faces.

It was half-past eight when they alighted at the hotel, and they were ready to do ample justice to the breakfast that was waiting for them. At the table they met Captain Charles Thompson, master of the steamer Kisanga, homeward bound from the coast of Africa. His steamer had come in during the night, and as it was to take on coal and water, as well as cochineal and bananas, it would not sail before evening. He brought the latest news from the "Coast," as this part of the Dark Continent is always called; but as it was mostly of a personal nature, our young travelers were not much interested in it. To the Ogowe Band it appeared to consist mostly of fevers, deaths, and "went home" on such and such a steamer. They were somewhat relieved to hear that the "Coast" was healthy at present; that is, there was nowhere any epidemic. When old coasters return to the shores of Africa with somewhat of dread, those who are making their first voyage may be excused for being a little nervous.

Captain Thompson appeared to be a most pleasant and agreeable gentleman, and Judge McGee invited him to join the party in an excursion among the mountains. To this the Captain gave his consent, and he proved to be in every way a delightful companion. He had a houseful of young people at home, and he knew just how to interest and amuse the young folks.

After breakfast they adjourned to the court of the hotel, opening out upon the garden, and a merrier party was never seen at Las Palmas. The two Captains told of their early adventures in various parts of the world, and the boys began to wish it had fallen to their lot to be sailors too. Both gentlemen had sailed to almost every part of the earth, and one of them had lived nearly a year in America. Conversation flowed on in a steady stream, and in the meanwhile Judge McGee went with the hotel proprietor to make arrangements for the coming excursion. In half an hour he returned and reported that all was ready.

Five open carriages, each drawn by three horses harnessed abreast, were in waiting in the street. The Judge assisted Lulu Wright and Grace Thompson into the first one, and then got in himself; upon the seat with the driver was the son of the hotel proprietor in the capacity of guide and interpreter. Captain Davis, Jessie Williams and Laura Reed occupied the second carriage; Captain Thompson, Mamie Belville and Hattie Clark, the third; while the boys followed in the two remaining ones.

When all were embarked, the drivers whipped up their horses and the procession rattled along at a lively rate. They passed the public square and through several of the principal streets, crossed a small river, now nearly dry, and were presently upon the outskirts of the town. The road, which was macadamized, was in splendid order, and followed the little stream as it flowed down its rocky bed in the narrow valley. Terraced gardens were built against the steep hillside, and these were planted with pine-apples, bananas, figs, oranges, lemons and grapes, as well as with many kinds of garden vegetables and flowers. A little further on the valley widened and there were many small fields of bananas with palm trees growing close by the river banks. The bananas were of the short variety, with many dark leaves, but they bore enormous bunches of fruit, and the young tourists thought it would be nice to have a few of them growing in the back yards of their homes in Philadelphia. The date palms filled them with wonder and admiration. Here, right before their eyes, were the trees they had read of in the Bible. It was just such trees as these that grew in Egypt, in the desert, and in the Jordan Valley.

It must be confessed that a palm tree, when one stands close by it, is not a specially beautiful object; but when seen at a little distance, so that some of the details are lost in the general outline, it is one of the most graceful and striking objects in the vegetable kingdom. When one who has spent some years in the tropics returns to his northern home, after all else is forgotten, the graceful palm waving its feathery arms in the brilliant sunlight, will be constantly before the mind, its enchanting beauty luring him to return.

The road again crossed the stream and began to ascend the mountain side. The sun was hot, but the pure fresh air from the ocean tempered the heat and made the ride most enjoyable. The steeper hillsides were bare of vegetation excepting a few coarse shrubs, but the gentler slopes had been terraced and planted with various crops. In many places the cliffs had been tunneled and houses cut out of the solid rock. These usually had a door and one or two windows next the road; how many rooms there might be in the cave dwellings our young friends could not tell. Provided the cliff faced the north, one might readily imagine these houses to be cool and comfortable in a hot climate.

Upon the roofs of some of the houses in the valley below them, were large bunches of some material of a deep orange color, evidently spread out to dry. None of the party could imagine what it was, but the guide told those in the first carriage it was Indian corn. "In this island," said he, "but little grain of any kind is raised, and the people value this corn very highly for feeding to their animals."

Judge McGee asked why they did not raise bananas, sell them, and buy corn with the money, as in this way they could get fully ten times as much from the ground.

The guide replied that he could not tell, but perhaps it was because ships seldom came over from America.

They were now approaching the summit; to their surprise the character of the soil improved, and it was everywhere carefully cultivated. The road was no longer steep and the increasing number of houses indicated a considerable population. To the amazement of the party, here upon the mountain heights a little stream went dashing along the road, singing merrily as it leaped by in the bright sunlight. It was a useful little stream too. A channel had been cut for it in the solid rock, and here, standing up to their knees in the rushing water, were the wives and daughters of the mountaineers washing their own clothes and those of the town people.

Jolly, merry groups they were, laughing and talking as they soaped the clothes and pounded them down upon the stones. In many cases the children were with them; those who were old enough had to help with the work as they were able, while the babies lay kicking up their heels in the shade of a bush or tree. They eyed the procession curiously as it passed, and no doubt wondered where all these fine people came from, and what brought them to their island home.

The girls were astonished at the way the clothes were pounded on the rocks and thought they would be hammered all to pieces. Hattie asked Captain Thompson if they had no wash-boards. He replied that this was the common way of washing clothes in many parts of the world, and that it did not wear out clothes faster than our fashion of rubbing them, provided a little care was used, and the stone was perfectly smooth. "In some countries I have visited," said he, "they beat the clothes with a club or mallet; this injures them far more."

The top of the mountain was a broad table-land, and the road was nearly level, so they rattled away at a good pace. There were vineyards on either side of the road, and occasionally a grove of fig trees. The vintage was past, but a few late clusters had been left on the vines, and now hung ripening in the autumn sun. The harvest for figs had of course long since passed, although plenty were still to be found in the markets. Several fields of thick-leaved cacti were seen; women were at work in the fields, and as nearly as the Ogowe Band could make out, they were cutting off the broad, heavy leaves and laying them in the sun to wilt. The guide told Judge McGee that the women were feeding the cochineal insects. When the cochineal was ready for shipment it was worth two dollars a pound, and was sent mostly to the continent where it was used to color candies. "It is a great deal of trouble," said he, "and not much of it is raised."

On the very top of the mountain was a village and here the carriages stopped while the horses were watered and recovered their wind a little. Beyond the village the road declined some and then gradually ascended to the next summit. The table-land in the interior of the island was more pleasing than the hillsides toward the coast. The land was all carefully cultivated and presented many charming scenes of rural beauty. The number of cave dwellings increased and in some places the hillsides appeared to be honeycombed with these primitive houses.

The procession came to a halt before a large iron gateway which opened into the grounds surrounding a fine country home. The guide wished to show them the flowers and fruit trees. The family were not at home, so they were not annoyed by such a host of visitors. Several fine orange trees attracted attention; they were not much larger than good sized peach trees, but the limbs did not branch so near the ground, and the tops were much thicker. The leaves were very dark green, and as some of the fruit was coloring, the contrast was a pretty one.

Willie inquired if these were the apples of gold, spoken of in the Bible, and Judge McGee replied that he thought they were.

A red-tailed parrot in a large cage near the house was a great attraction to the girls. It talked just like a person, but as it only spoke Spanish our friends could not make out what it said.

While the girls were engaged with the parrot, the boys were looking at some tame rabbits. They were just as pretty as they could be and held up their ears in a very knowing way. After visiting the garden and gathering all the flowers they cared to carry, the Judge gave the gardener a couple of shillings, and some sixpences to his children, and then the party resumed their ride.

After crossing another ridge they descended into a broad valley, and here, beneath the shade of some low trees, with a little mountain brook just across the road, the Judge called a halt and invited them all to alight and have a picnic. The rest of the party wondered where he would get his provisions, but at a word from him, the guide removed the seat from the first carriage, and, with the aid of the driver, drew forth a large, well-filled hamper.

Exclamations of surprise were followed by commendations of the Judge's thoughtfulness, and the girls went to work at once to "set the table." They made the boys stir around lively and help them, and they were soon as busy as possible. And yet, with all their activity, it was not so easy. There was no grass, and when it comes to "setting the table" on a lot of stones, it is not so readily accomplished as one might wish. Captain Thompson, who was skillful in every emergency, came to their assistance, so that at last all was ready and they sat down.

The carriages had been sent to a little village not far ahead, where the horses could eat and rest; thus leaving them more to themselves. The fresh air, and excitement of the ride, had given them an appetite, and they gave undivided attention to the good things Judge McGee had provided. By and by they began to look about them and note in detail the features of the novel landscape spread out before them. "The style of building in this part of the island," said he, "reminds me strongly of Syria."

"Yes," responded Captain Thompson, "one might readily imagine he was in one of the ports of Asia Minor."

"I have read," said Laura, "that some of the cities of Arabia are cut out of the rock; are the houses in those cities anything like these?"

"Yes," answered the Judge, "but very much more e.aborate. They had temples, palaces and other public buildings, while these are only private dwellings, and very humble ones at that."

Jessie desired to know what the Bible meant to teach when it said, "The righteous shall flourish like the palm tree."

"I suppose it means," replied the Judge, "they shall grow in beauty and usefulness."

"Why does it say they shall bring forth fruit in old age?" asked Robbie.

"The palm," continued he, "bears its heaviest crops when old. It does not begin to bear until it is some size, and then the bunches of fruit are small and poor, but as it grows older it yields better fruit and larger bunches. So a Christian is not expected to bear fruit at once; it is enough for him to live and grow; but when he gets old, if he has 'been planted in the house of the Lord' he should bring forth abundant fruit."

Grace thanked the Judge for his explanation and said it was so much easier to understand when the tree stood right before them.

"I think," remarked Willie, addressing Captain Thompson, "I heard you say at the hotel you were going to take on board a cargo of bananas."

"Yes," responded the Captain, "I will take on a deck load. I am full of palm oil and other African produce, but I will call at Havre, and so will carry as many bananas as the deck will hold."

"I should think they would be washed away," said Johnny.

"Each bunch," continued the Captain, "is carefully put up in a long narrow basket, well stuffed with the

DATE PALM, GRAND CANARY

dried leaves, and a canvas cover sewed over the end, through the centre of which the stem protrudes. Packed in this way they will bear pretty rough treatment without injury."

"How much do they bring?" asked Frank.

"They will average," replied the Captain, "at least a dollar and a quarter a bunch. We get twenty-five cents for freight; another twenty-five may be set down for the cost of the basket, packing, and commission; leaving seventy-five cents to be divided between the shipper and the grower."

Grant desired to know how long it took them to grow.

The Captain did not know exactly, but he thought it was somewhat more than a year.

Lulu inquired whether there were any wild canary birds on the island.

The guide said there were, but he thought not very many. "When the island was discovered," said he, "it was covered with trees and bushes, and there were many canaries; but now the trees are cut down and the ground cultivated, so there are few places for them to hide. Those that are offered for sale in the shops are raised in captivity, which is easier and cheaper than to try and catch wild ones."

The carriages now returned from the village and were followed by a number of brown-faced children who doubtless wanted to have a look at the strangers. They were too timid to come very near, but stopped a little distance down the road and gazed with undisguised admiration at the young tourists, perhaps wondering if that were the sort of people who lived in the lands beyond the sea. However, it is quite as likely they did not think anything, for in this priest-ridden country the common people are kept as ignorant as the dumb beasts who share their labors.

Two women came with the children, each bringing a bunch of fresh dates. The Judge sent the guide to buy them and then distributed the fruit among the party. They were sweet and good, but did not taste very different from the dried ones at home.

The Ogowe Band were sorry to leave their camping-place; it was so pleasant, and the little brook, singing merrily as it hurried on its way, had quite won their hearts; but the sun was turning toward the west, and both Captains were anxious to get back to their ships. The horses were refreshed by their dinner and willing to make good speed homewards, and by four o'clock they were rattling through the streets of Las Palmas, and soon drew up in front of the hotel. Here they had a cup of coffee while they rested a little, and then walked down to the boat-landing, for Captain Thompson had left word for his steam-launch to meet him there with his boat in tow, at five o'clock. The boat would not hold so large a number, but by transferring the boys to the launch, and steaming slowly, they went along nicely enough.

Captain Thompson left his friends at the Nubia, and after expressing his thanks for the pleasant day he had spent, and wishing them a hearty "bon voyage," he went over to his own ship.

CHAPTER V.

TROPICAL VOYAGING.

THE Nubia sailed from the harbor of Las Palmas a few minutes before sundown. As they passed the Kisanga she was just heaving anchor, and she followed close behind them. Captain Thompson was on the bridge and he waved his hand at the young voyagers as they passed. The two steamers kept near each other until they reached the Point, when the Nubia turned to the right down the eastern shore of the island, and the Kisanga headed for Cape Finisterre on the Spanish coast.

The Ogowe Band had enjoyed a full day, and were quite disposed to act upon the Captain's suggestion to go to bed early. During the night the island was lost sight of, and next morning nothing was to be seen but sky and water. The ship was steaming nearly parallel with the Great Desert and was heading for Cape Blanco.

The young voyagers were up early, and after a good romp and a hearty breakfast, they settled down in their comfortable chairs beneath the awning and talked of the great sandy desert along which they were sailing.

"Is it all nothing but sand?" asked Hattie.

"No," answered the Judge, "some portions of it are fertile, and again other portions are stony, and there are many hills."

"What is such a great barren waste good for?" inquired Mamie.

"It must be admitted," replied the Judge, "that it is not very valuable, and yet it is made to serve some useful purposes. Quite a good many people live there; it is a great natural stove warming the Mediterranean and the Southern coast of Europe, and it serves as a Northern rampart to protect the great negro nations who live in the central portion of the African continent."

Laura desired to know what the Judge meant by his last remark, and so he continued: "If you will take a map of Africa and look at it carefully, you will see that God has hedged in the negro nations in a way truly wonderful. On the north is the Great Desert, on the northeast the Nubian Desert, and on the south the Kalahari Desert. Both the east and west coasts are devoid of good harbors, the rivers empty by deltas that are not easily found, and the climate is so unhealthy that no colonies can be successful. Such a combination of circumstances cannot be found anywhere else in the world. Design is plainly evident in all this, and God undoubtedly has an interesting and important future in store for the black race."

"What do you think this future may be?" asked Robbie.

"I do not know," was the reply, "but I think it means at least the preservation of the race. In America, all portions of which are reasonably healthy, the native races are melting away before the advance of the Caucasian,

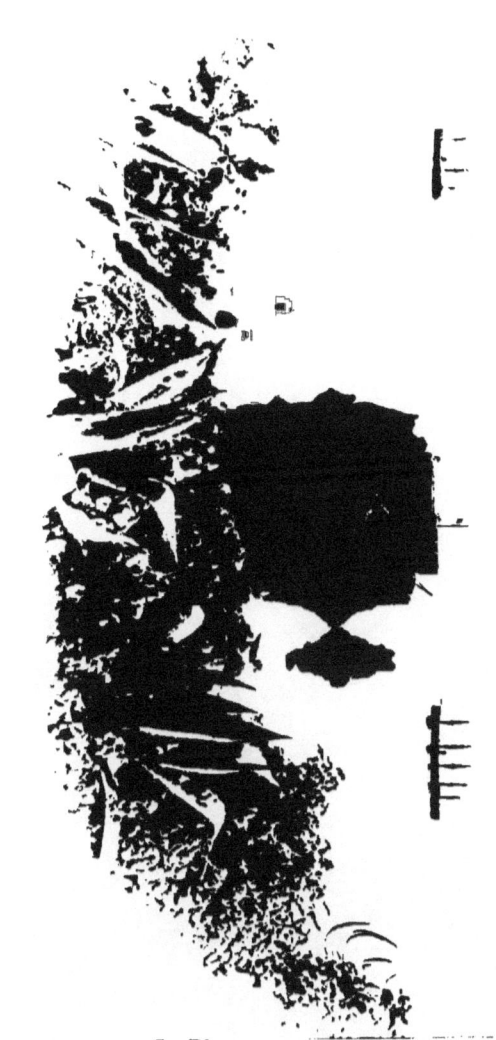

LOU ROCK, MADEIRA

but unless climatic conditions change, the negro will remain to the end of time."

The Captain now joined the party and Grace told him they were talking about the desert.

"Were you ever there?" inquired Jessie.

"Some few years ago," said he, "I called at a place nearly opposite to where we are now, to land some cargo, mostly provisions and other supplies. A French company were trying to cut a channel through the sand so as to let the sea flow into the desert and fill it up."

The Band gave an exclamation of surprise. "Fill up the desert with water! Now that's an idea," laughed Lulu.

The Judge said he had heard something of this before, and requested the Captain to tell them what he knew of the enterprise.

"Well," was the reply, "you know of course that a portion of the desert is below the sea-level, indeed much of it was once an inland sea. This sea, like the Mediterranean, was connected with the Atlantic by a narrow strait. The surf on this part of the coast is very heavy, and in course of ages this strait was gradually filled with sand; when it was entirely closed, the water that was left in this sea was evaporated and became the sandy waste we now find there."

"When did this take place?" inquired Frank.

"Since the Christian era," was the reply, "for there are records to show that in the time of Constantine there were lakes or reedy marshes in the southwestern portion."

"Only think," exclaimed Hattie, "if the canal were finished, we might pass through and sail direct to Timbuctoo!"

The Band thought that would be just jolly, but the Captain told them he thought they would have to wait awhile, as the enterprise was abandoned and not likely soon to be resumed. He then explained to them that the work was a very expensive one and not likely to bring large returns, as the traffic passing through would not be great, at least for a long time to come.

While they were talking, there was a flash of light through the air that made them start, and a bright object fell at their feet. It was a fine plump fish about ten inches long. The large pectoral fins spreading out on each side like wings, showed the new-comer to be a flying-fish.

The young voyagers were delighted; they examined the fish carefully, and were greatly pleased with its silvery appearance.

"It looks like our Delaware river rock-fish," exclaimed Johnny.

"It is lighter colored than a rock-fish; see, it has no stripes on the side," replied Saxe.

The Purser, who had just come up stairs, joined the party, and informed them that it closely resembled the African mullet.

The Captain told them that flying-fish often came on board at night, being attracted probably by the headlight; but that many more came on board sailing-ships than on steamers, perhaps because sailing-ships traveled more slowly and quietly.

"Would he be good to eat?" asked Hattie.

"Yes," answered the Captain, "they are excellent eating, and you shall have this one for breakfast to-morrow. He then blew his pocket whistle as a signal to the quartermaster who was working about the saloon-deck. The man promptly responded with a respectful "Aye, Sir," at the same time tipping his cap, and Captain Davis told him to give the fish to the steward with instructions to have it nicely cooked for the young ladies' breakfast.

The girls wanted to know more about these wonderful fish. The Captain told them they were everywhere plentiful in the warmer regions of the earth.

"Why do they fly?" inquired Jessie.

"To get away from their enemies," was the reply. "When they are chased by larger fish, they leap from the water to escape pursuit."

Laura asked whether in flying they flap their wings like birds, or only sustain themselves in the air by the impetus of their leap.

The Captain said he could not tell; he had never seen any motion to their wings, but as these were nearly transparent, especially when wet, it was a hard matter to determine whether they moved them or not.

The conversation now turned upon fishes and fishing, a subject in which both boys and girls took a deep interest. The Purser told them there was a species of fish that had a soft flat head of such a nature that it could, and did, attach itself to the sides of ships and thus be carried along with the vessel without any effort of its own. "These fish," said he, "will attach themselves to the bottom of a steamer and hold on there until something is thrown overboard, when they will go and eat what they can of it, and then come back to the ship again. In this way they can make a long voyage with us."

"Come now, what are you giving us?" exclaimed Willie.

"We may be young," observed Grant, "but we want a better bait than that on the hook before we bite."

The Purser asked to be excused a moment, and he soon returned with a large handful of breadcrusts from the pantry. After looking intently over the side, he called the young folks to come and look too. "There," said he, pointing down in the water, "do you see that fish?" Some of them saw a break in the water close to the ship's side, and a few feet below the surface; but most of them could distinguish nothing owing to the waves. "Now," continued the Purser, "you watch closely while I throw some bread in the water." He went forward a little and then threw half of the bread overboard; as it struck the water a large fish, perhaps three feet long, darted from the ship's side and swam for the bread.

Exclamations of surprise burst from a dozen young throats, and even the Judge was somewhat taken back. Presently the Purser threw the rest of the bread, and this time two fish were plainly seen to swim for it.

After this lesson the Ogowe Band were less skeptical, and the Captain tried his hand at a fish story. "There is," said he, "in the beautiful bay of Loanda, in the province of Angola, a fish that is certainly remarkable. This fish grows to a length of several feet, and it has a habit of coming beneath vessels that are at anchor and making a doleful noise, as of a man in great pain. Oftentimes the crews of sailing-ships are not able to sleep for these noises, and must get up in the night and splash on the water to drive them away."

"Do you tell that for a fact?" queried the Judge.

"Yes sir," replied the Captain, "it is a fact." The sailors say the fish put their backs against the vessel when they make these noises, but how that is I cannot say."

"Do sharks ever come near the steamers?" inquired Grace.

NATIVE WOMEN, GOLD COAST

"Yes," said the Captain, "the water is full of them."

"O my!" exclaimed Mamie, "to think that we are surrounded by sharks!"

"Well," responded the Captain, "they won't hurt you as long as you stay on board the ship."

Frank desired to know if sharks really could tell when there was a dead body on a ship.

"I cannot say," answered the Captain, "but it seems to be at least probable. They do seem to know if there is a serious case of sickness on board. I have known a shark to follow a ship for days when a man has been sick. Sailors bear a shark no good will, perhaps as much for this reason as any other."

"Are sharks good to eat?" asked Saxe.

"Not very," responded the Captain, "the meat is dry and coarse, and not of good flavor. I have eaten a young shark that tasted pretty fairly, but perhaps it was because we had been eating salt meat for a long time."

"I have heard that sharks will swallow almost anything," observed the Judge.

"Indeed they can," said the Purser. "I remember I was once in the West Indies when a shark was washed up dead on the beach. He was an enormous fellow, full eighteen feet long. Such an occurrence is very rare, and the natives naturally flocked to the shore to see it. They examined it carefully, and there was much speculation as to how it came to its death, for there were no marks of violence upon it. Presently one of the more thoughtful ones opened its mouth, which was as large as a trap-door, and looked in. To his surprise he saw a half-barrel full of fish; a careful examination led them to conclude that an empty half-barrel, with one head out, must have been floating on the water. The shark no doubt supposing this was a man or some other dainty morsel, swallowed it, and was unable to spit it out again. The open end of the half-barrel being up, after that all the fish he caught went into the half-barrel, and he starved to death."

The Judge thought he detected a certain air of improbability running through the story, but he said nothing, and just then the bell rang for lunch, which put an end to story telling.

When they came on deck again a large school of porpoises were coming near the steamer. They were a little distance ahead, and they were coming so as to cross the steamer's track. There were a great many of them, apparently several hundreds, and they were constantly leaping in the air as they hurried forward.

The Ogowe Band were delighted, and quite excited too, for the sight of so many wild creatures leaping in the air, and so near to them, was calculated to warm older blood than theirs. It was not long before the steamer was close up to them. They did not appear to be at all afraid of the vessel, for some dived under it, while others swam right alongside, not six feet away, and acted just as if they were trying to race with the ship. It was indeed a wondrous sight; one which even old travelers view with delight. The water was so clear that those that were near the Nubia could be seen as they put forth all their energies to keep up with the steamer. They would be swimming along some feet beneath the surface, when, without any warning, they would leap in the air, make a blowing noise, and dart down again into the sea.

Robbie asked why they made the noise.

The Captain told them the porpoise was not a fish like a shark, but a warm-blooded animal like a pig, and he needed to come to the surface to breathe quite as much as a whale. "They have a blow-hole," said he, "on top of their heads near the eyes; when they leap from the water they blow out the air from their lungs, take fresh breath and then dive down again."

"I thought," said Lulu, "they just jumped for fun."

"No," continued the Captain, "they come up to breathe, for they cannot remain long at a time under water." The porpoises were plucky fellows, and kept up the race for some time. But they were not a match for the tireless arms of the engine, and so by and by they dropped astern.

The Ogowe Band sat down and begged the Captain to tell them about porpoises. He was always willing to oblige his little passengers, and besides was not averse to spinning a yarn.

"The sailors," said he, "call the porpoise a 'sea-pig,' because it looks much like a pig when it jumps from the water. When I was a boy in a sailing ship, we did not have so many kinds of preserved food as we have now; indeed we had little else but salt pork, salt beef and hard tack. Then, too, our voyages were much longer than they are now, and we were glad enough to get a bit of fresh meat of any kind. It often happened that porpoises would come about when we had but little wind and the ship was almost motionless in the water. At such times one of the sailors would go forward on the bowsprit and when a porpoise came near, harpoon it. As soon as the porpoise was struck he would splash about at a great rate, but soon his strength would be exhausted and the poor fellow would be hauled up on deck by plenty of willing hands whose only thought was of the good dinner in store for them. The skin is an inch thick; when shaved quite thin it makes excellent leather. Underneath the skin is a layer of fat from which oil of a fine quality may be extracted. The flesh is dark colored and full of blood, and we sailors used to think it was excellent eating. Perhaps we might think differently now, although I must say I should like a nice porpoise steak to-day."

The Band thanked him for the information, and the Judge added that in former times the flesh was highly esteemed and reckoned fit for the table of royalty. In the time of Queen Elizabeth it was still used by the nobles of England, and was served up with bread-crumbs and vinegar. The young folks thought they would like to have some, but the Captain said he could not afford to stop a steamer for the sake of catching a porpoise.

The ship's Doctor now came on deck and stood by the rail looking out over the sea. Turning to our young friends he asked if they had seen the "Portuguese men-of-war." They did not quite understand him but they went to the side of the ship and the Doctor pointed to some delicate pink shells that were floating on the blue waves; these, he told them, were the nautilus, or as the sailors call them, "Portuguese men-of-war."

The little mariners held up two arms that had broad hands spread to the wind and answered very well for sails, while other arms rested on the water and were doubtless used as paddles. The shells appeared very delicate, and perhaps large enough to hold half-a-pint. Hundreds of them were in sight, all sailing before the wind, and apparently enjoying the warm air and bright sunlight.

The young folks asked the Doctor to tell them about these little fish that sailed along so jauntily in their beautiful pink yachts.

He replied, "The nautilus belongs to an interesting order of mollusca now reduced to a few species, but which were very abundant in some of the geological periods. They are found only in very warm climates. The shell is divided into sections, and the animal lives only in the outside one. The inside sections may be filled either with air or water, as the owner desires. It commonly inhabits the bottom of the sea, walking about in search of its food which consists of small shell-fish. It has a beak something like a parrot, with the edges notched, so that it can hold on to shells and break them.

"At certain times they come to the surface to sail about in the bright sunlight, as you have seen them to-day."

Johnny told the Doctor he had heard the chief officer say something about the "trades" not being strong, and he desired to know what that meant.

The Doctor explained to them that they were now in the northeast trade-wind region, that the sailors call these winds "the trades," and that what the chief officer wished to say was that these winds were not strong this voyage.

"The great heat in the equatorial region," said he, "causes the air to rise; the colder air from the temperate regions rushes in to fill the vacuum. If there were no disturbing elements this would produce a due north and south wind coming directly toward the equator from either side; but the earth is turning rapidly from west to east, more rapidly indeed than the air does; the conseqence is that these air currents are given a westerly direction, and become in the northern hemisphere a northeast wind, and in the southern hemisphere a southeast wind. These winds, to some extent, follow the sun; the northeast trades sometimes come up as far as Madeira, and then again their northern limit is a day's steaming south of the Canaries. Sometimes, too, they are stronger than others, but they always blow in one direction."

The Band thanked the Doctor, and then resumed their seats. They found the Judge and the Captain talking about the sea-serpent.

"Do you believe there is such a thing as a sea-serpent?" asked the Judge.

"That is a direct question," responded the Captain, "and I am not able to answer it directly. It is the fashion of the time to laugh at any one who thinks he has seen what may be a sea-serpent. On several occasions ship-captains have come forward to make oath to what they have witnessed, and their chief reward has been ridicule by the newspapers. These papers have suggested that the Captains were tipsy when they thought they saw the great snakes. For this reason mariners are reluctant to testify to what they have seen, through fear of being treated as impostors. I have never seen the monster myself, but I recognize the fact that the testimony of one man who has seen a thing, is worth more than that of a thousand who have not seen it. Many hundreds of persons, in different parts of the world, have seen the sea-serpent, and I do not see why the truth of its existence may not be considered established. If the size of these monsters causes you landsmen to be skeptical, you should remember there are inhabitants of the deep that quite equal them in bulk. Whales that exceed eighty feet in length are not uncommon, and when we consider their great thickness we can easily have enough to make a first-class sea-serpent, and leave a few tons to spare."

"Fossil remains of reptiles that lived ages ago in your own State of New Jersey have been found," said the Doctor, "that could swallow a full-sized man as easily as a frog swallows a fly. This has been proved by geologists beyond a doubt. If such things have lived, why is it impossible for some members of this reptile family to be still prowling about in the depths of the ocean?"

The Judge replied that he considered this evidence to be of a somewhat negative character, and that for the present he would withhold his decision; but he would say this, if any of the reptiles the Doctor referred to were still living, they must at least be aged.

The party now broke up; the girls went down stairs to prepare for dinner, and the boys took a stroll forward among the men. Their minds were full of what they had just heard, and Frank asked the boatswain if he could tell them anything about the sea-serpent.

"Sure and is it the sea-sarpint ye would be after inquir'en of me about?" said he. "Won day in forty-nine, when we men were comin' from Californy, we were becalmed in the West Ingies, and the Cap'en, he sez to me, sez he, 'Mike, what is that pint o'land on the lee bow?' sez he. Sez I, 'wait till I clap my weather eye on it Cap'en,' and when I looked I tole him, I be blowed if I knowed. That pint o'land was all covered with scales like, intromingled with long hair, and its eyes flashed fire and smoke at interwals. By and by it begun to sink and it kep' on a sinken fur three days hand-runnin, and if that ain't a sea-sarpint fur ye I don't know what is wun."

The boys listened with awe to this story of the ancient mariner, and they went back to the cabin without asking any more questions.

In the evening, as they all sat upon the deck enjoying the beauties of the night, the Judge told his young companions about the cochineal they had seen the women gathering at Grand Canary.

"Cochineal," said he, "consists simply of the bodies of a species of insect that feeds upon plants of the cactus family, particularly upon one known in Mexico as the Nopal. This plant is nearly allied to the prickly pear. The insect is a small creature of a deep red color, and has white wings. It is calculated that it takes seventy thousand of them in a dried state to weigh a pound. The gathering of the cochineal is very tedious and is accomplished by brushing the branches of the cactus with the tail of a squirrel or other animal. The insects are killed either by boiling water, or by heating them in ovens. It is cultivated in the Canary Islands and Mexico, but has never succeeded in the East Indies.

The Captain told his young passengers that as they had now reached the warmer waters of the tropics, it would be well for them to come out every morning at sunrise when the decks were washed down, and have a bath under the hose. They accepted his suggestion, and after this, as long as they remained on the Nubia, they came out every morning when they heard the sailors scrubbing the decks and had a good shower bath and a frolic. A strong pump, run by the engine, throws a stream of salt water through the hose and is an excellent means for giving a man a ducking. The girls did not care to get up quite so early and when they were ready they had a salt water plunge in the bath-room.

The Captain had a large goat named Billy. He was a great favorite among the men who had much rude sport with him. Billy was strongly inclined to strike things with his head. When he wished to make an examination of any strange object, his fashion was to rear high on his hind legs and come down against it with his head with all his force. The sailors thought this was very funny

LADY OF HIGH RANK, OLD CALABAR

and they looked upon him as one of the crew. There was one sad trial in Billy's life. Every morning when the decks were washed down, Billy had to be washed too. Four men were detailed for this job. They skirmished around the deck until Billy was caught and then led him, a defiant but unhappy prisoner, to a place near the after hatch where he was lashed "fore and aft" to the side of the ship and the hose turned on him. When he was thoroughly soaked a sailor came carefully up to him and soaped him all over, and then he was thoroughly rinsed again with the hose. Poor Billy was not fond of his morning bath; sometimes he tried to hide, and at other times he showed fight and was only captured after a lively tussle, but in the end he would be forced to submit and take his regular washing.

Among the sailors was an old man, who, by some means had been taken as one of the crew. He was not well when the steamer left Liverpool, and had grown gradually worse until half-past three, when he died; the body was sewn up in a sack and laid on a grating. The funeral took place two hours later on the main-deck in front of the Captain's room. An empty pork barrel was covered with a flag and one end of the grating was to be laid on this, and the other end was to rest on the bulwark. When all was ready, the bell was tolled, the engines stopped, the body on the grating brought aft and laid in its place. The passengers, together with as many of the ship's company as could be spared, gathered around while the Purser read the burial service. Then one end of the grating was raised, the body slid off into the sea, the Purser read a prayer and the benediction, and all was over. At the Captain's command the engines were started "full speed ahead," and the ship resumed her voyage.

It was a solemn scene, and the little voyagers shuddered as they thought of the possibility of one of their own number being thrown overboard.

"Poor old man," said Lulu, "I wonder if he had any one to love him!"

"Very likely he has an old wife," responded Laura, "who will be expecting him when the ship returns, and then she will hear that she will never see him again."

The voyage lost some of its charm after the death of the old sailor, and the Ogowe Band were not sorry, when, seven days after leaving Las Palmas, they saw they were approaching land. The water was no longer clear as it had been, and to the eastward, as well as ahead, a low, dark line of vegetation appeared above the water; this was their first sight of the great African continent.

Early in the afternoon the shore line began to take on a definite form and they saw they were steaming into a bay, the shores of which were low and covered with a thick growth of trees and bushes. Ahead of them, on a low, rocky cape, was a tall light-house that marks the entrance to the harbor, or, rather, river of Sierra Leone. By 4 P. M. they were abreast of the light-house; and, turning sharply to the left, they steamed up the river to the anchorage in front of the town.

The young travelers gazed with intense interest upon their first African landscape, and they felt almost oppressed by the rich, dense verdure which crowded upon their vision. Groves of oil-palms, their feathery arms like great ostrich plumes, waving in the gentle breeze; and tall cotton-woods, covered with a wealth of vines completely hiding the trunks and converting them into great columns of living green, especially attracted their attention. Beneath the palms and almost hidden from view were clusters of little brown houses, the homes of the native Africans. Upon the water were small canoes in which men were engaged in catching fish, while larger canoes were sailing by, doubtless returning home after having disposed of their produce in the town.

The air was very warm, and there was a steaminess about it that was distinctly noticeable, and which made them disinclined to any exertion, or, as Hattie expressed it, "It made them feel like a wet rag." The town is twenty miles above the light-house, and they came to anchor just before sundown, giving them an opportunity to get a little idea of the place before it was time to go below for dinner.

Freetown is beautifully situated at the foot of a mountain three thousand feet high, on the south bank of the Sierra Leone River, and is surrounded on the east and south by a magnificent amphitheatre of hills and mountains. The slopes of this mountain are covered with a tall, coarse grass, with here and there a few trees; and, for some distance up, is dotted with neat little villages, and the country residences of foreign merchants. Along the water a heavy wall has been built, with a pier where passengers and cargo may be landed. In a sheltered cove is the coaling station, and on the hillside above the town are the barracks for the troops. Our friends were surprised to find the town so solidly built, and having such an appearance of civilization in this out-of-the-way corner of the world. Many of the buildings were of stone, and from the steamer's deck appeared solid and substantial.

In the evening as they were seated upon deck the Judge told his young companions something of the history of Sierra Leone. "During the war of the revolution," said he, "a large number of blacks ranged themselves under the British banner. At the close of the war they followed the army to London; and, when that disbanded, they found themselves strangers in a strange land. The Government determined to colonize them on the coast of Africa, so they were brought out here and founded the present city of Freetown. In 1807 the slave-trade was declared piracy by England, and a squadron was stationed on the coast for the purpose of suppressing it. All the slaves taken by the British cruisers have been brought to this colony and discharged here; this has been the main source of its increase of population."

The Captain added that there was a good system of common-school education, together with some higher academies, and that the language spoken was English. He also told them that the Governor was an Englishman, but the rest of the civil officers were black men; the troops too were natives, with a few white officers. The Purser informed them that the Sierra Leone people were great scamps, an opinion they afterward found everywhere prevalent on the coast.

REGENT STREET, SIERRA LEONE

CHAPTER VI.

SIERRA LEONE AND LIBERIA.

HE next morning the Ogowe Band were out early, for the decks were washed soon after the change of the watch at four o'clock; and before this work was finished they took their usual bath under the hose, so they were quite ready for coffee and toast at six o'clock.

It was a glorious morning. A shower had fallen during the night, and, as the sun rose above the "Lone Mountain," its beams were reflected from millions of tiny drops, which still covered the grass and leaves like liquid gems. The air was deliciously soft and sweet with the fragrance of the luxurious vegetation; yet, with all its freshness, it induced a lassitude that disinclined one to active exertion. The inclination was to sit down and quietly enjoy the scene, moving about with any animation requiring a conscious effort.

Several boats had already come alongside the steamer, and the Judge engaged two of these to take the party ashore. The Captain was busy with a number of things that required his attention, and could not go with them.

The heavy stone steps of the pier made an excellent landing; and, as there was no surf, it was an easy matter to step ashore from the boats. Quite a crowd of loafers and idlers were sitting and standing about, but there were no beggars as at Madeira. At the market-landing a little distance away were a number of large country boats unloading plantains, bananas, yams, and other farm produce. These boats were quite good-sized and had four rowers seated in the middle to use the oars when there was no wind.

Our friends ascended by a broad flight of steps to the level of the town, and then passed along the street, first of all to the market-house. This was a large stone building and arranged inside very much like the old markets in the streets of Philadelphia. In the open space in front of the market a great number of women were seated beside small piles of fruit and vegetables which they had brought for sale. Customers were solicited in loud tones to purchase, and the din of the traffic was heard everywhere. Most of the bargaining was carried on in what, to our young tourists, was an unknown tongue; but occasionally English was heard. The principal articles of trade seemed to be plantains, yams, bananas, peppers, limes, and a number of strange looking vegetables and fruits of which our young friends did not know the name. Ginger-cakes, pies, and other articles of cookery, were also displayed, and eagerly purchased by the hungry countrymen.

From the market our young friends passed through the streets of the business portion of the town. The shops contained a fair asssortment of the cheaper varieties of dry-goods and various nick-nacks; and, on one of the corners they saw a really excellent grocery store. Most of the shops were kept by black people, but occasionally a white face was seen; these were very pale and had a deathly look which quite startled our young tourists.

They had not gone far when, on turning a corner, they met a procession which proved to be a funeral. The body was in a decent cloth-covered coffin, carried upon the shoulders of four men, and was followed by a long train of well-dressed men and women. After the funeral cortege had passed, the Judge and his young companions continued their walk. They were surprised to find the streets so clean and in such good order, and the houses and stores so substantially built.

"There is a photographer's," observed Lulu. "Perhaps he might have some pictures to sell."

"I think it would be well for us to go in," responded Mr. McGee, and so in they went.

The stock of ready-made pictures was not large and they were mostly either buildings or groups of faces. The artist informed them there was but little demand for pictures of tropical scenery. "Most of the people who have pictures taken," said he, "wish to send home a likeness of the house they live in or the store where they work, and that is all they care for." The prices were high and the Judge bought but few,—more to have some little souvenirs of Sierra Leone than anything else.

They now visited the residence portion of the town. The houses scarcely came up to the American idea of beauty and comfort, and yet, for a tropical town they were well built, and quite suitable for a hot climate. Most of them had small yards with a few coarse flowers; and the boys noticed chickens and ducks, with occasionally a pig, and a good many black babies.

The Judge now proposed that they visit the fort, and to this his young companions were quite agreed. A fine broad road wound by gradual ascent up the hillside and presently brought them to the parade ground. The commander of the fort happened to be on the piazza of his house, and seeing they were strangers, he sent an orderly to invite them to call upon him. The invitation was gladly accepted for the sun was getting very hot, and our friends were in a dripping perspiration from their exertions.

The commander received them cordially and led the way to a balcony where they had an excellent view of the town and harbor. As our friends politely declined wine, coffee was presently served, and in the meanwhile the commander gave them a graphic description of the country. He told them the country-people were quite distinct from the town-people. "These latter," said he, "were brought here by British cruisers and call themselves Englishmen; yet they are inferior in many respects to the native races, who indeed lack education, but are a sturdy, manly set of people." He also informed them that Great Britain claimed the ownership of the interior, but that practically the native tribes were independent except those who lived in the neighborhood of Freetown; the difficulties of travel were so great, and the climate so unhealthy, that the back country was simply left to itself. "There is no such thing as systematic cultivation," he continued, "but the bush-people gather the spontaneous products of the forest, and these are brought to town by native traders. As a consequence, the trade of the port is small, and if it were not for the money the steamers, the government, and the missionary societies, spend, the town would be poor enough."

The Judge inquired if missionary operations in the colony had been successful, and what were the visible results.

The commander replied that this was a difficult question to answer; that much had been accomplished but that much still remained to be done. "There is a very general disposition on the part of foreign residents," said he, "to cry down missions, and proclaim them failures, but I have observed, that as a rule the private life of such persons will not bear close inspection. On the other hand, there are some missionaries sent out who are not worthy to be such; some are quarrelsome, and others are unwise in their methods, but a goodly proportion of them are earnest, devoted men, and are a real blessing to the country. Of one thing I am sure, it is much easier for me to govern this mixed population than it would be if there were no missionaries. Whatever the individual faults of these men may be, their influence is always on the side of law and order.

"Now, as to the visible effects of their work, there is, first, an entire absence of human sacrifice and devil worship. Second, several churches in which well-dressed and devout congregations assemble every Sabbath. Third, a higher grade of morality, and a higher public sentiment than there would be without them. On the whole, the missionary movement, while it has failed to accomplish all that some had hoped for, may yet, in my opinion, be called a success."

It was now eleven o'clock and the commander invited the Judge and his party to have some breakfast with him, which invitation they thankfully accepted. At the table there were several junior officers and their conversation soon became animated and general.

"I think this is a very hot country," said Grace, speaking to a young Lieutenant beside her.

"Not so hot as it is sometimes in Senegambia," he replied; "that country, as you know, borders on the Great Desert, and occasionally they have winds called the Harmatan, which blow for two or three days and feel as if they came from a furnace. It dries up everything and makes the country appear as if scorched; even the skin cracks and blisters from the extreme heat. During its prevalence all business is suspended, and the people devote themselves to keeping cool."

"I don't see how they can do it," responded Grace.

"The best plan that has yet been discovered," continued the Lieutenant, "is to sit in jars. Large earthen jars about five feet high, with a stool or a low seat in them, are kept in the house. When the Harmatan begins to blow, the house is closed and each of the inmates gets in a jar and remains there until it has spent its force."

"Those must be family jars," observed Jessie, who had been listening attentively.

"Might we not call them preserving jars," answered the Lieutenant, "since they preserve their contents from the heat?"

"Do you have any telegraphs in Sierra Leone?" asked Saxe of a lively young orderly next to him.

"No," he replied, "it is torn down as fast as we can build it up."

"How is that?" inquired Saxe.

"It is all because of the monkeys," pursued the orderly. "A monkey is as full of curiosity as a girl, and as mischievous as a boy. As soon as the men put up the line and move away, the monkeys come about to see what the men have been doing; of course they find the poles and wire, and, after a careful inspection, they conclude it must have been put up for them. They evidently intend to show their entertainers that they appreciate their efforts. For they go at once into the forest and call all their friends and acquaintances and then have a jolly time together. They climb the poles and jump and play upon the wires to such an extent that both wires and poles are dragged down and the line destroyed. As fast as we can replace the poles and wires the monkeys tear them down, and so we have given it up for a bad job."

Saxe listened to the young Englishman's narrative with intense interest and then informed him that a somewhat similar experience had occurred to the company that first put up a telegraph line across the plains to California.

"There are no trees on those plains," said Saxe, "and the buffaloes had no way to scratch their backs; but when the poles were put up they thought they were just the thing, and crowded about them so eagerly for their turn, that the poles were thrown down. To remedy this the company sent to St. Louis, Chicago, and indeed all the cities, and bought up all the brad-awls they could find, and put these in the poles as high as the back of a large buffalo. But if the buffaloes were eager before, they were just frantic now, and fought their way through the mass of animals in order to get up to the poles, for the awls only barely reached through their thick coats, and the poles were thrown down more than at first."

"What did they do then?" eagerly inquired the orderly.

"Greased the poles," responded Saxe; and then there was a good laugh.

After lunch the party repaired again to the balcony, where the gentlemen smoked, and all drank coffee and had a good time talking about the country and its many objects of interest. At three o'clock the Judge and his young companions bade their kind entertainers good-bye and wended their way down to the landing. The sun was still very hot, but the sea-breeze coming in tempered the heat and the walk was a pleasant one. The Captain was glad to see them back again, for he hardly knew what had become of them.

At five o'clock the Nubia sailed, and her decks presented a more animated appearance than when she came in, for she had taken on board over fifty passengers. These passengers ate and slept on the deck, and, as Jessie truly observed, they did not want for fresh air. They found out afterward that a part of the company was an additional crew, which was shipped here to work the cargo while the steamer was on the African coast, and would be landed here again when the ship was homeward bound.

That evening as they sat upon the deck enjoying the cool breeze, Captain Davis told them it was so hot upon the coast, and especially in the rivers, that if the white crew did all the work, several of them would likely die; and so it was the custom for all vessels that sailed along the African coast to take on a crew of native men to do the heaviest work. "These men," said he, "get a regularly prescribed ration of rice and beef, and a shilling a day as wages, besides some extra allowances to the smartest of them." He told them they were called Kru-boys, had a language of their own, but all could talk a kind of pigeon-English which was universal on the coast. He also told them that in Africa native workmen and servants are always called "boys," no matter what their age or size might be.

Beyond the lighthouse were large banks and rocky reefs that compelled the Nubia to make a long detour in order to get around them. The next morning they were off the Liberian coast and at sundown passed Monrovia without calling. From the upper bridge, with the aid of glasses, the town could be distinctly seen; indeed it was near enough to be seen quite well with the naked eye. The town is small, the wooden houses scattered about apparently at random, and the large number of palms give it a pretty and picturesque appearance.

After dinner, as the party sat upon the deck in the quiet moonlight, the conversation turned upon Liberia, its history and present condition. The Judge told his young companions about the American Colonization Society and its effort to form an independent African Republic out of the negroes sent from America; while the Captain told of its utter failure.

"Your government made a great mistake," said he, addressing the Judge, "in sending out those negroes and then leaving them to care for themselves; colonial history everywhere shows that young communities in foreign lands need the fostering care of strong home governments. They need it just as much as an infant needs the care of a parent. Liberia was colonized with a better class of people than Sierra Leone, but it amounts to nothing; there is no freight, mail, or passengers, to be landed there, and so far as we are concerned, it might as well be a desert."

The Judge asked how all this came about, and he replied: "When the American negro came here, he felt himself quite above work and was content to be nothing less than a government official, a college professor, or a preacher; the native races would have nothing to do with them, and so they were just a pack of gentlemen together. No true success could come to such a people and they have been a hindrance to the native tribes rather than a help to them."

The Judge desired to know what was being done in the way of education, and in reply he learned there were a few small primary schools, some of which were called colleges, although the students might only be learning to read and spell; besides these there were a few small schools supported by various missionary societies.

"Does the country produce nothing for export?" inquired Frank.

"Almost nothing," was the reply; "a little coffee and cam-wood is about all."

"What is cam-wood?" asked Johnny.

"It is a tree that yields a valuable red dye," answered the Captain; the roots and stumps are the parts most used."

The Doctor now asked that he might read a few words about Liberia written by Professor Chase of Atlanta, Ga. Professor Chase made a personal inspection of the missions in Liberia, and he writes as follows: "In this connection allow me to make a remark about sending freedmen in large numbers to Africa. When they reach that shore there is no work for them to do; no one needs laborers. Although they may find plenty of land they cannot raise anything to sell; and after spending the little money they carry with them and wearing out the clothes on their backs, they must build mud huts, tie a handkerchief about their loins and feed on cassava. This, without exaggeration, is the present material status of the mass of the people, and must continue to be until Christianity and philanthropy teach them how to dig from the soil the accessories of a civilized life."

"That is just it," chimed in the Purser, "let them dig for a living, what do they want an education for, anyway? The better you educate a nigger the more able he is to cheat and steal."

"My friend," replied the Judge, "have you ever noticed that precisely the same is true of the white man? Is it not true that the 'American Colony' in Canada, of forgers and defaulters, are all educated men? Is not education a power which may be turned to good or evil accordingly as it is used? If education has been good for you and me, why may it not be good for these people? If it should be withheld from the African because he does not use it rightly, why should it not be withheld from us because a multitude of our race have by its means been able to injure others?"

The Purser did not attempt to combat this argument, but he asserted that: "Educate an African as much as you please, he will remain an African still," and so the conversation for the night closed. The following day they steamed along the Liberian coast at a distance of some three or four miles. The shores were low and covered with a rich forest growth. Every two or three miles were villages of the aborigines, the round pointed roofs forming a pleasing contrast to the heavy wall of living green. About these villages were great numbers of cocoanut trees, showing that the people were fond of its fruit. Canoes were drawn up on the beach in front of the houses; and many more were dancing on the waves, while their owners were engaged in drawing the finny denizens of the deep from their watery home. Occasionally great rocks were seen protruding from the water, against which the waves dashed with great force, throwing the spray high in the air. The Captain told them this was a dangerous coast, and that several steamers had come to grief on these rocks.

At four P. M. the steamer turned toward shore and anchored in front of a large native village called Sasstown, having first fired the cannon on the forecastle as a signal to the people to come off. The Judge inquired if cargo was to be put ashore here, and was told the stop was only made to get Kru-boys.

Presently a large number of canoes were seen coming off from land, and it was not long before they were alongside and their owners clambering upon deck. They were tall, handsome, finely developed men, with dark brown skins, woolly heads, and frank open faces. Most of them could speak the pigeon-English of the coast, and by this means were able to converse with the Captain. Some of the older of them had "books," or orders from traders further down the coast, to bring gangs of men with them, and these orders stated that the makers of them would pay the passage of such gangs to any captain who would bring them.

The Kru-boys were respectful but noisy, and had a great deal to say to one another and to those who had come on board at Sierra Leone. The canoes were not more than two feet wide and sometimes not so much as that, and they were turned up a little at each end. There were no benches or seats in them, but the Kru-men sat flat upon the bottom with their legs stretched out in front of them. Of course a good deal of water came in, mostly over the top, and the Ogowe Band were astonished to see the men bail it out with one foot, at the same time using the paddle with their hands.

"His foot is so flat it is as good as a scoop," observed Willie.

MISSION HOUSE, AXIM, GOLD COAST

"Yes," responded Johnny, "when they were climbing up the side I saw them take hold with their feet just as if they had been hands."

These were the first real wild Africans our young friends had ever seen, and they watched them with intense interest. Among the brown houses on shore, with the aid of a glass, the mothers and children could be seen moving about, and the young travelers wished they could go on shore and see this real African village and learn something of the life of its people. At sundown the Nubia resumed her voyage with about fifty of the Sasstown boys on board as passengers.

That evening, after dinner, the Captain told them that the Kru-men were the coolies of West Africa. "Strange as it may seem," said he, "there is everywhere on this coast, excepting just here, a scarcity of laborers; not because there are so few people, but because they will not work; consequently traders and others who employ labor must send here for men. These Kru-boys we took on board this afternoon go to different ports of the coast to work on a one year's engagement. Each gang is in charge of a headman who is responsible to the employer for the conduct of the men, and to the people in his native village for the safety of those under his care. A master seldom gives an order to one of his boys, but to the headman, and he sees that the work is done. So, too, when punishment is needed, the master pronounces sentence and the headman carries it into execution. Formerly it was not so, and in those days it was no unusual thing for traders to tie their men up and whip them to death; or to trice them up by their thumbs and so let them hang for hours in great agony. These practices are now rare, and as a rule the Kru-boys are treated with kindness and consideration. They receive as wages from one to two pounds sterling per month, and a regular daily ration of rice and meat, while on Saturday they get in addition a head of tobacco and a bottle of rum. Besides this they receive a new piece of cloth on the first Sunday in every month, which keeps them supplied with clothes, so all their earnings can be saved and taken home. Their employers pay the passage both ways, and altogether the Kru-boys have a very comfortable time of it."

"What do they do with their wages?" inquired Robbie.

"They use them mostly to buy wives with," said the Captain. "The old men are the rulers of the country, and in point of fact they own not only the property but the women and younger men as well. They compel the boys and younger men to 'go to sea,' as they express it, and when they return their wages are taken from them. If the boy is still young, he is given a little of the tobacco and rum and allowed to enjoy himself for a few days and is then shipped at the first opportunity under the care of some headman who is a friend or member of the family. When the boy has grown to man's estate, a wife is purchased for him and he is allowed to retain an increasingly large proportion of his wages, until by and by he himself becomes one of the governing class. I once asked a young man why it was the young men put up with such conduct on the part of the old men, and he answered that they hoped to do the same way when they got old."

Hattie wished to know what kind of food these people had to eat, and the Doctor told her it was usually rice. "Fish are not very abundant along here," said he, "and while there is some game in the bush, it is hard to get; so they have but little in the way of flesh, and are obliged to use palm-oil instead. When the rice is boiled, the rich yellow oil is poured over it and it makes a wholesome, and to them, palatable dish."

Frank asked how the rice was cultivated and the Doctor replied that when a piece of ground was selected the jungle was cut at the beginning of the dry-season and allowed to lie until the commencement of the rains. It is then burned and the rice is planted in little bunches among the stumps, and grows very readily. "It is the close of the rainy-season now," said he, "and the rice will be ready to harvest in a few days." The conversation continued until a late hour, for it was so pleasant upon deck that our friends were very reluctant to go to bed.

The steamer proceeded "dead slow" all night, and the next-morning they came to anchor at Grand Cess, which they found to be a large Kru village much like Sasstown. Some more Kru-boys were taken on here, and then the Nubia went on to Cape Palmas which place she reached in the afternoon.

Cape Palmas marks the southern boundary of Liberia and presents an inviting appearance as seen from the deck of a ship. A lighthouse stands on the extremity of the low rocky promontory and back of it are the houses of the Americo-Liberians. These are well built, mostly of stone, and give the place the appearance of a considerable degree of civilization and prosperity. In the beautiful bay to the north of the cape, is a large steamer high up on the sand. She was anchored too near in and with the turn of the tide she struck a rock which knocked a hole through her and she was run on the beach to prevent her from sinking. A wall of sand was soon thrown around her by the waves, and now she cannot be moved from her position.

Although Cape Palmas appeared to be a place of considerable importance, yet no cargo was put off here, and but few passengers were taken on. The Judge thought he would like to go ashore, but the Captain said the surf was too heavy, and besides there was scarcely time.

ELMINA, GOLD COAST

CHAPTER VII.

IVORY COAST AND GOLD COAST.

THE Nubia ran "dead slow" all night and the next morning made land near the Kavali river at a place called Taboo. She did not anchor but hove to under steam and fired a gun as a signal to the people on shore; it was not long before a fleet of canoes was seen, coming in answer to the summons.

Less than two years before this, the steamer Senegal was passing this part of the coast in the night, when by some mischance she ran ashore and was plundered by the natives. At first they contented themselves with robbing the ship; but when rum was found in the cabin, they all got drunk and were abusive to the passengers. These unfortunates were stripped of their valuables, and a finger was cut off the hand of one lady in order to obtain a ring which did not slip off easily. There is no telling what might not have happened to the unlucky passengers had not a passing steamer presently picked them up. The Senegal was homeward-bound and full of palm-oil and other African produce. The Kru-boys of course knew perfectly well how to work cargo and as soon as they sobered a little they set to work to rig up a spar and get out the oil. As each cask was hoisted over the side it was towed ashore, rolled across the narrow sandy beach, then towed across the lagoon and taken to the Kru-towns on the main-land.

Here on this lonely coast, an old Frenchman has a trading-post, and when the excitement about the wreck had quieted down the oil was brought and sold to him, and he made most of the profit out of the transaction after all. His trading-house, on a little bluff that jutted out into the sea, could be plainly seen from the ship.

The loss of the Senegal brought on a conversation about this part of the coast. The Captain told them that one of the most remarkable features of the geography of this part of the country is a long narrow lagoon extending from Cape Palmas to Cape Three Points, and separated from the ocean by a mere bed of sand seldom more than half a mile wide. This lagoon forms a sort of reservoir or back-water for the many streams that come down from the Kong mountains, and affords an excellent means for inland navigation without the risk and danger of passing through the surf to the open ocean. Some of the rivers that empty into this lagoon are navigable for canoes to the very foot of the mountains, and the country is rich in all natural products, but so unhealthy that white people can hardly live there.

This part of Africa, as far as Cape Appolonia, is called the Ivory Coast, but at the present time very little ivory is shipped, the trade being almost entirely in palm-oil and kernels. Some more of the Kru-boys were taken on board at Taboo, and the Nubia steamed away to the eastward.

All day long they were in sight of the shore which, though low and flat, was covered with a dense vegetation forming a dark line of living green that was wondrously beautiful as the brilliant sunlight of the tropic skies streamed down upon it. Every mile or two little brown villages lay embosomed among the rich cocoa-nut groves that in many places lined the beach.

The decks of the Nubia now presented an animated appearance as there were more than two hundred black passengers who had to eat, sleep and lodge there. All of these men had English names by which they were known among the white men, as their own native names were in many cases unpronounceable. The muster-roll showed the most common of the names to be Brass Pan, Jolly Nose, Sea Breeze, Tar Bucket, Snow Ball, Flying Jib, Salt Junk, Cod-Fish, Wool Pate, Bottle of Beer and other curious titles. Of these fine names they were very proud, quite as much so as white men are with Honorable, or Doctor of Divinity; and yet it was somewhat startling to inquire of some tall, handsome fellow what his name was, and have him answer with a proud smile of satisfaction, "My name, he be Pea Soup, sir."

The Ogowe Band were greatly interested in the way these people were fed. Rice was placed in large stationary kettles and cooked by steam supplied from the boilers. When done, every grain stood out distinct by itself and the whole mass looked wondrously white and attractive. Each head-man received an amount of this rice proportioned to the number of his men, and also a small piece of salt beef or pork. Each group then sat upon the deck, encircling its pan of rice, and watched in silence while the leader cut up the meat and handed each his little share. This was, to them, an important matter, and they looked on with a seriousness that indicated their appreciation of the gravity of the occasion. Each received his portion of meat with an evident sigh that it was not larger and prepared to make the most of the little he had. If it was a lean piece he carefully bit off a small portion, or if it was a piece of fat he sucked off a little of its richness, just so as to get the taste in his mouth; every right hand was now thrust into the central dish and a large handful of the steaming white rice taken and firmly pressed into a solid ball. The head was then thrown far back, the mouth opened to its greatest extent, the great ball of rice dropped in, the jaws closed—the patient was then ready to repeat the operation.

This is the way a native African dines, and as Lulu observed, "it may be called the natural method."

"Yes," added the Judge, who overheard the remark, "and this is the natural man. How do you like him?"

"I think I should prefer the artificial variety," responded Laura, and it was quite evident the rest of the Band agreed with her.

In the afternoon the steamer called at Little Bereby, and at Grand Bereby, and at each place took on a few more boys. There were now more than three hundred deck passengers and the ship appeared to be fairly alive with people.

Just before sundown they called at Jellah Coffee for a few fresh provisions. This is the only port on the coast where chickens, ducks and other fowls can be obtained; the people of Jellah Coffee make it their specialty, and from all appearance they do a thriving trade. This poultry is obtained from the towns on the various rivers that empty into the lagoon already referred to, and is sold to the steamers at reasonable prices for cash. In addition to the

CEMETERY AT ELMINA, GOLD COAST

poultry trade, the people gather up and ship by homeward-bound steamers many kinds of wild animals to be sold to menageries and zoological gardens. All wild animals have a market value, and may be consigned to commission houses the same as palm-oil and ivory.

One more day's steaming brought them to Grand Bassam, a rather desolate looking place with a glaring, white sandy beach, belonging to the French. Here there is an opening through the sandy beach into the lagoon; by means of a small steamer, vessels are towed in and out, and may thus load their cargoes in quiet waters. The French possessions here extend to the Assinee River, but they are neither large nor important. The unhealthiness of the country not only prevents colonization, but also retards commercial enterprises, and this century will probably witness little change on the Ivory Coast.'

The next port was Axim on the Gold Coast, where there are several gold mines just being opened up by English companies. Very little could be learned by our friends on the Nubia about these mines; after considerable inquiry they came to the conclusion that there was an abundance of gold, but owing to its inaccessibility, and the unhealthfulness of the climate, much earnest effort would be needed and some sacrifice of life to make its mining profitable; and that the present companies paid more attention to selling stocks and drawing salaries than they did to digging out the gold and reducing the ores.

The Gold Coast extends from Cape Appolonia to the River Volta and presents as much richness and variety of scenery as can, perhaps, be found anywhere in the world. Hills of every conceivable form and outline rise from the water, and verdant fields in graceful undulations stretch away toward the interior; while forests of palms and other tropical trees lend variety to a landscape which is a constant delight and of which the eye never tires. It is indeed a beautiful land, and, if adapted to the constitution of the white race, could be made almost a paradise.

The general aspect of the towns and villages on this part of the coast is scarcely less striking and varied. We find no more circular huts such as we saw on the Kru coast, but comparatively large quadrangular houses with clay walls, occasionally two stories in height. The appearance of these towns is rendered still more imposing by the presence of large European forts in their immediate vicinity. These forts were built more than three hundred years ago by the Portuguese, Dutch, Danish, Prussian and English governments, and number altogether not less than twenty-five. These forts were erected to protect the trade in gold-dust and slaves, the latter of which was particularly profitable. Only a few of these forts are now kept in repair and they have nearly all passed into the hands of the English who have established a sort of protectorate over the country.

These remarks apply only to the coast, for nowhere have towns or stations been formed in their interior, and such a thing as a carriage road or a railway does not exist. Missionary operations are carried on almost solely by English and German societies, and with fair average success. If the climate were such that missionaries and their families could live in the country for a lifetime, and their efforts were not counteracted by the lives of irreligious white men, in a century or two the whole continent might be converted to Christ. This, however, is supposing what cannot be, and so the influence of the Gospel, though it is sure to prevail in the end, will conquer only by slow, and oftentimes by painful degrees.

There was no opportunity for our friends to go ashore at Axim, but they were so fortunate as to secure two photographs by a native artist, which appear in this volume.

The people of the Gold Coast are quite different from the natives of the Grain and Ivory Coasts. They have not the fine muscular development, the manly, independent gait, or the frank, open countenance of the Kru-men; but they have more of a mechanical turn, and possess more of the comforts of life. Thus, while the Kru-men go in gangs to various parts of the coast to act as porters and day laborers, the men of the Gold Coast go in smaller numbers to work as carpenters, blacksmiths, stokers, tailors and jack-washers.

Slavery exists not only here, but everywhere upon the West coast; and as society is now constituted, it is a necessity. Here, as well as in Christian lands, there is a criminal population; the Christian nations build prisons and shut the vicious up in them; the Pagan African sells him for a slave, where he can have a certain amount of freedom, but must do some work and submit to the will of another. Of course, while African slavery is not so severe as American slavery, yet it is an evil and gives rise to many abuses. One of these is the system of pawning, now very general wherever that trade is carried on. It is not the genius of the African to buy and sell on his own account, so as to be the absolute owner of the goods he deals in; but rather to get goods on trust from some white man, trust them out to his friends, and they in turn to their friends, until at last the producer is reached; even he gets the goods first, and goes to gather the oil and rubber afterwards.

Now, when a white man makes a loan he wants collateral; just so the black man. The white man gives bonds, mortgages, stocks, or the name of his friend; the black fellow gives a wife, a child, or a poor relation. Like collateral in civilized lands, these may not be sold until the debt becomes due and there is small chance of repayment; in the meantime the human security is called a "pawn," which is virtually the same as slave. Sometimes a man even pawns himself in order that he may obtain an advance of goods. Slaves, if well-behaved, are permitted to marry and have their own homes, and even to own other slaves themselves; and so long as they are worked moderately and treated kindly they have little cause for dissatisfaction with their lot.

The next morning the Nubia anchored off Elmina, a town founded by the Portuguese in 1471, twenty-one years before America was discovered, and called Oro de la Mina, or the Gold Mine, because the natives brought so much gold for sale. It afterwards passed into the hands of the Dutch, and quite recently has been transferred to England. The town was once well built, but has now fallen into decay and presents many picturesque ruins which are well worthy of a visit. Our friends would gladly have taken a little run ashore, but there was scarcely time to do so, and besides it was Sunday and they did not feel it was right to go sight-seeing on the Sabbath.

Eight miles farther on was Cape Coast Castle where passengers as well as mails were to be put ashore, and also a few parcels for the governor. The surf here, as elsewhere on the African coast, is very heavy and is justly dreaded by strangers, especially those who do not enjoy a drenching. Mr. Stanley, in his "Coomassie and Magdala," says, "It was no light matter to have forgotten the oil for the engines, neither was it a light matter to send a boat back through that awful surf, which the English

CAPE COAST CASTLE, GOLD COAST

have left to be a curse and an annoyance to all who seek this part of the Gold Coast. In coming through the frantic surf we had both been drenched to the skin by a vicious wave, which had simply wetted us for spite, though it might have drowned us had we submitted the boat to its power."

The same writer, in speaking of the town of Cape Coast, says, "I have been wandering through Cape Coast Castle. Now, behold the town of Cape Coast, like a smouldering volcano, blazing and burning and smoking in the hollows between the seven hills, domed by a sky of brass seven times heated by fire." Upon the unprotected parts of the Nubia's deck the sun shone with blistering force, but under the double canvas, fanned by the gentle breeze it was most delightful to sit in the comfortable willow chairs and read or sleep as one might feel inclined. Our friends were quite willing to remain upon their floating home, and they concluded that very likely Cape Coast looked better at a distance than it might upon a nearer acquaintance.

Cape Coast is the port of entry for the great negro kingdom of Ashantee which lies some distance in the interior beyond the Prah river. After lunch the Captain joined the Ogowe Band upon the deck and related some reminiscences of the Ashantee war in 1873-4. "During the time the war was in progress," said the Captain, "we were so full of passengers we scarcely knew where to put them, and indeed several of our ships were chartered to bring nothing but men and stores for the army. Those were busy days and profitable ones, too, for the steamers; but we had more passengers coming out than going home, for many a fine young lad fell a victim to the fever and dysentery and never saw home and friends again.

Although our side was victorious, the war was fruitful of no good results. The Ashantees ought to be our allies and not our enemies; with them we might penetrate to the heart of the Soudan, and by building a railroad we might bring down an immense quantity of produce, while at present we get almost nothing. A little gold dust is brought from Ashantee, and some palm-oil from the coast districts, but the amount is small."

"Coomassie, the capital of Ashantee," added the Doctor, "is one hundred and sixty miles from the coast, and is built upon the side of a large rocky hill of ironstone; and, with its suburbs, contains one hundred thousand inhabitants. More than half of this number reside in plantations within two or three miles of the town, as the higher classes could not support their numerous followers (or the lowest their large families), in the city, and therefore employ them on the farms, where they can raise food both for themselves and for their masters.

"Coomassie is more than four miles in circumference, with streets crossing at right angles. The King's compound is situated on a long and wide street running through the middle of the town, and is enclosed by a high wall which runs back to a marsh. There is a large market-place and back of this is a small grove called Sammonpone, or the Spirit House, because the bodies of all the human victims are thrown into it. The bloody tracks, daily renewed, show the various directions from which they have been dragged, and the number of vultures on the trees indicate the extent of the sacrifice. The stench is almost insupportable, and the place is nightly visited by panthers and other animals. Over one thousand slaves are butchered annually 'for custom,' as the Ashantees say, while upon the death of some great personage as many as two or three hundred are killed at one time. One of the common sayings of the king is, 'By the slaughter of one hundred shall I be able to produce a thousand.'

"The markets in Coomassie are held daily from eight A. M. to sunset. Among the articles offered for sale are the flesh of the wild-hog, deer and monkey; also yams, plantains, rice, peppers, bananas; and salt, dried fish, and smoked snails."

The Judge thanked the Captain and the Doctor for their information, and remarked that he was quite satisfied to do his marketing in New York.

Frank inquired if gold was found as far up the country as Coomassie, and the Captain replied that it was. "There are valuable mines in the hills near the city," said he, "and even the sands of the streets are full of small particles of gold."

"Are the Ashantees brave soldiers?" asked Grant.

"Yes," said the Doctor, "give the Ashantees the same weapon, such as the breech-loading Sniders which the English troops have, and they will find them a foe worthy of their best efforts."

Toward the middle of the afternoon the Nubia steamed away from Cape Coast and at sundown anchored at Accra.

One of the unpleasant experiences in traveling by steamer is that there is no Sunday; work goes on just the same as other days. It is true some captains try to have less washing and scrubbing done, and give their men a little time to themselves; but when working the ports there is no distinction made between the Sabbath and the other days of the week. When crossing the ocean of course the ship must keep right on, but when coasting or lying in port, the reason usually given is the true one, viz: that the ship costs so much per day and they must work on Sunday to save that day's expense.

It may be a question worth considering, whether God's blessing may not be worth as much in dollars and cents as the sum total of the work done on Sunday. In a certain town in New Jersey there were three principal mercantile establishments; one of these closed up tight on Sunday and would not sell five cents' worth of tobacco to accommodate the best customer the concern had. The other two would open the back door "just for accommodation," and this sometimes was pretty often. Nothing happened for some years, but in the end the first concern made money and has it yet; of the other two, one broke and paid twenty-five cents to the dollar and never was able to start again; the second dwindled down to nothing and went out of existence.

It may, at first sight, seem strange that such results should follow from such apparently slight causes; but let us suppose there is an ever present personal Spirit, who sees all things and takes a keen interest in human action. Suppose, too, this personal Spirit to be an active, moving agent in all second causes, working in them and through them with resistless power, yet slowly and silently, to accomplish His purposes. Suppose He has given certain rules to guide human conduct and is very jealous of the way in which His commands are received and treated by men. Suppose one of these commands is to "Remember the Sabbath day to keep it holy"; will it pay to obey such a command? Will it be safe to disobey it?

It was a lovely Sabbath afternoon, and Accra presented an inviting appearance as the setting sun threw its rays aslant the white cliffs and whitewashed walls of the

ACCRA, GOLD COAST

town. The land about Accra is singularly devoid of vegetation; from the face of the cliff upon which the town is built, the ground slopes back to a lagoon. This strip of plain country is covered with bunches of cactus, thorns and grass. There is a scarcity of good drinking water in Accra, and large cisterns are built to catch the water during the rainy-season and preserve it for use during the rest of the year. The town is ill-planned and many of the buildings are going to decay. The trade is in palm-oil, gold-dust and gum-copal, with a few monkey skins and other products of the forest.

Away to the right in a cocoa-nut grove is the Basle Mission, the best known of any mission on the African coast. This Mission has undertaken to civilize as well as Christianize the African. Pupils in their schools are taught carpentering, blacksmithing, brick-laying, and other handicrafts, as well as reading, writing and arithmetic; and trade is carried on with the natives as well. There is a store or shop where workmen are paid in goods; and cloth, tobacco, soap and other necessaries are exchanged for palm-oil, monkey skins, etc. Much good is doubtless done in this way, but very naturally the secular department absorbs most of the time and attention. Those who place a high value upon civilization as distinct from Christianity, are loud in the praises of these industrial schools; but those who value more highly spiritual results, have not been found so favorably disposed toward them.

These Swiss and German brethren have some customs that may appear to us a little singular. The men are obliged to come out unmarried; when, after a residence of a year or two permission to marry is obtained, the selection is made by the Society at home from a list of "waiting, willing ones," and the fair candidate is shipped by the first steamer, consigned to the head of the Mission. Immediately on arrival she must marry the man for whom she was intended, whether she likes him or not, and this without any previous acquaintance. Occasionally these hasty unions turn out to be happy ones, and in any case they must make the best of it, just as people must do everywhere else in the world.

The Judge and his young friends desired very much to attend the evening services at the Mission, but the surf is so extremely dangerous that the Captain was not willing they should go ashore.

Early on Monday morning canoes and surf-boats came off to the steamer bringing passengers for ports farther south; these were mostly carpenters, masons and jack-washers, many of whom had received their training at the Basle Mission. A few of these were accompanied by their wives, but mostly they left these behind and formed temporary alliances with others in the places where they went to work. Here then was one of the fruits of industrial schools; it created a surplus of mechanical labor, which went abroad to seek employment and in doing so destroyed home life.

Captain Davis did not wait very long, but as soon as he could get his passengers on board he steamed away for Whydah, the port of the kingdom of Dahomy, which place was reached soon after sundown. Dahomy is the rival of Ashantee among the negro kingdoms, and is if possible more brutal and cruel than the latter nation. Its army is composed largely of women, who are even more fierce and bloodthirsty than the men. It is not an inviting country and our young travelers were not sorry to hear the Nubia was to remain but an hour or so.

Next morning at breakfast-time the steamer came to anchor off the entrance to Lagos, a large town built on a low marshy island in a lagoon that is connected by back creeks with the Niger delta. It is an English colony and has a large and flourishing trade. The houses can scarcely be seen from the anchorage which is a long way out, for the bar is the most dangerous one on the West coast and is justly dreaded. A small steamer, built expressly for the purpose, comes out at a certain stage of the tide and takes off passengers and freight.

Lagos was once the head-quarters of the slave trade for the Niger region; but this nefarious traffic has now ceased and palm-oil and kernels have taken its place.

Inland from Lagos is the kingdom of Yoruba, of which the capital is Abeokuta, a city surrounded by a wall and possessing a considerable degree of civilization. This city is the scene of labor of Bishop Crowther, a very uncommon man, both on account of his eminent piety, and his high intellectual qualifications. He is a native of this country and was sold as a slave at Badagry, in 1822. The vessel on which he was embarked was captured by an English man-of-war and taken to Sierra Leone. Here young Crowther received a good education, was converted, and became a minister of the Gospel. After a time he returned to his native country and has ever since been most active in preaching and in organizing churches among his fellow-countrymen.

After mails and passengers had been put on board the small steamer that came out from Lagos, the Nubia resumed her voyage, and on Wednesday morning crossed the bar at the mouth of the Bonny river, and anchored abreast of the English trading stations.

CHAPTER VIII.

BONNY AND FERNANDO PO.

THE great Niger river forms a large delta and empties through six smaller rivers into the Gulf of Guinea. These are called the Opobo, Akassa, Brass, Benin, Bonny and New Calabar; of these the Bonny is perhaps the best known and has the best bar at its mouth. The entrance to the Bonny river is simply a break in the sandy key which acts as a breakwater against the heavy surf; inside, a vast swamp stretches away on every side. The low islands, covered with a dense growth of mangroves and other water loving trees, are surrounded by wide reaches of water which expose mud-banks at low tide, but with a deep, crooked channel winding among them.

Until recently it was not thought possible for white men to live on shore, and trade was carried on upon what were called "hulks." Ships that had grown too old to be safe in rough weather, were purchased at a low price and sailed out in the summer season; on arrival they were stripped of sails and spars, covered with a roof and used as a permanent trading-station. The necessity for more

CANOE ON THE BONNY RIVER, NIGER DELTA

room at length compelled the largest firms to try what might be done ashore. Piles were driven in the mud so as to enclose a space, and ship-loads of sand and gravel were brought to cover the mud and fill in this enclosed space, and on this "made-ground" buildings were erected. Three establishments are now on shore, and two still occupy hulks.

The shore stations are surrounded by a sea of black mud, except on the side next the river, where the mud is of course covered with water. Strange as it may seem, this apparently pestilential spot is less unhealthful than Sierra Leone which seems to be so delightfully situated. There is a wide-spread opinion prevalent upon the African coast, that standing water absorbs the malaria, and this opinion appears to be borne out by facts. It is thought to be much better to sleep on ship-board than to sleep on shore; yet in places like Bonny, where some sleep on hulks and some on shore, no perceptible difference is seen in the health of the two classes.

The whole subject relating to malaria is a great puzzle, and the probabilities are that no one knows what it is, or what is the cause of it. True, wiseacres are not infrequently met, who can tell you all about it and lay down iron-clad rules for its operation in any given set of circumstances; but facts are usually against them, and besides that, they do not agree among themselves.

Until this time no cargo had been taken from the Nubia; mails and passengers had been landed, together with a number of parcels, but now the real business of the voyage was to begin, and our young travelers watched with eager interest the preparations for hoisting the cargo out of the hold and putting it over the side. A heavy spar was rigged to each mast in such a way that the upper end was directly over the hatchway. A small steam-engine called a "winch," turned an iron drum over which a heavy chain was tightly wound; this chain ran along the under side of the spar, and then over a wheel at its end, and so hung down through the hatchway into the hold.

The ship's Kru-boys were divided into two gangs, one of which worked the forward hatch, and the other the after hatch. These nimble fellows clambered over the piles of bales and boxes in the dark hold, selecting such as were marked for Bonny, and fastened them to the chain which drew them forth and deposited them on deck. The rattle of the steam-winches and chains, the shouts of the workmen, who always do best when making a noise, and the bustle and excitement of working cargo, made an animated scene that was highly entertaining to our friends.

As soon as the Nubia came to anchor, boats put off from the trading-posts, to bring the agents on board to get their mails and hear the news. These gentlemen were dressed in white linen and their faces were bleached by the fever as white as their clothes; they were polite and gentlemanly, and were men of ability and experience. After a private chat with the Captain they returned to their places of business, and soon their white assistants came off with surf-boats and large lighters to get the cargo.

These lighters can carry as much as six or eight tons, and are not propelled by oars reaching out from either side, but two or three oars extend over the stern, and are worked back and forth in a fashion known as sculling. Our friends were surprised to see such great boats forced through the water by what appeared to be wholly inadequate means. When these boats came alongside, the cargo was hoisted over the side and let down in them, and when they were full they were towed ashore.

The tide is strong in all the African rivers and the time consumed in sculling a loaded boat ashore is so great that not more than two loads a day is taken by each boat, and oftentimes when there is some detention, not more than one. To save time the steamers now carry a small steam launch, which is put over the side at every port and is used to tow these heavy laden boats ashore; by this means four loads a day may be taken by each boat.

But other visitors came besides the traders. Quite a fleet of canoes was presently gathered around the good ship. Their owners brought plantains, bananas, yams, pine-apples and dried fish for sale to the native passengers; and mats, baskets and other curiosities to sell to the white ones. These baskets and mats were wholly of native manufacture and were quite interesting and curious. The Judge thought it well to buy a few table mats, as they could be packed in their trunks without taking too much room, and so each of the Band took a dozen. The pineapples and bananas were not of a good quality, and as they are not thought to be altogether wholesome, especially for new-comers, it was decided to let them entirely alone. The Doctor told them that, strange as it might seem, peppers were more wholesome in Africa than pineapples.

The men who brought the mats for sale spoke English fairly well, and in answer to an inquiry from the Judge they stated that they had been educated in the mission school; indeed the Judge had already noticed that at all the ports where they had called, English was the medium of communication between all the passengers and the coast natives.

While bargaining for the mats a great drumming was heard, and on looking out over the water a large canoe full of men was seen approaching, with flags at either end, and a great umbrella of many bright colors, in the middle.

"O, what a gorgeous umbrella!" exclaimed Mamie.

"It reminds me of Joseph's coat," responded Robbie.

The canoe bore down on the steamer with much beating of tom-toms and wild singing of the crew, until it came alongside the ladder, when the owner came on deck and introduced himself as one of the head men among the people. He was not the "king," as the most influential chief is called, but the head of one of the leading families, and a trader.

He spoke good English, and in answer to inquiries from the Judge he said he had twenty-seven wives, over fifty children, and he did not know how many slaves, but more than two hundred. He said most of these slaves lived on little plantations in charge of his wives, and that they raised the food needed for the entire family. For himself, he spent most of his time on trading expeditions. He took powder, guns, rum, gin, tobacco, and other goods, in a large canoe and then his slaves paddled two or three days' journey up the river to the town of one of his friends, and there he remained until enough oil was gathered to purchase his stock in trade; when he returned, sold the oil to the white men, rested awhile in his town, and started away on another expedition.

In reply to the inquiry as to what he did when his slaves would not obey him, he said he killed them when they needed it.

"Why don't you become a Christian?" asked the Judge.

"Yes, I Christian now, this time," he replied, "no more, I be trade-man too."

TRADING HULK, BONNY, NIGER DELTA

The Judge expressed his surprise and the man continued. "What's the matter, you white men you no be Christian and trade-man all same time?"

Hereupon the Judge explained some of the requirements of the Christian life, but this representative of one of the "leading families of Bonny" remarked that, "white man was not all the same like black man," and thereupon took his departure.

A little while after lunch a very intelligent and gentlemanly man came on board and was introduced by the Captain to Judge McGee as Archdeacon Crowther. After an hour of pleasant conversation the Archdeacon invited our friends to take a little run ashore and pay him a visit, and the invitation was promptly accepted. The Captain placed his gig at the disposal of the Judge and sent them away in tow of the steam launch.

The cool sea-breeze was now blowing and it tempered the heat so that the trip was a delightful one, although they found it much warmer on shore than under the awning on the ship. It was about half tide and much mud near the shore was exposed, sending up a strong effluvium as it lay exposed to the sun's rays. Upon arriving opposite the mission landing the launch went back to its work, and the Kru-boys got out and carried each passenger through the water and mud to the shore, as if they had been so many babies.

It was rather startling to see so dignified a gentleman as the Judge carried like a child, and it certainly destroys all appearance of dignity; but it is better than wading through the water, and so is the usual fashion on the coast. Some sit on a Kru-boy's shoulders with their legs astride his neck, and hold on to his wool to balance themselves; but it is an unsteady position and new-comers are safer to be carried in arms, as our friends were on this occasion.

The mission premises are not more than a foot or two above the water-level and the ground is soft and springy. Mrs. Crowther, like her husband, a native African, gave her guests a cordial welcome and made many inquiries about their journey. She was a highly cultivated and refined lady, and, with her husband, a good example of what the African race may become. Presently tea and sweet crackers were served and then the Archdeacon took his guests out to see the fine new church recently erected. Mr. Crowther told the Judge the house was filled every Sabbath, and that mission work was making commendable progress, not only in Bonny, but up the Niger river. Yet the light penetrates slowly, for the depravity of the negro races is great, and the principles of Christianity are opposed to the degraded instincts of the African savage.

After inspecting the church Mr. Crowther led the way along a narrow foot-path, that in some places was little better than a quagmire, to a village of the Bonny people; it was inexpressibly filthy and they did not remain long. It was a matter of surprise to the Ogowe Band that any one could live in such dirt and be a Christian, or, as Laura expressed it, "I don't wonder these people are heathen."

The Archdeacon told them the villages up-country were much better than this one, and that the people they saw to-day would be away on the farms in a week or two, and others would come and take their places for awhile. "This town is kept up," said he, "mainly because it is near the trading stations."

On their return, the Judge and his party bade the kind Archdeacon and his wife adieu, and were carried out to their boat and went up the river to have a look at the trader's houses. They landed near the end of a large covered wharf and walked up to the yard where men were hooping palm-oil casks. Here they met a very pleasant gentleman who told them he was the head of the telegraph corps and he invited them into his house.

The Judge was quite surprised to learn that Bonny was connected with Europe by a sub-marine cable. This obliging official ordered coffee to be brought in, and then explained that the cable extended from St. Paul de Loanda to St. Thomas, thence to Bonny, Lagos, Cape Coast Castle, Sierra Leone, Senegambia, Canary Islands, Madeira, and so on to Lisbon and the rest of Europe. Not very many messages were sent and the line did not pay, but it was hoped it might by and by. Our friends thought of cabling home, but the expense was so great that the idea was given up.

The Ogowe Band went into the operating room and were surprised to learn that messages were not sent by sound, but by sight; as Hattie expressed it, "Real, true flashes of lightning."

The Superintendent explained that the amount of power needed to operate a sounding machine was more than to transmit a flash, so the electric spark was made to pass before a small mirror, and by observing the length of the flashes, and the intervals between them, the operator could read the dispatch. This seemed very wonderful, as indeed it really is. If men, possessed of such feeble power as we know they are, can send messages for thousands of miles, what may not free spirits be able to do in the boundless realms of space? Who can say they may not send messages to our dear ones in the "far-away home of the soul?" So thought our young friends as they watched the little sparks of electric fire flash from the positive to the negative pole of the delicate telegraphic instrument.

It was now sundown and the Judge and his young friends bade the kind director good-bye and returned to the Nubia. The cargo that had been unloaded during the day had consisted of guns, powder, cloth, crockery, iron-pots, rice, salt beef, and rum, gin, and other intoxicants. These latter compounds had made up about one-half in bulk of the whole. The Judge had read much of the rum trade in Africa, but he was surprised to see so great an amount of the vile stuff unloaded from so respectable a steamer as the Nubia.

In the evening, as they sat upon the deck enjoying the cool sea-breeze, he asked Captain Davis to tell him something about the rum traffic. He was not long in finding out this was an unpleasant topic. So much has been said about the iniquity of the African rum trade that the firms at home, who are men of great respectability in the communities where they live, are irritated and annoyed, and all those who are in any way connected with this trade prefer to keep very quiet about it, especially in the presence of those whose sensibilities are shocked by the disclosures that might be made.

The Captain himself was a teetotaler, but he preferred to talk on some other subject than the rum traffic, although it was not difficult to see what he thought of it. The Judge determined to keep his eyes open, see what he could for himself, and make further inquiries of his friends when he reached Gaboon.

He was not required to wait long for an example of what effect it had upon the white-man. Just across the passage way from his room was a state-room occupied by a trader who had lived for some years on the coast. This gentleman, with some others, went to one of the hulks to spend a social evening with friends. Late in the night he fell overboard and for some unaccountable reason did not sink, but floated away with the swift ebb tide. The Kru-man on watch on the hulk half a mile below, saw a dark object coming down the river, and went down the ladder to have a nearer view of it as it passed. It came so near that he was able to catch it with his hand, and by exerting all his strength he drew it out of the water on the grating. He gave the alarm and when the trader who lived on this hulk was aroused from his sleep, he ordered out his gig and the unconscious visitor was rolled into it and taken to the Nubia; even when carried into his room and bundled into his berth, he was so drunk he did not know what had happened to him! A more wonderful escape from a watery grave perhaps was never known.

Why men should drink so heavily upon the West Coast of Africa, is hard to tell. At one of the ports a trader was dying. In the evening, when work was finished, all the other traders came to see him, and as there was no hope of his recovery they decided to "give him a good send off." They got him out of bed and bolstered him up in the arm-chair at the head of the table and made him "drink to the occasion" with them. They kept on drinking until one by one they slid off their chairs under the table in a drunken mess together, and the poor dead one was left sitting upright, the only sober one of the party.

Stanley, in his "Congo," says: "The evils of brandy and soda in India need only to be remembered to prove how pernicious is the suicidal habit of indulgence in drinking of alcoholic liquors in hot climates. The West Coast of Africa is also too much indebted to the ruin effected by intemperance." One would think there were dangers enough in African life without inviting sure destruction by indulgence in so pernicious a habit.

The agents at Bonny desired a portion of the cargo put ashore at another post farther up the river called Boogahmah, and the next day at noon the Nubia started on her way. The channel was crooked and wound about among mud banks, and islands covered with a thick growth of mangroves. Sometimes the steamer went so close to the trees that the sides almost touched the end of the branches. It was a strange experience to be steaming along through the forest and the Nubia seemed to have forgotten her wild ocean home as she picked her way through the thick waters, among the muddy islands of this great African swamp.

The Ogowe Band were delighted, for although the scenery was desolate and depressing to older minds, yet to these young people it was novel and full of interest. They peered among the mangrove roots and into the forest shades in hopes of seeing a few stray crocodiles; occasionally the enormous vines hanging from the trees would appear like giant pythons or boa-constrictors. Now and then a canoe was passed hugging the bushes closely so as not to be too near the great ship, and the half naked negroes would look up in wonder at the great vessel that had invaded their domains.

A mangrove swamp is a wild, wierd, desolate waste, with pestilential odors of decaying matter, and abandoned by all save reptile life; it is a very land of the shadow of death; without any order, and where the light is as darkness—a fit emblem of that land of everlasting night where all the filth of the universe is to be drained to fester and ferment throughout the eternal ages. Such a land is the fit abode of the evil one, and our friends were not surprised at the stories of the cruelty which these black people practice on each other, told them by two of the Bonny merchants who had come on board to go up to Boogahmah with them.

Sometimes in turning a short corner the Nubia's engines would be stopped in order to give her time to swing around, and the lead was kept going all the while, but they got along without any accident, thanks to Captain Davis's skill as a navigator, and at sundown cast anchor before the trading-posts of the village of Boogahmah. The young men stationed here were glad to see the steamer for it is not often one comes up so far, and they came off at once to hear the news and have a chat with the steamer people.

Boogahmah, like Bonny, is situated in a swamp, and our friends had not been there long before the mosquitoes discovered the arrival of the strangers, and came on board to pay their respects. No one has yet been found who appreciates the attention of this frolicsome little insect; he may sing his cheerful song never so sweetly, so bewitchingly, his absence will yet be more appreciated than his presence. Africa is no more afflicted with this troublesome pest than many other countries, perhaps even less so, but at Boogahmah at least they were abundant and they made it lively for all hands throughout the night.

Friday was spent in landing cargo and on Saturday morning, much to the relief of our young friends who saw few attractions at Boogahmah, the Nubia returned to Bonny, and late in the afternoon turned her prow seaward. It seemed good to be once more on the broad ocean, with the pure, cool breeze sweeping the deck, bringing life and vigor to the languid frame, and feel that the swamps and their malarious exhalations had been left behind.

Sabbath morning dawned calm and bright. The sun rose in majestic splendor from behind the lofty range of the Cameroons, lighting up the vapors about their summits with a glory of crimson and gold. From the gorgeous coloring of the skies it might be thought that some bright-winged embassy from the Spirit-land had come down to earth with glad message of peace and good-will to men. Looking heavenward along the shining pathway, one could fancy that "thinly the veil intervened between the fair city" and this lower world.

On the starboard bow was the peak of Fernando Po, lifting its forest-clad head more than ten thousand feet above the sea.

Notwithstanding the throbbing of the engines a solemn hush had settled down over the sea as if the calm and silence of the eternal world had touched the earth to give a slight foretaste of the Sabbath of Heaven. A long time did our young friends remain on deck, lost in the beauty of the scene, nor was the enchantment broken by any word or remark.

At noon the Nubia came to anchor in Clarence Bay on the northeast corner of the island of Fernando Po. This bay is small, but the water is deep and the vessels can lie close in to shore. The town of Clarence is an insignificant place, little more than a clearing in the jungle, and has a reputation of being more than usually unhealthy,

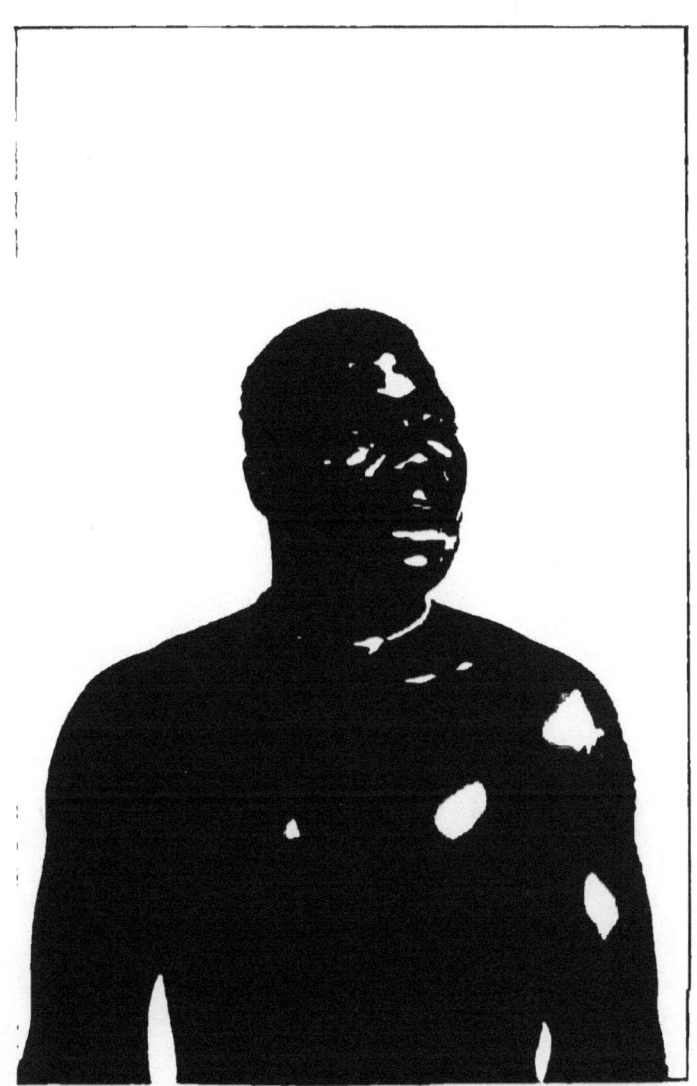

especially for ladies. Everywhere the vegetation is the richest and most luxuriant that can be imagined; the cliffs that skirt the bay are covered with palms and vines in the greatest profusion.

An hour after the steamer's arrival the Rev. Mr. Luddington came off and after an introduction from Captain Davis and a friendly chat, invited the Judge and his party to come ashore and spend the afternoon with him. The invitation was thankfully accepted and, as the Captain loaned his gig, all the young folks were soon safely landed on the beach. There was a short covered pier with steps, which made the landing easy, and a road was cut in the face of the cliff which led to the town situated on the level land above. The Governor's house, Holt & Co.'s factory, and the Spanish mission, are the most pretentious buildings; the English Primitive Methodist Mission-house is a pleasant home-like structure of wood and galvanized iron.

Not far away was the church and our friends were glad to hear that the second service was to be held at four P. M. and they would be able to attend; several weeks had passed since they had worshiped in God's house and now the opportunity had come in this far off island of the sea. Mr. Luddington informed them he had changed the time of the second service from evening to afternoon, so that he might have the evening for rest, otherwise he was not able to sleep that night.

Mrs. Luddington received her American guests with true English hospitality, and the girls, for their part, were glad enough to be in a real home once more. Mrs. Luddington showed them around the house and explained to them some of the mysteries of tropical housekeeping, and her management of her girls.

In the cool, pleasant sitting-room her husband was giving the Judge some account of the island, and his troubles with the Spanish officials, and so the time passed until the ringing of the bell announced the hour for service. About one hundred and fifty persons, "clothed and in their right minds," entered and reverently took their seats. Mrs. Luddington presided at the organ; the hymns were the well known ones of Moody and Sankey, and were sung with a heartiness too often lacking at home. All the services were in English, which is preferred by the people to Spanish. So similar were the services to those in our own fair land, that the travelers forgot they were far away from home and when the benediction had been pronounced they almost expected to look out and see the streets and pavements of their native city.

The people of Clarence are like those of Sierra Leone, a conglomeration from all parts of the coast, and call themselves Englishmen, although the island belongs to Spain; but the natives are Boobies, said to be the lowest and most ill-favored of all the human race. Some even of these have felt the power of the gospel, and are earnest, consistent members of this church. The Judge and his young friends were introduced to several, and it needed but a glance at their faces to see the Christian joy shining in their countenances, showing plainly they had been with Christ and had learned of Him. Mr. Luddington informed his guests that the church had over one hundred members, and that the mission work at all the stations on the island was prosperous.

Fernando Po is celebrated for its yams which are the best grown anywhere on the coast. For tea that evening they had several that had been baked in the ashes, which is much the best way to cook them. The Ogowe Band thought they were excellent, and they did full justice to them.

A gun from the steamer announced the fact that the Captain's boat had come for them and they bade their kind entertainers good-bye, little thinking that in a few short months good Mrs. Luddington would be in her grave.

So it ever is in Africa.

CHAPTER IX.

OLD CALABAR.

WHEN the young travelers awoke on Monday morning the Nubia was steaming toward the broad mouth of the Old Calabar river.

Away on either side was a dark line of mangroves converging toward some point far ahead; while in mid-channel was a fleet of canoes, whose occupants were engaged in drawing the denizens of the muddy waters from their turbid home. There must have been at least two hundred of these canoes, as the water for a mile or more was thickly dotted with them. The way they fished was by planting two long poles in the mud, and stretching a sort of basket between them. Each canoe had several of these nets to attend to, but after all, the number of fish taken was not very large. A few of these are sold fresh in the Old Calabar market, and the rest are smoked over slow fires and taken far up into the country to be sold where fish are scarce.

By and by the banks of the river drew nearer and the Nubia crossed from side to side as it followed the

FOREIGN SETTLEMENT, OLD CALABAR

deep channel; sometimes the ship almost touched the leaves of the mangroves. The boys kept a good lookout and were rewarded by seeing two crocodiles, lazy, slimy fellows they were, appearing to be more than half asleep; the girls saw a family of monkeys,—two old ones and three smaller ones scampering away among the branches of the trees. The Band were quite excited by the sight of the crocodiles and monkeys, and felt they had now reached Africa and no mistake.

At ten A. M. they rounded the Nine Fathom Point and as they did so, they fired a gun and blew the whistle as a signal that they were coming, and a little later a turn in the river brought the town into view. Far ahead on the left bank of the river was a long line of foreign houses close to the water-side, while the hillsides were covered with the native villages.

Shortly before eleven the Nubia came to anchor, and in a few minutes handsome gigs were seen coming from each factory, the strong arms of the rowers making them leap through the water. All along the coast of Africa the traders take great pride in their boats and crews. The "gig," as this kind of boat is called, is long, narrow, and of a fine model; and each man's gig is painted a different color. So, too, the cloths and caps of the crews are different, each trader having his own style or color, as our base-ball clubs have at home.

The traders were all dressed in white and their pale faces showed plainly the traces of Africa. They gave Captain Davis a hearty greeting for he was an old friend, and then they assembled for the transaction of very important business. The mate had brought up the mail sack and this was now opened out on the deck and each pair of eyes sought eagerly through the pile for messages from home and friends or business firm. When the division had been made, each took his share and returned to his place of business, and it was not long before surf-boats and lighters were alongside and the work of unlading cargo begun as at Bonny and at Boogahmah.

Among those who came on board for letters was Albert Gilles Esq., of the firm of Taylor, Laughlin & Co., Glasgow, who may easily be called the leading merchants of Old Calabar. Mr. Gilles had traveled in America and he recognized Judge McGee as one of a party of gentlemen he had met in Philadelphia; he was greatly surprised to see him in such an odd corner of the world, and gave him and his party of young folks a most pressing invitation to make his factory their home while in Calabar.

The Judge thought it best to sleep on board the steamer as he had been told it was unwise to sleep on shore when making a journey, and so it was arranged that when the sea-breeze came in, and tempered the heat somewhat, Mr. Gilles should send his gig for them.

Old Calabar is forty miles up the river and is a very hot place; this was not the hottest time of the year but still at noon the heat was oppressive, more especially to those just from the cooler North.

The river here is about five hundred yards wide; the right bank is low and covered with a jungle of mangrove, palm and other trees, but the left bank is high and in some places rises abruptly from the water. Where the slopes are more gradual, the ground is occupied by native villages, while at the foot of the bluffs are located the trading-stations of the great foreign firms. To increase the available area for building purposes, as well as to afford better landing facilities, piles have been driven in the mud of the river-bed and the enclosed space filled with gravel.

Duketown, as the settlement at Old Calabar is called, is the greatest palm-oil market in the world; in the season from five hundred to eight hundred casks, each weighing nearly a ton, have been shipped in a single week. The town contains several thousand inhabitants and the head-men possess a large amount of barbaric wealth; several of these live in large handsome houses of wood and galvanized iron, that were made in England and then brought out at a cost of several thousand dollars each. These houses are fitted up with fine chandeliers, mirrors and other furniture, and when the owners entertain a white guest the table is spread with a linen cloth and adorned with real china, and the food provided is largely imported from Europe. Of course polygamy and slavery prevail, but a stranger visiting the town as our friends were doing, would see little or nothing of either. The streets of the town are narrow and crooked and not particularly clean, but as the white people travel almost entirely by water, it does not make so much difference.

The Ogowe Band sat upon the deck in the shade of the friendly awning and feasted upon the strange and varied scenes around them. The trading establishments along the river were scenes of busy activity; coopers driving down the hoops upon the great oil casks with a deafening din; Kru-boys turning the handles of the stationary iron cranes, to draw up the cargo from boats, and the casks of oil from the canoes; women paddling home after a morning of toil in the plantations; and large canoes with casks of palm-oil seeking among the traders for the best market. Children splashed about in the shallow water near shore as naturally as white children at home.

Slaves came down to the river to wash great baskets of yams and manioc to be cooked for dinner for their masters' families. Great clumps of feathery bamboo growing upon the steeper hillsides, hung like enormous ostrich plumes quivering in the noon-day heat. Upon the hill-top, a little back from the river, the buildings of the Scotch Presbyterian Mission stood amid the cool shade of wide spreading fruit trees, looking from a distance most home-like and inviting; over all was a rich flood of tropical sunlight so brilliant and dazzling as almost to pain the eyes.

At three P. M. Mr. Gilles's gig drew up beside the ladder, and the Judge and his young companions tripped lightly down the steps and got in; as the one boat would not hold so many the Captain sent his gig too, and a jolly party they were as the two boats raced down the river.

Mr. Gilles met them at his wharf and conducted them through the large open shed to the broad stairway that led to his comfortable home. Tea was served upon the wide veranda, and the conversation, wholly upon African subjects, was most interesting to the young travelers.

Mr. Gilles's house was a very large one, built like most factories on the coast, in two stories. The ground floor is used as a shop and the general place of business, while the second story contains the living rooms. The shop is fitted with a counter and back of this the goods are piled up in regular order, much as in a wholesale store at home.

Two kinds of trade are carried on, the wholesale and the retail. For the retail trade, brass rods are used as a medium; these are passed out in certain proportion upon every cask of oil purchased and are then used as money

INTERIOR OF PALM OIL FACTORY, OLD CALABAR

among the people. These rods cost more according to their selling price than any other article and the traders are glad to get them again in exchange for other goods; so when a Calabar mother wants a cloth for herself or a cap for her little boy, she takes some brass rods to the factory and buys it. The wholesale trade is the principal one and consists in the exchange of bales of cloth, barrels of rum, casks of tobacco and other goods, for casks of palm-oil and tubs of kernels.

Calabar is the only port on the coast where the credit system has been wholly done away with, and this was accomplished but recently here. When a man has one or more casks of palm-oil to sell he puts them in his canoe and his slaves paddle it to one of the factories. Here it is hoisted up on the wharf, the bung drawn and the oil sampled; an offer is then made which is either accepted or the owner is free to try his fortunes at another factory, in which case his cask is carefully lowered into his canoe again. When a bargain is made, a due-bill is given for the amount, which may then be taken to the shop and exchanged for goods, or it may be kept until a future time, being always good until used.

Kernels are sold at so much a "tub" which holds about a bushel and a half; the price for kernels is uniform, but as oil is of many different qualities, the price varies considerably. This is one of the few rivers where white men have not tried to go up the river to trade, and it is one of the few rivers where African trade is now profitable. In every case where white men have pushed up toward the interior the result has been to raise the cost of the produce and increase expenses without augmenting the volume of trade. It is better to let the coast people collect the oil, kernels, or whatever the country produces, than for white men to try to do it themselves; such at least has been the experience of trade as Mr. Gilles explained to the Judge.

Mr. Gilles also said the greater part of the oil came from the tide-water region and the level country immediately adjoining; that in the hilly districts of the interior the oil-bearing palm was not so abundant and that most of the nuts were used for food.

"I do not exactly understand what you mean by kernels," said Johnny.

"The palm-nut," replied Mr. Gilles, "has a fibrous pulp on the outside which contains the oil; inside this is a very hard nut or stone, and in this nut is a kernel which has a black skin but the meat is pure white and contains a fine oil."

"It must be a great deal of work to crack so many pits," observed Lulu.

"You must remember there are a great many hands to do the work," responded Mr. Gilles.

"Where do the Calabar people go to get the oil?" asked Willie.

"They go to what they call the markets," replied Mr. Gilles. "Everywhere throughout this part of Africa there are towns where markets are held on certain days; everyone goes who has something to sell or who may possibly wish to buy, and of course pretty much the whole neighborhood are there. Our Calabar people fill their canoes with goods and go to these markets and buy the oil and kernels and bring them here to us to exchange for goods again. The oil is brought to these markets for sale in earthen jars, and sometimes in kegs and small barrels and is not put in the big casks you see until the Calabar trader has purchased it."

"Are oil and kernels the only things brought to these markets for sale?" inquired Grace.

"No indeed," was the reply, "almost everything you can think of; and, by the way, if you do not mind I will tell you a little story."

"By all means," chimed in the other girls, "we want to hear it."

"Well, then," continued Mr. Gilles, "there was once a man trudging along to one of these markets carrying three hoes on his shoulder; they should have been made of iron, but this fellow had them made of clay and thought he might sell them to some one who did not know any better. By chance he came up to another man who was carrying a basket with three crows in it and was going to the same market.

"'Well, my friend,' said the first man, 'what have you got in your basket and where are you going?'

"'I have three chickens in the basket,' said the second, 'and I am going to the fair at Kirasa to exchange them for three hoes.'

"'How fortunate!' replied the first, 'for I have these three hoes that I am taking to the same market to buy me three fowls; now why should we go further? let us make the exchange here,' and so they did.

"'Now,' said the second one, 'these fowls are very wild; I have only just caught them and they are not accustomed to being confined in a basket; I would advise you not to open the basket until you get home, for they might fly away.'

"'And I,' said the first, 'have only just made these hoes and they may be a little soft yet, and perhaps you had better not try to use them until they have had a little time to harden.' So they made the exchange and each one returned to his home. When the first got there he opened his basket to look at his fowls and out flew the crows. The second thought he would try his new hoes, and they broke at once and he found they were of clay.

"The next time they met one said, 'See, we have each been trying to cheat the other, now why should we do this any more? Let us go together and cheat others and then we will soon get to be rich men.'

"So they went on together and by and by they came to an old lady who was tending goats, and they said to her, 'Mother we see you have had a hard time of it with these goats;' and she answered, 'Yes, they are always wandering away and I must run after them to bring them back, and I am so old and stiff it is too much for me.'

"Then these rascals said, 'We are truly very sorry for you and we will try to help you so you can have an easier time of it.' Then they took long cords and tied one end of each to a goat, and the other ends around the old woman's waist, and they said to her, 'Now mother, you just sit quiet, and when one of the goats wanders off this way, you can take hold of the cord and draw him back; and when one wanders that way, you can do the same thing, so you will be able to sit quietly all the while.'

"The old woman was very grateful to them and blessed them, so they went their way but presently returned with a dog and set him at the goats; this frightened them so much that they rushed away in all directions and tore the old woman to pieces. Then these wicked men caught the goats and took them away and sold them; and so they kept on deceiving the people, but by and by they were found out, and their heads were cut off and their bodies were thrown in the river."

The Judge observed that this sounded to him like an African story, and Mr. Gilles replied that it was one that was current among the people and had been told him by a chief.

At six o'clock the factory bell rang and all hands quit work and went to their quarters to rest after the labors of the day. Mr. Gilles had invited some friends to take dinner with him and meet his American guests; these now arrived and were introduced to the Judge and his young companions.

Messrs. Lyon and Munroe were prominent traders, each in charge of important factories; Mr. Holmes was a contractor who had come out from England to put up a large house for a native chief; Captain Davis came from the Nubia, and there were Mr. Sleigh and another of Mr. Gilles's assistants.

The dining-room extended all the way across the house and was all needed to seat so large a company. A punka over the table created an agreeable breeze and made the dinner more enjoyable. It was surprising to come across so much comfort and even elegance on the coast of Africa, for the dinner was served with as much grace and style as in many a pretentious home in good old England.

Our friends gleaned a large amount of useful information from these gentlemen concerning the country and the customs and superstitions of the Calabar people. Mr. Gilles had lived in former years on the Gaboon and a deep scar on his face attested his bravery in an encounter with the cannibals.

Among the many good things on the table were two dishes new to the American travelers; these were palm-oil-chop and Avagada pears. Old Calabar is noted for its palm-oil-chop, which is blacker and hotter than elsewhere on the coast. What they had for dinner this evening was made by a wife of one of the chiefs and was so hot with pepper it fairly burned like fire, and the Ogowe Band were obliged to desist from attempting to eat it. This dish is a great favorite with "old coasters," and is both wholesome and nutritious. It is made of palm-oil and the pulp of the palm nut, fish or chicken, yams, and a whole handful of small chilli peppers, and tastes, as Saxe expressed it, "like concentrated African sunshine." The best of all meat to put in it is monkey, although crocodile or hippopotamus meat does very well; some of the native people use snake-meat cut up into suitable lengths.

Avagada pears are much larger than any pears we see in the market at home, and are more of a vegetable than a fruit. The outside is a purplish brown and inside is a large stone or pit; the flesh is yellowish green and of the consistency of custard. It may be served in a variety of ways, but the usual fashion on the coast is to cut the pear in half and in the cavity occupied by the pit, pour vinegar, oil and mustard, with a little salt and pepper (some add Worcestershire sauce) and scrape out the pulp with a spoon. The pear has a peculiarly rich, buttery taste, and this, combined with the condiments already mentioned, is greatly relished by those who have acquired the taste.

Our young friends partook of them sparingly, and indeed it may as well be stated at once that tropical fruits, such as they are, do not taste good to a Northerner and are really very poor, compared with those of the temperate zones. It is true a few hundred years of careful, scientific culture may so change them, as it has our own fruits and vegetables, as to make them really luscious, but at present their excellence exists mostly in the imaginations of those who have never seen them.

The evening proved a most enjoyable one, and it was time to go all too soon; by ten o'clock our friends had thanked their kind entertainer for his hospitality and were on their way to the Nubia, having first accepted an invitation to spend the next day with Mr. Lyon. This gentleman is an early riser and his gig was alongside next morning before the Ogowe Band had breakfasted, but they did not keep it waiting long and were soon on their way up the river.

Hope Factory is the furthest up the river of the long line of trading-posts and is well situated for business, as all the canoes coming down the river must pass it first. Mr. Lyon met them at the wharf and showed them all the factory buildings and the manner in which palm-oil is prepared for shipment. The casks are lifted from the canoes by an iron crane at the end of a long, covered shed and are rolled to one side out of the way. All the buying is done in the morning; in the afternoon comes the work of preparing the oil for the home market. It is all taken from the casks in which it came down the river and put in great caldrons heated by steam, and boiled to clear it from impurities; it is then ladled out into clean new casks, bunged tightly, and the casks whitewashed and rolled into the store-room.

Kernels are carried up from a landing on shore and measured in tubs, and are thrown in a bin where a belt, with tin buckets on it, carries them to another bin in the second story; from here they come down a chute into sacks, which are then sewn up and piled to await shipment. A steam engine furnishes power for running the endless belt, and also saws wood and pumps water, as well as makes steam to boil the great oil kettles. A railway track runs from the store-houses to the end of the pier and so makes it easier to handle so much heavy weight. Everything was in perfect order and the quietness was remarkable, considering the amount of work accomplished.

In the back yard were many kinds of trees, and here our young friends first saw coffee growing and ripening on the trees; Mr. Lyon had some served after lunch and it was excellent, fully equaling the best Java. There was a large chicken-house, a pigeon-house, duck-pond, and goat-house. The quarters for the workmen were clean and tidy and so were the kitchen and laundry; the girls came to the conclusion that Mr. Lyon was a good housekeeper.

After a careful inspection of the premises the party sat down on the front veranda to rest and enjoy the lovely view on the river. As Hope Factory is located on the bend of the river, there is a clear view of the entire water front of the foreign settlement, and with a good glass everything moving on the water may be seen.

The Judge had been surprised to see so large an amount of rice unloaded from the steamer; he had expected to see rice exported rather than imported. Mr. Lyon informed him that the coast people, especially in large towns like Duketown, would rather buy their food than raise it, for they thought it was easier to spend some of their profits from the oil trade in purchasing provisions, than to dig in the ground and grow them. What was most surprising was that none of the interior tribes attempted to supply this demand for food, but left it for white men to import from abroad. Hundreds of tons of rice, hard bread, salt beef and codfish are sold in the oil rivers every year. Many of the wealthier men purchase

MISSION HOUSE, OLD CALABAR

flour, butter, tea, sugar, coffee, sardines, and other tinned provisions—paying for all these things in palm-oil.

In the yard in front of the house were twenty-seven great hogsheads of American leaf tobacco, giving good evidence of a love for the "fragrant weed" by the dark sons of this tropic land.

While they were conversing a great drumming was heard up the river, with shouting and wild songs, and presently canoes came in sight around the bend. They were such as our friends had seen at Bonny, many of them larger, and were full from stem to stern with a double line of men paddling with all their might and singing at the top of their voices, while the drummers beat their tom-toms furiously, and a medicine-man in each canoe, dressed in a most fantastic manner, was dancing and throwing his body in grotesque attitudes.

Mr. Lyon explained there had been a great "palaver" or council up at the markets, about the price of oil, and the Calabar people were now returning. It was a wondrous sight, for there were more than forty canoes and perhaps two thousand men; the canoes had great quantities of fetiches trailing in the water from bow and stern, and the great chiefs were arrayed in a gorgeous regalia of monkey skins, feathers and paint. A street parade of a circus is tame compared with this barbarous pageant of negro savagery; these men were all devil-worshipers and it was easy to believe they were in league with the powers of evil.

In speaking of factory life, Mr. Lyon explained that factory people are astir early. Usually by the first dawning light, a servant brings a cup of coffee and a piece of toast to each one, either to the dining-room or to his own room as he may choose. The factory bell is rung and all hands "turn to" and the business of the day is begun. Native people are also astir early and most of the produce is bought by nine o'clock. At ten A. M. the shop is closed and the white men have breakfast. At noon the bell is rung for all hands to "knock off" and a rest is given until two P. M., when work begins again; at six o'clock the labors of the day are ended, and quiet reigns until the morning.

At Old Calabar, by agreement among the traders, (an agreement faithfully kept) no work is done on Sunday, and as a matter of fact, the Sabbath is more strictly observed on this wild African river than in our own home cities. Who knows but Africa may yet teach by example the so-called Christian nations of the world!

The Judge was greatly interested with this information and made inquiry concerning the Scotch Mission and its work among the people. He was informed that it was for many years a power in the community and had done great good, but that dissensions had crept in, and, at Duketown at least, had destroyed its influence. Mrs. Ross has an independent church with a Sabbath congregation of six hundred, and she enjoys the respect and esteem of both natives and foreign traders. Younger missionaries have recently been sent out by the Scotch society and these have gone up the country and are busy building stations and doing other preliminary work, and it is hoped that substantial advance will be made in educating and Christianizing the people. There is quite a strong force at Creektown, a few miles up the river, and a large church has been built entirely by subscriptions of natives and traders.

The Duketown mission was in full sight from Mr. Lyon's house and looked so cool and inviting among the trees, that Mr. McGee expressed a desire to visit it. Mr. Lyon replied that he would be most happy to accompany him, and at five o'clock the whole party were on their way down the river. They landed at the wharf at Mr. Gilles's factory and climbed the steep path back of his house, that led up to the mission premises. The hill kept off the sea-breeze and the walk was a warm one. The location of the mission was a pleasant one when it was reached, but our friends felt it was a mistake to put the mission on top of a hill where it was somewhat difficult of access, when the river is the natural highway for natives and foreigners alike; but little work appeared to be going on and our young travelers did not make a long stay.

An excursion to Creektown had been arranged for our friends next day, but it rained and they could not go.

On Thursday morning at five o'clock the anchor was hoisted from the muddy bed of the Old Calabar river, and through the mists of the early dawn the Ogowe Band saw the white houses of their trader friends fade away in the distance. As they doubled Nine Fathom Point the sun's rays began to pierce the dull gray vapors with streams of soft white light, fit emblem of the Sun of Righteousness which even now is rising ó'er this dark land, bringing life and immortality to light through the gospel, growing brighter and brighter unto the perfect day.

Chapter X.

KAMERUN AND ELOBY.

AFTER the Nubia had passed the bar at the mouth of the Old Calabar river, Captain Davis joined the Judge and his young companions, and the conversation was very naturally upon the sights and incidents of their stay at Old Calabar. The Captain called the attention of the Judge to the peculiar geographical location of Old Calabar, and in order the better to illustrate what he was about to say, he sent to his room for a chart.

"Now," said he, "you will see by this chart that the Kong mountains, which thus far have been the coast range, end near the Calabar river in rather low foot-hills, and the Cameroons range lie distinctly to the south of it; this gives a free pathway to the interior. You will notice too that this is the nearest point on the coast to the heart of the great Soudan. For myself I do not believe in a healthy interior; I do not believe there is anything healthy about Africa either morally or physically, but if there is any healthy interior anywhere it lies to the north and northeast of Old Calabar.

GOVERNMENT HOUSE, KAMERUN, SOUTHERN GUINEA

"We know that this vast region is well watered, has a fertile soil, is largely an open grassy country and is certainly free from the dense, damp forests of the equatorial region and the coast-line. It may be that some extensive region can be found where white colonists could live, which would afford a favorable outlet for the surplus population of Europe; or, a second India might be made there of Hindoo coolies and other Eastern nations. A railroad of but a few hundred miles in length would extend to Lake Tsad and would drain a far more productive country than the Congo. I believe that to-day the world presents no more inviting investment for capital than such a railroad."

As the Judge examined the map, he was convinced the Captain was right, and he felt sure such an enterprise, if carefully managed, would be a real success.

At four P. M. the Nubia arrived at Victoria, at the foot of Mt. Albert of the Cameroons range. This mountain rises from the sea to a height of 13,800 feet, and its bold form was strongly outlined against the sky. It is a volcano and smoke may sometimes be seen rising from its summit. A few years ago the side of the mountain opened about half way up and mud and water burst forth. It is clothed with a dense forest growth, and as the evening sun shone upon it, it presented a striking and beautiful appearance.

The bay of Victoria is full of islands which rise rather abruptly from the water, and are covered with a solid mass of vegetation of the most brilliant green, making them appear like gigantic emeralds set upon the bosom of the sea. Upon one of these islands is a large house belonging to the English consul; but he is seldom at home, for most of his time is spent in traveling up and down the coast within the limits of his jurisdiction. On shore, at the foot of the mountain, are four or five European houses near the beach. One of these is the Protestant Mission where the beloved Robert Smith lived and died. No man on the African coast was more widely known and loved than he. There is a large native population, not gathered in one town by the water-side, but scattered in small villages through the forest.

Victoria is exceedingly rich in tropical vegetation, but it is rather out of the steamer track, and is a lonely place. There was but little to put ashore here, but as the Kamerun river was but a comparatively short distance away, the Nubia remained at anchor through the night, giving every one a fine opportunity for a good sleep. When at anchor in the rivers, the nights on an African steamer are not favorable for sleeping; the heat is great, the state-rooms close and confined, and mosquitoes are sometimes troublesome; it is usually considered unsafe to remain on deck, and so every one is thankful for a quiet night outside.

At four A. M. the Nubia was again under steam and by breakfast time was entering the delta of the Kamerun river. This delta is quite extensive although not nearly so large as those of the Niger and Ogowe rivers. There is an inland navigation almost to Victoria, and also for some distance to the south. The water of this river is very muddy, perhaps more so than that of any river on the coast.

The foreign settlement is on the south side of the river, about twenty miles up, on the first solid land above the mangroves. Here a clay cliff, some thirty or forty feet high, faces the river; at the foot of this cliff are the factories and store-houses, and upon its top are the government buildings, mission station and native villages. The river is narrow and at low tide exposes large mud-banks to the sun; opposite are low islands covered with mangroves, and, with the exception of here and there a dry spot, these same trees extend up the river to the foot-hills of the Cameroons range. On a clear day Mt. Albert is plainly seen rearing his giant bulk far above the line of fleecy clouds; as a rule, however, a clear atmosphere is a rarity in the coast region; there are not many rainy days, most of the rain falling at night, but the air is so charged with moisture as to present a slight hazy appearance, as though one were looking through a thin, white, gauzy veil.

The Nubia pushed her way steadily against the turbid tide and at ten A. M., anchored between two hulks abreast the town. There are several of these hulks used as trading-posts, and they are all fast in the mud close to shore, to which they are attached both fore and aft by heavy chain cables. Notwithstanding the mud-banks, the general appearance of the place is good; nowhere else had our friends seen so many oil-palms, nor such fine specimens as they saw here.

Coming up the river the first object to strike the eye is Government House, built of brick and painted a fine shade of terra cotta. It is modern in style, as may be seen in the engraving, and presents a pleasing contrast to the glaring white houses so universal on the coast. Next to Government House are two galvanized iron houses used as offices by the government officials; these are all on the level ground on the top of the bluff and are surrounded by lawn and gravel walks. Good concrete steps lead down to a covered iron pier which forms an excellent landing-place. This part of the coast, from the

Campo river on the south, to a point near the Old Calabar river on the north, is a German Protectorate ruled by a governor appointed by the Imperial Government. The Germans took possession in 1885 after a hard fight with the natives, and have been active in the work of improvement, and will doubtless do much to develop and civilize the country. A free school has been established and the native tribes are kept in subjection, so that trade and commerce may flow on unimpeded. It may well be doubted, whether on the whole, foreign colonial enterprises are beneficial to Africa, but there can be no question that the English and Germans are far superior to the Latin nations in their influence upon the natives.

The Nubia was anchored close by the mission landing and soon two of the brethren, Rev. Messrs. Arntz and Bastian, came off and were introduced by Captain Davis. These brethren very cordially invited the Judge and his young friends to visit the mission and they promised to do so toward evening.

Among the traders who came for their mails and to hear the news, was Mr. Kudeling, agent for the great Hamburg firm of Jantzen and Thormahlen. When he heard that the Judge and his party were going to Gaboon, to be the guests of his friend Mr. Reading, he gave them a pressing invitation to make his factory their home, as he felt he could not do too much for any one in whom Mr. Reading was interested. As his factory adjoined the mission-station, the Judge decided to take lunch with Mr. Kudeling and walk up to the mission in the afternoon, and it was not long before he and the Ogowe Band were seated in the front room of the factory, through which the breeze passed on its way up the river, making the room comfortably cool.

A BIT OF THE KAMERUN BEACH, LOW TIDE

Mr. Kudeling gave the Judge a long description of the palm-oil trade, and the habits and customs of the natives. He informed his guest that the Kamerun was made up of a number of small streams that drained the southern slopes of the Cameroons range and were navigable for canoes as far as the foot-hills, after which they were obstructed by rapids. No one had succeeded in fully exploring these rivers, nor the country beyond them, owing partly to the dense jungles, and partly to the jealousy of the natives. At a point some distance south of the Kamerun there had been greater success, one explorer having penetrated for a distance of twenty-three days in a northeasterly direction. From what he saw it was quite certain that after the belt of dense jungle, some two hundred miles in width, was passed, there was a fine country thickly populated, but at present raising little that was valuable for export.

Referring to the possibility of a railroad, as suggested by the Judge, Mr. Kudeling thought the natural difficulties to be overcome would be very great, owing to the mountains and the jungle; still, if the first two hundred miles could be gotten over, and some of the navigable affluents of the Congo reached, it might open a wide extent of the interior to German influence.

The Judge shared the opinion, common in civilized lands, that if the narrow belt of country between the coast range and the sea (covered with jungle, containing a sparse population, unhealthful, and cursed with the rum traffic), produced so much oil, rubber and ivory for export, what might not be expected from the vast interior when once put in communication with the sea; an interior not only of immense extent, but with a large population all eager for the comforts which civilized nations stood ready to furnish.

Mr. Kudeling remarked that this was a delightful dream, but a mistaken one. He called Judge McGee's attention to the fact that the oil palm is only found in commercial quantities in the sea-coast region, and on the low lands of the Congo Basin; that rubber grows only in deep, dense forests where but few people can live; that elephants can exist in a wild state only where the country is comparatively uninhabited; that wherever there is a fine open country the people have little or nothing to sell; that the greatest amount of produce is sent from those rivers where the white men remain near the sea; and that the opening up of the interior has decreased the shipments, as is true of the Ogowe and the Congo.

The Judge admitted the African riddle was a complicated one to solve. "The volume of African trade," observed Mr. Kudeling, "will not greatly increase until the native people learn to cultivate the soil and obtain from it those products that are needed in our home-lands, such as sugar, coffee, cocoa, and spices; this at present they will not do."

The idea of colonizing Africa with Chinese, Hindoos and other industrious nations was then discussed, and Mr. Kudeling informed the Judge that the most intelligent among the traders believed it might be a success if the plan were wisely carried out. While Mr. Kudeling and the Judge were discussing these weighty problems, the Ogowe Band were out on the piazza [seen in the picture], with their eyes opened wide to drink in the novel scenes of the strange land they were visiting. It was now low tide and the river-bed was exposed to view for a long distance from shore. The towns-women were coming down the

the path with great baskets of dark brown roots on their shoulders; these baskets were held in place by a broad band that passed over the forehead. The loads were heavy and the poor women were bent nearly double sometimes by their great weight. Little children trotted by their mother's side, full of life and fun, all unmindful of the life of toil and privation in store for them.

The Band watched with eager interest to see what these women were going to do. They saw them go out upon the exposed river-bed until they came almost to the water's edge; then they began to dig with a short-handled hoe, something like a small adze. The soil here was gravel and the scrape, scrape, scrape, from many hoes, attested the energy of the diggers.

"What are they digging for?" queried Mamie.

"Let's wait a little and see," suggested Laura. When a good big hole had been made, the women took banana leaves and lined it neatly and then peeled the roots and placed them carefully in the leaf-lined hole; after this the gravel was carefully heaped in a conical mound over the covering of leaves, and the work was complete.

"I wonder how each one can tell her own mound when she comes to open it?" said Jessie.

"Why," said Lulu, "I saw one of them pull out an end of a leaf and fix it very carefully along the side of her mound; I would not wonder if they put a little private mark on them in that way."

"These must be cassava roots," added Hattie, "and I remember hearing Mr. Reading say one time when he was in America, that they contained a poisonous juice, and must be soaked a few days before using; I should not be surprised if this was what the women were doing."

When the women had finished burying their roots, they went to other mounds, and, opening them, took out the large white roots, carried them to where the water was knee-deep and washed them clean, then piled them on round wooden trays, and balancing them carefully on their heads, picked up their baskets and hoes, called the little ones to them, and trudged along homewards no doubt to prepare dinner for a hungry family.

Poor heathen mothers! how carefully, and may be lovingly, you provide for your husband and your little ones, just as thousands of gentle, loving mothers do at home; do you know there is a beautiful world of light where you may rest when your earthly toil is ended? Have ever hopes of a better life entered your dark breasts to cheer your hearts and help you along life's weary way? Do vague longings for a better land sometimes steal over your soul? Who can tell? Are we not taught that you are feeling after the loving, infinite One, if haply you might find Him, though He be not far from any one of us? Who can estimate the joy of making known to these toiling ones that dear Saviour who is the great Burden-bearer as well as Redeemer of mankind?

The boys were greatly interested in some half-grown youngsters who were fishing. Whenever you want to wake up a boy all over, show him some one fishing. But not only were those boys fishing, but they were pursuing their finny prey after a novel fashion. They had taken several long banana leaves and fastened them end to end so as to form a length of several yards; the thin part of the leaf hung down from the mid-rib and did duty as a net, and was not such a bad substitute in the shallow water. One of the boys would start out from shore with an end of the banana-leaf net, and then he would circle

A BIT OF THE KAMERUN BEACH, HIGH TIDE

round and the two would drag the impromptu net quickly up on the gravel, bringing crabs and little fishes with it. A third boy carried a wooden bowl in which the game was put, and they appeared to enjoy the sport as much as some members of the Band would have done.

At four P. M. the Judge and his young friends walked up the path that led to the mission. This mission was begun many years ago by the English Baptists and was in many respects very successful. When the Germans desired to annex the country they asserted that these English missionaries incited the natives to resist them; be this as it may, the Germans were not long in possession of Kamerun when the enterprise was transferred by the English Society to the Basle Society, a German-Swiss organization, and it is now under their management. They are trying to establish stations at various points up the river, and it is to be hoped their efforts may be productive of good; but, belonging as they do to the conquering nation, they do not as yet stand well with the people.

The Ogowe Band were very kindly received by the brethren at the mission, and also by Mrs. Leitzer who had recently been left a widow, and who was now acting in the capacity of housekeeper. Coffee was served, and then Mr. Arntz took our friends around to inspect the premises. The house is two storied, built of brick made on the premises, and is covered with a galvanized iron roof. All the buildings, including the church, are of the same materials. The grounds are small, and the Judge thought the brethren made a mistake in allowing the bananas to grow so near the house, forming a barrier to shut out the sea-breeze and all view of the river, and making the house damp and unwholesome.

After supper Mr. Arntz took his guests up to the veranda of the second story, and here, above the broad banana leaves, was an extensive view of river and marshy islands. The veranda extended around the house, and on the land side the brown houses of the people were seen clustered beneath the oil-palms, presenting interesting pictures of African home-life. After spending a pleasant evening Mr. Bastian took our friends back to the Nubia and bade them good-night.

The next morning the Judge and his young companions went to visit the Governor. They landed at the neat, covered pier and climbed the concrete steps to the level plain at the top of the bluff where the government buildings are. The grounds were tastefully laid out, and many trees and other plants were seen that were new to their eyes.

Baron Soden, the governor, received them cordially, without any fuss or parade, and soon made them feel quite at home. They had a pleasant chat and found him to be in every way an accomplished gentleman. He regretted their short stay in the German possessions, and hoped they would arrange for a longer visit before their return to America.

On their way back to the Nubia our friends called at one of the trading hulks to pay their respects to Captain Dayas to whom they had letters of introduction. The Captain was an "old coaster," and told them many incidents of former years, before steamers had brought Africa into such close communication with the rest of the world. He showed his visitors over the hulk, but it did not differ materially from the factories already described, except that everything was necessarily crowded. The Captain told them that business was not nearly so profitable as in former years.

In the afternoon when the sun had somewhat lost his power, and the sea-breeze had cooled the air a little, the Judge and his party went ashore and took a stroll through the native towns. All the leading men among the people had, when young, been educated in the mission school and so could speak English, which enabled our friends to go about without an interpreter as they could always find some one to converse with.

From the government buildings a well constructed road runs parallel with the river to the upper end of the island, for Kamerun is upon an island. This road wound among the groups of houses and beneath the shade of lovely palms, making a delightful promenade. The town is two miles long and nearly as broad; it is not built in continuous streets, but with short ones; or small groups of houses are separated by strips a few rods wide planted closely with bananas and plantains; each of these little settlements belongs to those of one family name, and its domestic politics is administered by the oldest man of that family name, who calls the small aggregation of houses, "his town." Between these "towns" are narrow footpaths among the banana groves, and now the wide government road makes a broad avenue through the whole. Most of the houses were oblong in form and built of bamboo; some were made of boards, and there were a few two storied ones of brick which the Baptist missionaries had taught them to make.

The people wondered greatly to see so many white folks walking through their town, and they were especially surprised to see the girls. The little children were much frightened at beholding so many pale-faces and ran crying to their mothers; indeed the sight of a white face everywhere in Africa creates consternation among the children; a white face in this land seems to be an unnatural object and even the wild beasts of the forest notice it quickly. All hunters find it expedient to black their faces before going in pursuit of game.

In front of some of the houses were quantities of light brown nuts exposed upon mats in the sun to dry. An old man explained that this was cacao and then going to a dense bushy tree with large, long leaves, he drew aside the foliage and showed them the golden fruits or pods that contain the seeds. The Judge knew at once that this was the bean from which chocolate is made. The old man said they gathered the fruit when ripe and dried the seeds in the sun, and then sold them to the traders for a six-pence a pound.

Near the farther end of the town they heard a great drumming and singing, and following the sound they came upon a dancing party. An open space surrounded by bamboo houses was filled with a crowd of lookers-on all critically watching the party in the centre. At one end of this square a fine large house was built on posts and our friends were invited to climb the short ladder to the front veranda where they were presented to the master of the house who was giving this ball in honor of some important family event.

From this piazza an excellent view was obtained of the dancing party which consisted of something over a hundred women standing close together in single file in the form of a circle. The orchestra consisted of several drums beaten furiously by stalwart negroes and to this were added the voices of the women chanting a wild song to which they kept time with their bodies; their move-

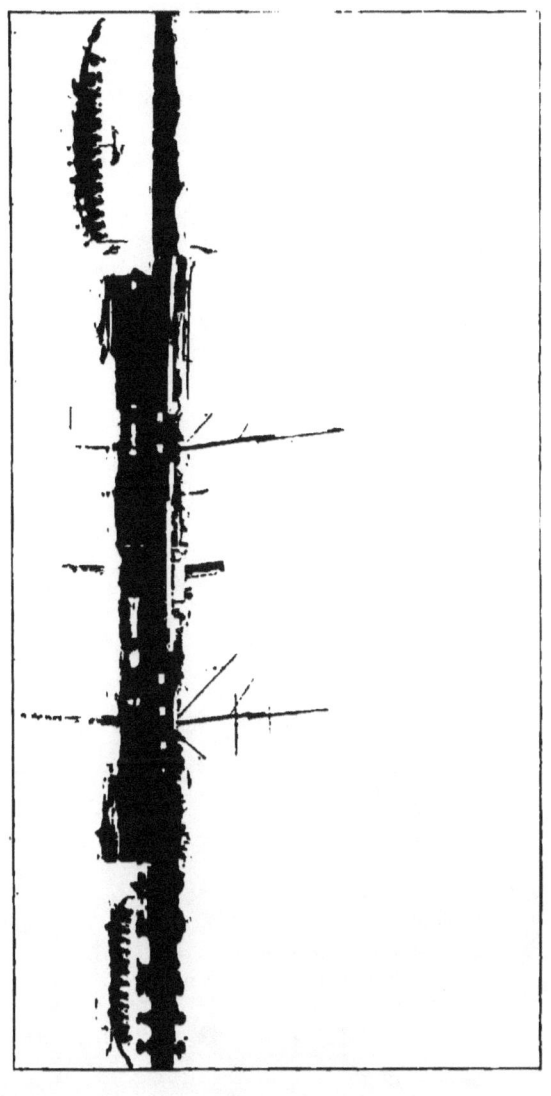
THE NUBIA AT ANCHOR IN THE KAMERUN RIVER

ments were oftentimes more energetic than elegant, but after all, perhaps not more objectionable than a fashionable dance at home.

The Ogowe Band soon had enough of it and going down the ladder they continued their walk. They were scarcely out of hearing of the drummers when they came upon piles of brick, and men squaring logs to make beams for some new building; a well dressed and intelligent looking black man standing near introduced himself as the "pastor of the church," and informed the Judge that the native congregation was building a new house of worship, making the bricks and doing the work themselves. He said this native congregation paid him his salary and also kept up several schools in the town and country districts, but they found it hard work to do so much and it required a great deal of sacrifice on their part. He walked along for some distance with the Band and gave them much valuable information about the people and the mission work, and when he left them he gave them into the care of a young man to show them through some of the byways of the town and then conduct them safely to the landing.

When they reached the steamer they were real tired, but a change of clothes and a good dinner rested them, and they enjoyed their chairs and the sea-breeze that evening, while they talked over what they had seen during the day, and it was a late hour before they retired for the night.

The next morning the ship was half way down the river when the tourists came on deck; it was a lovely Sabbath day, quiet and beautiful; one of those days when the calm and peace of Heaven enters the soul and we feel lifted above the worry and care of earthly existence—a day to do one good, restful and comforting both to body and mind.

At intervals during the day the coast-line was in sight, but far away to the eastward and not near enough to be distinctly seen.

On Monday morning the Nubia was headed for the shore, and when the Ogowe Band reached the deck after their coffee and toast, the dark, heavy mass of Cape St. John was on the left and the island of Corisco away to the right, while before them were the waters of Corisco Bay. This bay is some twenty miles in depth and the water in many places is shallow; as they passed in they could see quite plainly with the aid of a glass the American Presbyterian Mission station. Indeed this society had formerly three stations on this island, but there is now only one and that is in charge of a native man. It was thought that because this island was so small and so far out in the sea it would be healthful, but such did not prove to be the case as the well filled cemetery can testify, and now the efforts of the society have been transferred to the main-land.

At nine o'clock the Nubia anchored off the island of Eloby where the foreign settlement is. This tract of country about Corisco bay is claimed by the Spanish, and there is a Spanish military post on Eloby. This island is small and has no native population, being occupied entirely by the trading factories and the Spanish mission and military post. It is a lonely place in which to live and one needs a good flow of spirits to keep from getting the "blues" here.

On the main-land, four or five miles away, was a large English factory at the mouth of the Muni river which comes down from the Sierra del Crystal range. Mr. Armstrong, in charge of Holt & Co.'s factory, gave the Judge and his party a cordial invitation to take a little run ashore and visit his factory, which they did. The chief article of export is rubber, there being but little oil offered for sale in this neighborhood. Everything about Mr. Armstrong's factory was in excellent order showing him to be a good manager. He informed the Judge that each factory paid a tax of a thousand dollars a year to the Spanish Governor and that trade was slow and unprofitable.

At four P. M. the Nubia left Eloby and the American voyagers began to gather up their things and get ready to leave the ship in view of an early termination of their journey.

CHAPTER XI.

ARRIVAL AT GABOON.

THE Ogowe Band were astir with the dawning light. The Nubia had been running "dead slow" all night for when once out of Corisco Bay she had less than fifty miles between her and the outer buoy off the mouth of the Gaboon; as soon as the Captain could see the beacon on Sandy Point he had put the engines to "full speed" and this had roused our friends from their slumbers.

When the Judge and his young companions reached the deck they saw before them a wide expanse of water with the shore-line on either side barely visible ; away to the eastward, up river, nothing was to be seen but water; indeed the Gaboon river is more like an inlet from the sea, than a river, for its average width for the first thirty miles is at least ten miles. It had rained some during the night and heavy banks of mist hung over the land as if some of the clouds had fallen from the skies and were resting there.

ELOBY, CORISCO BAY

ARRIVAL AT GABOON

The Nubia was heading for the Point on the south side of the river; by the time she reached this and turned her prow toward the northern bank, where the foreign settlements are, the sun had burst through the mists and clouds and was shining brightly upon river and land. When half-way across the river Captain Davis ran up the stars and stripes at the fore, as a signal to the American Mission that he had passengers on board for them. There was considerable speculation among the members of the Band as to whether the signal would be seen and understood, but the Captain told them there was no doubt Mr. Reading was watching them for he had an unusually good glass, and it was the custom of those ashore to scan approaching steamers as soon as they were visible.

As they neared the northern bank they saw spread out before them the finest landscape they had yet seen in Africa; indeed the view from the usual steamer anchorage is one of the most beautiful in the world. Along the river-bank for two and a half miles are the factories and residences of the foreign settlement; about the government buildings this assumes the proportions of a good sized town, with large stone buildings, a cathedral, machine-shops, and a stone pier extending into the river. The brown roofs of the native villages are almost hidden by the broad banana leaves and the heavy masses of foliage of the mango trees. Back of the town are hills and grass-fields with little clusters of houses here and there, and in the distance are high hills covered with heavy forests. Along the beach is a fringe of cocoanut palms, their great fronds trembling in the morning breeze, while the river is alive with canoes, boats and steam-launches moving about, and larger vessels at anchor.

At the extreme upper end of this charming picture, upon a hill rather more than a quarter of a mile from the water, is the Baraka station of the American Presbyterian Mission. It is quite a little village of itself, with a grass-field on the slope next the river and a large orchard of fruit trees back of the houses. The new church, but recently completed, is a conspicuous object, and the dwelling houses look cool and inviting beneath the shade of the cocoanut and breadfruit trees.

The Nubia stopped her engines near a large white hulk anchored a mile from shore just abreast of the government buildings; this the Doctor told the Band was the "guard-ship." "We must remain here," said he, "until the health officer comes off and give us permission to pass." "Gaboon," he continued, "is one of the most troublesome places on the coast, we must get permission for everything we do, and the officials seem to take delight in humbugging us; the people on shore are slow to take away their cargo, we get little or no return cargo, and we steamer people have little love for Gaboon, I can tell you."

The Doctor had scarcely finished his discouraging narration when a boat was seen pulling off from the guard-ship and in a few minutes was alongside the ladder. The Purser handed the ship's papers to the officer in the boat, answered a few questions, and was then told it was all right; the boat returned to the guard-ship, and the Nubia steamed off a half a mile and anchored.

A few minutes later Captain Davis came down from the bridge and pointed to a boat heading for the Nubia which he said was the mission boat. The Judge and his companions watched this boat with eager interest as it drew gradually nearer; it was propelled at a good speed by six strong Kru-men, and in the stern was a short, stout

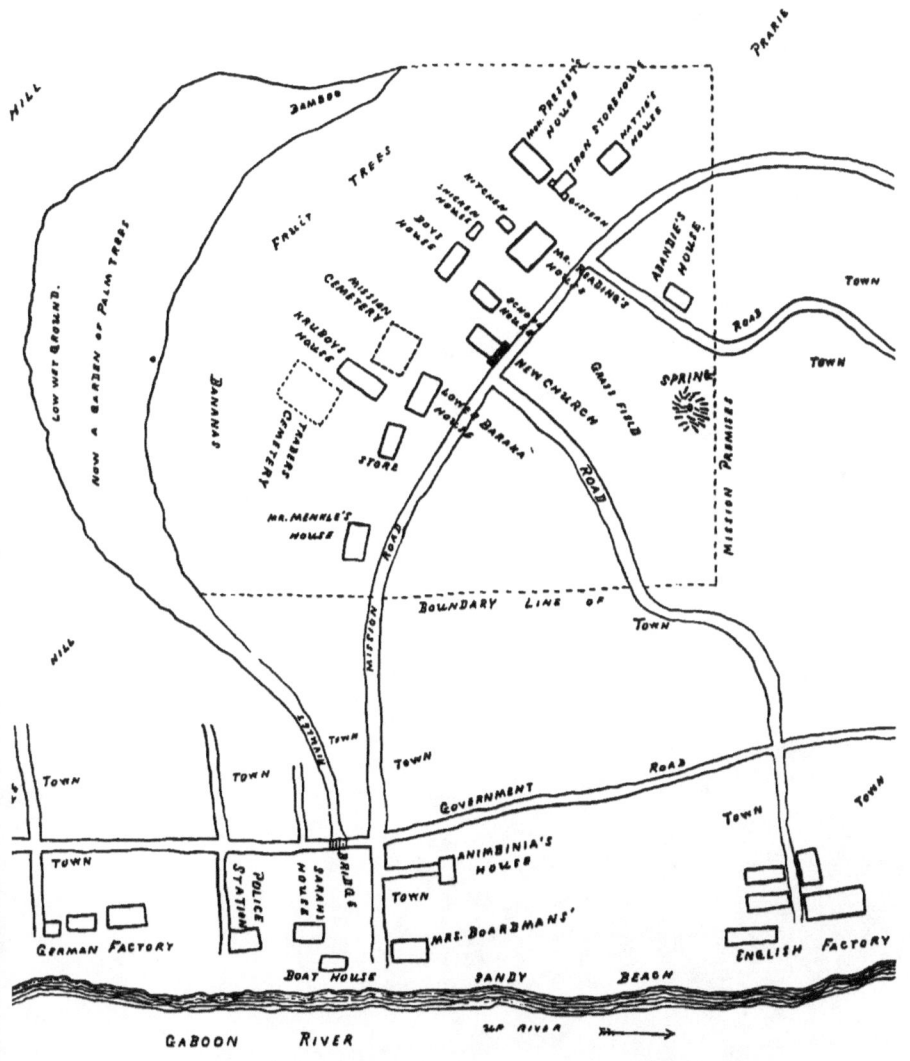

PLAN OF BARAKA MISSION PREMISES.   DRAWN FOR THIS WORK.

man of forty, with long side whiskers; this was Judge McGee's friend, Mr. Reading, missionary in charge of the Gaboon station. The Judge waved his handkerchief and so did the members of the Band, which was responded to by Mr. Reading by raising his hat; soon he was alongside and up the ladder, and he could scarcely believe his senses when he saw before him his old friend Judge McGee and a full round dozen of young visitors. This was the first time in the history of the mission that visitors had come all the way from America, and Mr. Reading felt himself extremely fortunate at being thus honored. Captain Davis inquired if he had seen the signal, and he said he had, and supposed there was some of his coast acquaintances on board who wished to see him.

It was now breakfast time and all hands repaired to the saloon, but there was more talking done than eating, for the events of the voyage had to be related, and the news from the shore told. Boats and canoes now began to gather about the Nubia, and a steam-launch brought a custom-house officer who was to remain on board until the steamer left, and without whose permission not a single article could leave the ship. The customs regulations at Gaboon are intricate, and it is not an easy matter to land a large lot of baggage; a small amount may be taken ashore at the police station near the mission landing, but larger quantities must go to the custom-house for examination.

The Captain placed his gig and steam-launch at the disposal of the party, and Mr. Reading proposed that they should all go ashore with the portmanteaus and smaller articles and in the afternoon he and the Judge would return for the trunks; this plan met the approval of the custom official and it was not long before the two boats were filled with the happy party and cutting through the water behind the steam-launch on the way to shore.

When near the beach they "cast loose" from the launch, and turning their bows toward the river so as to cut the breakers, they drifted ashore stern first until they began to bump and then the Kru-men jumped over the side, leaving one man in the bow to keep the boat facing the waves, and began to carry the passengers ashore. An official at once walked down from the station to see what was brought ashore, but he made no trouble for he knew Mr. Reading well, and a few words of explanation was all that was needed.

The Ogowe Band were delighted to be on land again; at all the other places they had gone ashore they were transient visitors and the ship was their home, but now the voyage was ended, they were cut loose from the steamer and the goal of all their journey was reached. They had often pictured in their minds what Gaboon must be like, but now they found it quite different from what they expected.

Mr. Reading's little carriage was in waiting at the boat-house; at his suggestion two of the girls got in it and were quickly wheeled away by four of the boat's crew, followed by the rest of the party on foot. Some of the mission boys were awaiting the boat's arrival, and these carried the portmanteaus and willow chairs. As the party passed up the street through the town the native people came to greet the strangers and inquire of Mr. Reading in their own language who they were, for they had an idea these were all new missionaries come to live among them; they gave many exclamations of surprise when they learned they were simply visitors.

BARAKA MISSION STATION GABOON

ARRIVAL AT GABOON

The four Kru-men with the carriage were soon at the top of the hill and Mrs. Reading, who came out on the piazza when she heard them coming, was not a little surprised at seeing two girls, almost young ladies, instead of the husband she was expecting. When she learned who they were and who were coming, it almost took her breath away, but she soon recovered herself and gave them a hearty welcome. Little Lizzie, the only child of the household, was glad to see them too, but she was bashful and kept close to her black playmates who had come in the house with her.

The news of the new arrivals quickly spread over the premises, and by the time Mr. Reading and his party had reached the house, numbers of black faces were seen everywhere trying to get a view of the strangers. After introductions all around, the Judge in behalf of the Band gave a short account of the journey and their reasons for coming to Africa, which were, to see the country, and learn what they could of the manners and customs of the people, and the progress of mission work among them. Mr. Reading commended the idea and promised to do all he could to assist them in carrying it out; coffee was then served and Mrs. Reading gave orders to her girls to prepare rooms for the use of the visitors.

After lunch Mr. Reading and the Judge rode to the beach in the little carriage and then went to the Nubia in the mission gig, to see about landing the trunks; at the same time the platform wagon was sent to the custom-house two miles away to bring them to the mission when they had been inspected. Before getting in the boat Mr. Reading went to the police station and informed the officials where he was going, and for what purpose. Nothing can leave the Gaboon beach, nor can anything be landed thereon, without a written statement countersigned at the custom-house, except personal luggage accompanying passengers. As nothing was being taken to the Nubia, except bananas and mangoes to the Captain, nothing was needed but simple permission.

The sea-breeze was now coming in and the waves getting high so that it took rather more than an hour to pull to the ship. Everything was in confusion on her decks, as is always the case when cargo is being worked, and it was some little time before the trunks were ready to go ashore. Captain Davis very kindly gave the use of one of his surf-boats and the launch, so that when once ready they were not long in reaching the pier.

The Judge thanked the Captain most heartily for all his kindness and courtesy, and Mr. Reading invited him ashore to dinner at six o'clock, which was declined, as he would get back to his ship too late in the evening, and this was now the rainy season for this part of the coast.

When the trunks arrived at the pier, the men who had come with the wagon carried them to the custom-house and they were opened, but there was little trouble; the Judge was asked to make a "declaration" of all articles that had not been in actual use, and when this was done, a duty varying from ten to twenty-five per cent was charged, the money paid, and the luggage was free.

The Kru-men now loaded the trunks on the platform wagon and departed for the mission, while Mr. Reading and his guest returned to the gig and an hour later were at the mission landing. As they were carried ashore a black policeman came to see if anything had been brought from the steamer, and when he found there was nothing, he returned to his chief to report.

While the gentlemen were away for the trunks, Mrs. Reading and the Band were not idle; the boys found an agreeable friend in Mr. Presset the French teacher, who took them to his room and entertained them with accounts of his African experiences.

The girls gathered around Mrs. Reading in the parlor and it was not long before they had a number of callers; these were mostly members of the church, who came to pay their respects to the young ladies; sweet-faced, intelligent women they were, and as they spoke excellent English, they could converse with the young ladies without an interpreter. Indeed the Band could not but confess a certain amount of disappointment, for, after their long journey, and many rude scenes by the way, here they were at their journey's end, and behold, a civilized community and well dressed, intelligent natives addressing them in English!

The house, too, looked wonderfully comfortable and home-like; to be sure it was without ceiling, open right up to the roof, but it had neat China matting on the floor, plenty of rocking-chairs, lounges, desk, and organ; while upon the centre-table were the same newspapers and magazines to be found in a well-to-do home in an American city. For lunch, too, the table looked as inviting with its white linen and silver as if their mothers at home were expecting friends, while the food was nearly the same as it might have been in Philadelphia.

"Never mind," said Mrs. Reading in reply to Mamie, "if you visit some of the country places, as I expect you will, you will experience enough hardship to satisfy you, I have no doubt. Mr. Reading and I have not always found it so agreeable. When we first came to Gaboon we were dependent upon sailing vessels for our food and we have known what it is to be hungry, and when we did have something to eat it was not always of the best.

"I remember one time I went up the Ogowe (the river that gives its name to your Band) with Mrs. Bachelor; Miss Dewsnap was there waiting for us, and both she and the two traders had run short of provisions; they sent her a little corn-meal and she scraped her own barrel to get the flour that stuck fast to it; of this mixture she made three small loaves of bread, one for each of them. They were eating this bread when we arrived with two barrels of flour, and I can tell you there was rejoicing. In our boat journeys on the Ogowe, and in the lakes, we have sometimes run short of provisions, and even when we had something to eat we could not take time to cook it, for it takes a long time to cook in the forest, and we needed to push on in order to reach our destination."

By this time little Lizzie had thrown off some of her shyness and had made friends with the girls, so while her mother went to see about tea, she took her visitors out to see her monkey and parrot. Polly was a nice bird, with grey plumage and a bright red tail; she had her liberty during the day and walked about the yard like a chicken, but her wings were closely clipped so she could not fly away. Every night the house-boys put her in a box until morning, so the rats should not eat her up during the night.

In Africa there are no flies as in our summers at home, but there are a great many rats. These rats might with propriety be called "bush rats," for most of them live outside and come into the house at night; they are very cunning and are not easily caught in a trap.

The girls wanted to hear Polly talk, but this she would not do, she turned her head and looked up at the

MRS. JOSEPH H. READING

strangers in an inquiring way, but she would not say anything. Lizzie told the girls Polly would talk only when alone, and that she could not speak English, but only Mpongwe.

"What is Mpongwe?" asked Grace.

"That is the name of this people, and the name of their language," replied Lizzie, "and I like it ever so much better than English, too."

"Do you talk the same as the black people?" inquired Hattie.

"Yes," was the reply, "I learned that first, and I know it best; my name in Mpongwe is Avanji." [Ah-van-nge]

"What a funny name," said Lulu, "I never heard such a name before."

Across the yard was the monkey, a bright little fellow with a white nose, and a very long tail; he had a little house to live in, and was fastened with a small rope. When he saw the girls coming toward him he jumped around at a great rate and made believe he was afraid, but as soon as they were near enough he grabbed Lulu's dress and gave it a little tear; that young lady promptly gave a good sized scream and the saucy little monkey sat up and laughed at her.

"That is just the way he goes when he gets loose," said Lizzie; "sometimes papa lets him loose just to see him run after the boys and girls; he bites them, too, sometimes, and makes them fear very much."

"What do you give him to eat?" inquired Laura.

"Just whatever we eat," was the reply, "but he likes most of all a piece of meat, or a dried fish; he likes bananas and palm-nuts, and everything."

The girls were inclined to be shy of the monkey, and they went to the kitchen to see how that was arranged. In the tropics there are no fires in the houses; there may indeed be an oil-stove for heating water in the night, in case any one is taken with a chill, but all cooking is done in a separate building some yards away.

The kitchen at Gaboon is built of bamboo, and has a mat roof. The stove is a number eight American cooking stove, and wood is used as fuel; the pipe does not run into a chimney, nor out at the end of the house, but stands straight up for five or six feet and then ends there, so all the smoke comes into the kitchen and must find its way out doors the best it can. The floor is clay, while the pots and pans are like those at home; Ntyndorema [En-chin-do-rem-mah] presided over this important department of the Mission establishment, and was a very good cook, as the Band soon discovered. He was a nice young fellow and devoted to Mr. and Mrs. Reading. They had taken him from the Ogowe Bush when he was as wild a little savage as ever paddled a canoe on that noble river; now he was an educated young man, a member of the church, a singer in the choir, and could cook as good a dinner as any one need wish to eat. Mrs. Reading did not need to go to the kitchen from one week's end to the other; an hour before tea, and two hours before dinner he appeared before her and received his orders, and he needed no further looking after, but when the appointed time came, all was ready. In the evening he came for orders about breakfast, and when bread needed to be baked he did it without being told.

"Do you have cows or horses?" asked Hattie.

"No, we don't have any," replied Lizzie, "the Governor has lots of cattle with great big horns; they go by here sometimes and they are so lean and look so poor; sometimes one of them falls down and cannot go any farther. He gets them in a ship from some place far away, I don't know where."

"What makes them fall down?" inquired Mamie.

"Oh this grass is not good except when it is young," responded Lizzie, "It gets to be very high and the cows won't eat it, any way not if they can help it."

"The grass is nice now," observed Jessie.

"Yes," continued Lizzie, "this is the beginning of the rains, and it has just commenced to grow; it gets to be higher than a man, and in the dry season it is all burned off and the ground is bare."

While they were talking a flock of wild parrots flew overhead, screaming and whistling and talking as they flew; soon another flock passed, and another; Lizzie told the girls they did so every evening; in the morning they went to their feeding-grounds and in the evening they returned to their town to sleep.

"Do the parrots have a town?" inquired Grace.

"I don't know," said Lizzie, "that is what the people say, and anyway there is an island up the river called Parrot Island and may be that is their town."

The girls came around the end of the house to where Mr. Reading had a little flower-garden; perhaps it would be more correct to call it a nursery, for he used it mainly to start trees and plants to be afterwards set out in different parts of the grounds. It was but a small place enclosed with a low bamboo fence, and just where he could look into it from his study window.

By the side of this little nursery was something the girls took far more interest in—two low trees covered with beautiful scarlet fruit, and very good to eat as well

ARRIVAL AT GABOON

as pretty to look at; these were Batangas, or African cherries, the best fruit that Africa produces. They were just in their prime, and the slight acid taste was most grateful to the young folks after being so many days at sea. Seeds of this delightful fruit have been brought to this country, and it is to be hoped they will grow in our southern States.

While the girls were eating the cherries, the two gentlemen returned from their excursion to the Nubia, and the young ladies followed them in the parlor to hear the news in regard to their trunks.

After resting a little, Mr. Reading proposed a short walk about the yard, as there was still half an hour before dinner would be ready. In front of the piazza were several beds of lilies, all native specimens, and these were now in full bloom; along the walk leading down to the church was a long line of dwarf marigolds just beginning to bloom. Mr. Reading explained that this, (the first of November), was the spring-time of the tropical year, the rains having begun a month before. The marigolds had been planted in boxes in the nursery during the dry season and carefully watered, which was why they were so forward. Across the field, at the foot of the hill, was a thick clump of East India bamboo; in the midst of this clump was the spring.

Mr. Reading informed the Judge that good water was not easy to get and that toward the end of the dry season there was a good deal of strife for what little water there was in the spring, although it was on the mission premises. The towns-people come in the early morning and even the French gunboats send their men for the precious liquid. "I have been so troubled," said he, "that I have been trying to see what I could do in the way of storing up rain water to last us during the dry season. I have been two years at it, and am now entirely successful; if you will come with me I will show you."

He led them to the upper part of the yard where there was a neat galvanized iron store-house, and showed them two covered cisterns, one on each side; they were nearly full of clear, sweet water, and were as nice cisterns as could be found anywhere. "When we were building the church steps," continued Mr. Reading, "we ran short of brick and would not be able to get more for nearly a month; I was afraid to let my mason go for fear I might not be able to get him again, as the government was doing a good deal of work then, so I set my men to quarrying stone and we built that large cistern you see unfinished over there by the kitchen. The food-house just beyond must have a new roof next dry-season, and then I will put on galvanized iron, raise the cistern walls, put on a roof, and it will hold water enough for all my people in July and August when water is so scarce."

From the top of the hill, just back of the storehouse, is an extensive view up river as far as the eye can reach; in the grass-field below are the pretty brown bamboo houses of the people, while back from the river, across the creek, are hills covered with a luxuriant growth of trees. Encircling the hill at the rear of the mission buildings is a narrow valley of rich soil; while walking along the hillside overlooking it, Mr. Reading said, "This valley was a jungle of wild growth when I came here. I cleared it out, and now, as you see, it is a garden of palm-trees; my men get enough nuts from it to make themselves palm-oil-chop nearly every day. This hillside too, was little better than a wilderness, and now I have growing on it at least a hundred young trees besides the bananas."

Mr. Reading exhibited the small cocoa-nut, mango, breadfruit and other trees, with a fatherly pride that told plainly of his love for them; and indeed the premises were so large and in such good order as to proclaim him an enterprising and successful gardener.

A messenger now came to announce that dinner was ready, and the dining-room was soon filled with a merry, happy company. A new dish on the table to the Band was fried breadfruit; this had much better be called "potato-fruit," for it is not at all like bread, while it exactly takes the place of the potato, and is cooked in the same way. It is not a native of Africa, and is only found in the gardens of Europeans, or occasionally in some town where it has been planted by a Christian native, for the heathen will not plant trees.

The fruit may be roasted in the fire, but it is usually boiled and eaten with gravy or palm-oil, and what is left is cut in thin slices and fried for the next meal; this is the way Mrs. Reading had it for dinner, and the Band liked it pretty well, but it has a sickish, sweet taste which is not altogether agreeable to a northern palate.

After dinner a few minutes were spent on the front piazza enjoying the refreshing sea-breeze, and then all adjourned to the parlor to spend a pleasant evening. Here at the equator the sun sets every night at six o'clock, and by half-past six it is beginning to get dark. As the young tourists retired for the night, the rustle of the cocoanut leaves and the patter of the rain-drops gave place in their consciousness to dreams of dear ones far over the deep blue sea.

LITTLE LIZZIE

Chapter XII.

BARAKA AND GABOON.

IN the tropics everybody is astir early; however late either natives or foreigners may have been up the night before, it is the custom to rise early in the morning and begin the labors of the day with the first dawning light; this was the case with the Gaboon household; and so by half-past six all were out of their rooms, had taken a small cup of strong coffee, and were ready for whatever the day might bring forth.

The sun was just peeping over the eastern hills, and the mists in the valleys were rising in response to his alluring warmth to float as masses of white cloud in the bright blue sky. The wild parrots were flying to their feeding-grounds, filling the air overhead with their shrill voices, and all animated nature was greeting the new day with expressions of gratitude and praise. Out on the river the fishing boats were seeking the finny inhabitants of the waters, and the noble ship that had brought its precious freight from the distant shores of happy England, was swinging lazily with the tide.

Just as the Band stepped out upon the front piazza, the bell rang, and the heads of the various working departments came to receive their orders for the morning.

The mission family take an informal cup of coffee immediately on rising, either in their rooms or at the table in the dining-room, as each one may choose. The first bell rings at six A. M., and the second at half-past six. When the second bell rings, all the native workers present themselves to Mr. Reading at the front veranda; causes of complaint, if there are any, and requests of all kinds are then presented, the operations of the day outlined, and the necessary orders given. The Kru-men have a head-man who receives all orders for the work they are to do, and who is responsible for its performance; the head carpenter receives his instructions, the head mason his, the young man who buys the native provisions his, and the one who transacts the business with the French officials his. The Bible reader and the two theological students have their tasks assigned them, and usually there are documents for Mr. Presset to translate and prepare in French.

But the missionary cannot get along by giving general orders to his people if he desires really satisfactory results; he must be perfect master of details, and not only direct what shall be done, but take hold and show how to do it. At this morning hour, and indeed all through the day, people from town will come with all sorts of requests, letters of inquiry relating to business affairs will be received from the factories, and policemen and other agents of the Government will bring notices and copies of new regulations of various kinds, all of which are to be signed. When all of these matters have been attended to, if there is any time left, the missionary attends to his private correspondence and does his writing for the press.

MISS SUSIE DEWSNAP

At eight o'clock there is breakfast, and after that the more active labors of the day begin; the missionary takes off his coat, rolls up his sleeves, puts on his broad-rimmed sun-hat, and sallies forth. All parts of the premises are visited, work inspected, trips made to the beach, and the factories; plantains, dried-fish, bush-rope, bamboo and other native produce examined and bargained for; all kinds of supplies passed out to workmen, and to people from town in payment of debts in the form of due-bills; goods received from the steamer and cared for, or packed and shipped to other parts of the mission-field.

At eleven o'clock a single stroke of the bell calls the caterer for each group of workmen or colored mission family, to come and get the provisions for the day. There is no regular supply of native food, and the mission must feed every one in its employ except the mission family itself, which must buy its own food or do without. Many plans have been tried at Gaboon for feeding its employees, but the one now adopted is to keep on hand rice and codfish, with a common grade of salt beef, all of which is imported from England. Plantains, eguma [e-goo-mah], and dried fish are purchased when they can be had, and when these fail the rice and codfish are given out, with a piece of salt beef on Saturday to those who have done specially well during the week. The ration for one person for one day is eight fingers of plantains, and two dried fish, which are like the little smoked herrings sold in the grocery stores of America. If there are no plantains, a cup of rice holding a pound and a quarter is given instead, and when there are no dried fish, a small codfish is given for each person for one week.

Rations are given out at Baraka for from thirty-five to forty people including women and children, and when visitors from other stations are there, the number of course is greater. Once a week, each mess, or family, is entitled to a plate of common coarse salt. When cocoanuts, breadfruit, bananas, or peppers can be spared, they are divided around; but this does not often happen, and when it does occur they are usually distributed in the evening.

At noon the bell rings and all work ceases; the men cook and eat their dinner, and the mission family retire to their rooms and rest for an hour, when dinner is announced. Unlike the traders, the heaviest meal of the day is taken at one o'clock; this is not a good plan, but it accords better with the work of the station.

At half-past one, the bell again rings, and the head of each department comes for additional instructions, if any are to be given. The missionary now settles himself at his desk, and brings forth the memoranda taken during the morning; books are posted, accounts copied, bills forwarded, letters of advice written, orders made out, and "declarations," manifests, bills of lading and other business papers prepared.

At 4 P. M. the theological students must have an hour's instruction, and then it is expected there will be a little breathing spell, but it seldom comes, and this closing hour of the day is spent in pastoral visits or some other form of light work. With six o'clock comes supper, and if there is no evening service the hours until bedtime are spent in study.

This is a brief outline of one part of an ordinary day's work at Gaboon, for the management of the household, and the work among the women, has not been mentioned; all of this, of course, falls upon the lady of the house. The school too, being entirely in the French language, is under care of Mr. Presset, who was sent out from Paris to take charge of it, in accordance with the Colonial Law. Mr. Presset is also invaluable in translating documents and facilitating intercourse with the various departments of the French Colonial Government.

Gaboon being the headquarters of the mission, there are seldom two consecutive days alike; the arrival and departure of steamers from England, France, Spain, Germany and Portugal, as well as to and from the various rivers and coast-ports, and of the mission sloop "Nassau," breaks in upon the regular routine of the station and often in an hour's time entirely changes the current of the day's operations.

Large amounts of merchandise are used by the mission in exchange with the natives, and the handling of this under the intricate and vexatious custom-house regulations, without horse or other draft animal, one-third of a mile from the beach and on top of a hill at that, and two miles from the Government offices, and still further sometimes from the steamer, with no wharf or hoisting appliances, and under an equatorial sun, consumes a great amount of time and sadly reduces the missionary's efficiency for spiritual work among the people. Then, too, all these goods are to be retailed out, and it not infrequently happens that the missionary holds forth one day the emblems of the broken body and shed blood of our Lord, and the next day is landing cargo or dickering with his congregation over a bar of soap or a head of tobacco.

As it is not the design of this work to criticise missionary operations, these and kindred matters, will not again be referred to, unless it be incidentally to keep up the run of the story.

Strangers arriving in Gaboon are expected within three days to call upon the Governor and obtain his permission to remain in the colony; this permit is issued by the Governor's Secretary and "viséd" by the Chief of Police, who records in a book for the purpose, all the facts of interest in reference to the new-comer. With such a large party it was only necessary that one person should visit the Governor as the representative of all, and so after breakfast Mr. Reading and the Judge rode away in the little carriage to call on him.

The sensation of riding behind human horses was a novel one, and while it might seem strange in our own home-land, yet in Africa it was easy to feel it was the correct thing as it harmonized perfectly with the surroundings, and the Judge thoroughly enjoyed it; it was surely much more comfortable than to be carried in a hammock, and much easier for the men. There was no danger of these horses running away, and no need of any lines; a word now and then was all that was needed, and the little carriage was so light it was just fun to pull it.

The French have made an excellent road, parallel with the beach, three miles long; this road, with a few connecting streets, is the only road nearer than Kamerun, on the north, and Congo on the south; all the vast interior is one great jungle with the waterways as the only open lines of trade and travel. French road-making is thoroughly done and is as expensive as preparing a road-bed for a railway. After the bush has been cleared way and the ground somewhat smoothed, a temporary narrow-gauge railway is laid along the section to be improved, and extended to a stone quarry. Heavy stone is then laid over the ground and filled in with broken stone, and so on until the desired grade is reached, when the top is carefully rounded and a

ROAD-MAKING IN GABOON

layer of gravel spread over the whole. Meanwhile ample preparation is made to carry away the drainage; the sides of the road slope sharply to the gutter, and are covered with a coating of lime and cement. Lime-stone is found near the river, and lime is burned in the kiln, seen on the right in the engraving.

Along the line of this road are three iron bridges which span as many streamlets which come from the hills. The larger of these streamlets separates Gaboon into two unequal portions; the larger of these portions is called the Plateau, or French settlement; and the one further up river is called Glass, or the English settlement. Formerly these were about equal in importance, but of late years Plateau has grown rapidly and Glass has diminished both in size and importance.

Gaboon was, but a few years ago, an important trading-station for ivory and rubber, but trade has now almost entirely fallen off, and is simply a retail business for the supply of the resident population. Drinking places and eating houses pay better than trade, and the number of small establishments has considerably increased of late.

The road to the Plateau does not present any striking features, but it is very pleasant, and many a bright picture of tropic life and scenery may be enjoyed as one rides comfortably along. The Government buildings are built of stone and are large, cool, comfortable and well adapted to the uses for which they are intended.

M. Ballay, acting Governor of the French colony of the "Gabun et Congo" is a quiet, pleasant, middle-aged man, under whose wise and energetic administration Gaboon has gone steadily forward in improvement. He has an enviable reputation as an explorer and has done much to open up the vast region now claimed by France. He and Mr. Reading were old-time friends, having lived together in the Ogowe, and he was greatly pleased to see the Judge and offered to do all in his power to make his sojourn in the colony agreeable and profitable. The Judge thanked him for his kindness and remarked that he might need his assistance by and by in his efforts to visit the Ogowe river.

After taking leave of the Governor the two friends went down to the telegraph station, and the Judge sent a cablegram to America announcing his safe arrival. This is rather expensive business, costing two dollars, ninety-six cents a word, including the address and signature; but it is wonderful to think that this remote colony in equatorial Africa should have a wire rope extending under the sea all the way to distant America. It takes from five to eight hours for the message to be transmitted, and as the difference in time is about six hours, it arrives at its destination at the same time of day it was sent.

Near the telegraph station is the Roman Catholic Cathedral, a large, plain, substantial building, kept in excellent repair, and an ornament to the town.

From the Cathedral to the French Catholic Mission, a distance of over half a mile, the road runs along the beach through an avenue of cocoanut palms, with houses and shops on one side, and the rolling surf on the other, and is as delightful a drive as can be found in any land. The Catholic Mission is a large and important one, employing some twenty priests and nuns, and enjoys the patronage of the Government. Its chief aim seems to be to make good citizens of the natives, and in this it has met with a large measure of success as it teaches handicrafts of various kinds. The spiritual results have not kept pace with the material, but in regard to these it may be that a Protestant cannot fitly judge. Its jealousy of, and opposition to, the Protestant Mission, seems to be its most unpleasant feature, and also its practice of giving rum to natives; indeed it has imported a still and is teaching the people to make rum from the mangoes; surely it can be no part of a religious system to teach the manufacture and use of a vile beverage that can produce only debauchery and crime.

The residence of the Fathers is built of stone, with tile roof, as is also the chapel which stands beside it. The grounds are extensive; much time and effort have been given to gardening and with a good measure of success; tomatoes, egg-plants, lettuce, radishes, spinach, squashes and other vegetables, are produced in limited quantities, as are also many varieties of tropical fruits. In the women's department, which is situated near the cathedral, the girls are taught to sew, make paper flowers, and other feminine accomplishments.

While the Judge and his friend were making their explorations about Gaboon, those who were left behind at Baraka were not idle; the boys had made the acquaintance of good old Elder Adande [ah-dan-dee], and went down to his house to see how a Christian African home looked, and hear his stories about hunting and fishing, while the girls gathered in the parlor about Mrs. Reading and begged her to tell them a story of the olden time.

"Fifteen years ago," said Mrs. Reading, " we sailed from New York for Liverpool on our way here to Gaboon. In the cabin of the steamer we were introduced to Miss Susie Dewsnap, a sweet-faced young lady, who was to be our traveling-companion and associate in the mission work. At Lagos we were all poisoned by bad water from the condenser, which was given us to drink because there was a quarrel between the stewards and the carpenter, and he would not give out the fresh water; nearly every one on board was ill, but Miss Dewsnap and I suffered the most. Five weeks after our arrival our little boy died, and Miss Dewsnap lined the little pine box and laid him in it so gently, for she had learned to love him almost as much as Mr. Reading and I. Then we went down to the other house to live, while she remained in this house with Mr. and Mrs. Bushnell. Five years after this, she went with us to the Ogowe to live with Dr. and Mrs. Bachelor, and we had some good times together while Mr. Reading was building a new station.

"One day Mr. Reading and I started on a journey up the river and left Lizzie in Miss Dewsnap's care. We had not been gone more than an hour when they were both taken sick. As no one thought the attack was going to be a serious one, a messenger was not sent after us, and we went on our way quite unconscious of any impending evil. When we reached home at noon of the third day we found them both very ill, and Lizzie delirious. We at once went to work to do what we could, for no time was to be lost, as the African fever develops with great rapidity.

"Mr. Reading and I took charge of Lizzie, and Dr. Bachelor and Mrs. Sneed of Miss Dewsnap, while Mrs. Bachelor managed the housekeeping and the station. In two days Lizzie was out of danger and Miss Dewsnap was dying. Before she died she became blind, which is always a fatal symptom. We were eating, and the door leading to her room was open; she thought it was night and asked us why we had put out the light; then she said, 'Do please light the lamp, it will do me no harm.' It was

MR. READING'S LITTLE CARRIAGE

noon time and the sun was shining with all the brilliancy with which it is shining now, and her window was open and she was looking right toward it, but to her it was darkness. She begged so hard for a light that I was obliged to go in and tell her she was blind, for neither of the gentlemen had the courage to do it; when I told her, she was quiet a minute, and then she said 'It is all right.' She knew it would not be long before her eyes would open to the light of that world where there is no night, but one eternal day. She soon went into a wild delirium, but just before the end she came to her right mind and called us to her one by one, and kissed us good-bye, and begged us not to be discouraged by her death. Just at the last a vision of the glorious future of Africa passed before her mind, but she could not tell us much of it, for her voice was hushed on earth to burst forth with rapture in the skies, and we were left alone. We sat there in the quiet afternoon looking out upon the lovely palms, and thought of the glad home-coming in our Father's House, of the welcome to His child; it seemed to us that we could hear, like distant music borne upon the summer's breeze, the triumphant songs of angels and we wished we were with them to share their joy. Her body was placed in a neat coffin and laid in a surf boat and towed to Gaboon, for she made us promise to lay her beside our little Arthur."

The girls thanked Mrs. Reading for the story and secretly resolved that they would one day be missionaries too, and live, and if need be, die, in this very land.

About the middle of the afternoon when the seabreeze had somewhat cooled the air, Mrs. Reading and the girls started out to see something of Gaboon; the girls were young and active and did not mind walking, so they followed Mrs. Reading and Lizzie who rode in the carriage. Instead of taking the road they went along the beach where the breeze was fresh and enjoyable, until they came to the Long Bridge and then they took what is known as the Old Road, which is shaded by large mango trees and passes the Botanical Garden. The gardener's house was beautifully overgrown with vines, and in the garden were many plants entirely new to the young ladies, all of which were described to them by the gardener. There were very few flowers, for in this land of brilliant sunshine, for some reason flowers do not thrive; the few there are grow on trees and are rather coarse. The gardener told them he had tried almost every kind of flower but he had not met with much success in their cultivation.

After leaving the garden the party turned to the right and passed along an avenue of cocoanut palms, with cosy little homes on either side nestling amid a wealth of shrubbery; occasionally a larger house occupied by some French official, or used as a shop or cafe, stood out in an open space, for, as a rule, foreigners do not care to have shade immediately about their dwellings. There were no lawns and no flowers, indeed the only lawn in Gaboon is at the American Mission.

On the way home they called at the house of Mary Walker, a young Gaboon woman, and in a few minutes quite a little crowd gathered to see the strangers. A few wore dresses, but most of the women had on what is called a "cloth"; this is made of five or six yards of wide calico or chintz, in the form of a sheet and wrapped around the body, with a little tuck under one arm for a fastening; this is the national dress, and is very becoming, but it would hardly do for the streets of Philadelphia.

Laura thought these cloths would all the time be coming undone, but the women told her they never had any trouble and that they were more comfortable to wear than dresses. A number of the women wore hairpins made of ivory, which formed a pleasing contrast with their jet-black hair. Some of the head-dresses were quite elaborate and Mrs. Reading told the girls that not unfrequently half a day is needed to arrange one of these heads. In order not to disarrange the braiding at night, the neck is laid on a narrow block of wood so that the head itself cannot touch the pillow.

This was the beginning of the mango season and everywhere they found both children and grown people eating the fruit; it is somewhat larger than a peach, and with a smooth skin like a plum; indeed the resemblance to a large plum is such that foreigners quite generally call them "mango-plums." They are of a beautiful golden color, with a red cheek, and look most inviting, but notwithstanding their attractive appearance they are not favorites with Europeans; the flesh is yellow and juicy, but to a northern palate rather insipid, and the skin is more than suggestive of turpentine. The native people think them delicious and during the season they grow fat upon them, but the tree is not a native of the country and is only to be found in the settlements along the coast. The girls liked them best when stewed, for then they taste much like apple-sauce, and Mrs. Reading told them they were good made into pies. They may be taken when half grown, peeled, and the flesh cut off and stewed like any other green fruit, or they may be used when nearly ripe.

Hattie asked Mrs. Reading to tell her the difference between a plantain and a banana; "Ever since I reached the coast," said she, "I have heard of plantains and bananas and I cannot tell them apart."

"The stalks are so nearly alike," replied Mrs. Reading, "that I cannot tell them myself, but I know a plantain requires a richer soil than a banana; bananas do well on the hillside back of our house, but plantains will hardly grow there. The fruit of the plantain is much larger and coarser than bananas, and is seldom eaten raw; besides, it has when cooked, a very different taste; I will have some of both fried for supper this evening and then you can see for yourself."

"How do you fry them?" asked Lulu.

"I cut them lengthwise into about four slices," replied Mrs. Reading, "sprinkle them with a little salt, and fry them just as I would potatoes."

When supper-time came the girls were on the lookout for the fried plantains and bananas; they liked them both, but as Mrs. Reading had told them, the plantains were the best.

Supper was a little earlier than usual as the weekly prayer-meeting is always held on Wednesday evening, and it is the rule that all who live upon the premises shall attend; there were thirty-five native people present, which, with the Ogowe Band and its leader, made forty-eight.

The exercises began with a hymn; a prayer of invocation, Scripture lesson, and remarks by Mr. Reading occupying about eight minutes, just to introduce the subject for the evening; two verses of another hymn, and then all the church members, including the visitors, were called upon to take part. As each one's name was called the person spoken to responded by reciting a verse of Scripture, starting a hymn of which one verse only was sung, making a prayer, or a short exhortation; the prayers were short and to the point, and remarks did not occupy more than from three to five minutes.

In this meeting everyone was free to use what language he pleased, and so it was that each spoke in his mother tongue, so there was English, French, Mpongwe, Benga, Kombe, and Banawkaw. "Good old uncle Adande," as the boys called him, was eloquent in his address, and the Band wished ever so much they could have understood what he said. Notwithstanding the babel of tongues the meeting was most enjoyable, and it did one's heart good to attend such a prayer-meeting in this far-off heathen land. The girls were surprised to see the women taking part as well as the men, and they were not a little dismayed too when Mr. Reading called upon them, but they managed to think of a verse of Scripture each, and so got through for this time.

When the service was ended there was a hand-shaking all around and the people were slow to go home, as in our country churches in America. The people from town carried lanterns to keep off the tigers, which sometimes came about and are very much feared; all the African people have a great dread of wild beasts of every kind.

CHAPTER XIII.

CHURCH WORK AT GABOON.

EVERY morning the good old Elder Adande went around among the villages and country hamlets to preach to the people, and urge them to turn from their heathen superstitions and worship and obey the living and the true God. Before starting out he came to Mr. Reading to receive any instructions he might have to give, and then he went forth, sometimes remaining away for several days. When he came on Thursday morning at the ringing of the bell, Judge McGee expressed a desire to go with him and see how the old man conducted his work; so Mr. Reading sent the little carriage, and the boys went too, taking turns in riding with the Judge, for the sturdy old African elder declined a seat, as he was accustomed to walking and did not mind it a bit.

They went back over the hills behind Baraka through grass now not quite knee-high, which looked like mowing fields at home, only the grass was in small clumps and not spread evenly over the ground. About half a mile beyond these they came to the crest of a ridge, and before them

"GOOD OLD UNCLE" ADANDE

lay one of the most beautiful landscapes that can be seen in any country; from where they stood the ground descended to a valley, through which ran a little stream bordered on either side by oil-palms; the slope beyond was covered with cassava bushes, with here and there clumps of broad banana leaves which nearly hid the brown bamboo houses of the "plantations," as these little country settlements are called. On either side were low hills, some covered with grass and others with trees, while far away rose higher hills clothed with a mantle of the richest green. Looking back, they saw the mission premises with its fruit trees and buildings, and beyond them the river and the deep blue sea; it was a scene to be indelibly impressed upon the memory and frequently recalled in after years.

Adande told them that all this broad land was once thickly peopled with the little Mpongwe nation, but now they were nearly gone, and their land was either waste, or was occupied by other people who had moved in from the bush. The Judge inquired why it was that they died off so fast, but Adande replied he did not know, but he thought it must be owing to rum and the new style of living which broke up family life. "Young men do not wish to get married now-a-days," said he, "they want to walk about all dressed up like gentlemen, and do not wish to be burdened with the care of a family; so there are few children and these bush-people are coming in to occupy our land and take our places."

After feasting for a short time upon the lovely scene, and taking long breaths of the fresh morning air, the party pushed their way down the hillside, across the valley, and up the opposite slope to the first plantation, where Adande was to hold a meeting. The little hamlet consisted of five houses, and as they stepped into the open space that served as a street a quiet scene of African home-life presented itself.

An old man was sitting on a short bench making a fishing net; beside him was his old wife twisting the fibers of the pine-apple leaf to make cord for him; a younger woman, perhaps his daughter-in-law, had a large bundle of these leaves beside her and was scraping away the pulp from them so as to get the fiber. A man had just brought up a basket of clams from the creek, and another was cutting the beautiful golden palm-nuts from a large bunch he had taken from a tree in the valley; two or three children were playing about, and a couple of women were peeling the cassava roots, while another one was sewing; a hen was scratching in the dirt for worms for her young brood, and a half a dozen large ducks and a mother goat with her kid completed the list of the street population.

The people were rather surprised to see so many white faces, but they knew Adande and greeted him with a respectful "Good morning." After some preliminary conversation, Adande began to speak to them of their lost condition and their need of a Saviour, and as he pursued his subject he grew quite eloquent, but as it was all in the Mpongwe language the Judge and the boys could only guess at what he said. After the exhortation came a prayer, and then there was more conversation.

In one of the houses, huddled over a smoky fire, was a poor old woman who was sick; she sat in the ashes with scarcely any clothing on, and her poor withered form looked more like a mummy than a living being, so covered was it with dust and smoke. Adande told the Judge this was the country fashion for old folks; when they got sick they hovered over the fire to try to keep warm and but little attention was shown them. Far away from Gaboon, beyond the reach of the gospel, it is the custom to throw such old folks in the river when they get sick and troublesome; or they are taken out in the forest and left to be eaten by the tigers; sometimes a little food is given them so as to enable them to linger for a few days, and occasionally one, more humane than the rest, will knock the poor old creature over the head with a club and so end the misery at once.

How different this from the treatment of aged parents in our own loved land ; truly the tender mercies of the wicked is cruelty. The one thing which principally distinguishes the heathen from the irreligious classes in Christian lands, is their utter absence of feeling toward suffering of every kind; in all other respects the difference is not so great as is commonly supposed—as the Bible fitly says [Eph. 4, 19], they are "past feeling" and no degree of human agony can move them in the least.

From this little plantation the party went on, visiting three others, and returning to Baraka by another road; the Judge and the boys were completely tired out and glad to stay at home in the afternoon and rest.

The women of the Gaboon church hold a prayer-meeting in town every Thursday afternoon under the leadership of Mrs. Reading; at three P. M. she and the girls, with Julia the Bible-woman, and the Christian women who live near Baraka, went down to the house of Animbina [ah-nee-mbee-nah], near the beach, where the meeting was to be held. The house was a very pleasant one, built of bamboo, with board floors, wide, cool piazzas, and wood-work neatly painted. There were curtains at the windows, nice furniture in the rooms, pictures on the walls, and a sewing machine near the door; altogether it was a comfortable home, neat and clean as any one could wish for, and the girls thought they would not object to just such a home for themselves. A number of women came in, some members of the church, and some heathen, until the house and front piazza were filled.

Mrs. Reading gave out a hymn and read a Scripture lesson, both in the native language, and then Julia, and others, made remarks and led in prayer. It was a meeting to warm one's heart, so earnest, so tender, and all in the wild language of a heathen tribe, some of whom had now learned to love that dear Saviour who had died that all tribes and nations might be brought home to His Father's House to become one great family in the heavenly home above.

The hour and a half quickly passed away, and when the meeting was over Mrs. Reading introduced her guests to the towns-women who gave many exclamations of surprise at their coming so far to see them, and made complimentary remarks upon their beauty and goodness; but as these observations were in Mpongwe the girls were quite ignorant of what they said, and smiled sweetly upon the old women in the most innocent fashion. It is quite a funny predicament to have persons comment upon your appearance before your face and not know what they say.

When the people had dispersed to their homes, Mrs. Reading sent Lizzie and five of the girls up to Baraka, and then went with Lulu to make a call on Sarah, one of the Christian women whose house was on the beach near by. Sarah is one of those comfortable persons who hold to the even tenor of their way whether the events of life are pleasant or otherwise, and who are always in a good humor. Sarah's life had been in many ways a trying one, but she had borne it all with such good nature that she was a favorite with every one; she was a model wife and mother, and a great worker although very fleshy.

The sun was now declining in the west, and the sea-breeze came in so cool and refreshing that when the carriage returned Mrs. Reading determined to take a little turn up the beach; it is a delightful ride when the tide is low, for the wet sand is smooth as a floor and it seems as if the carriage were running on rails. For half a mile the houses line the beach, and then a turn around a corner, where there is a bay, hides the town and shipping from view and gives one the feeling of having suddenly plunged into the wilderness; sand crabs are running around, birds flit about, and one would not be surprised to see a monkey or a snake; the last idea was not a pleasant one and Lulu asked Mrs. Reading if there were many snakes in Gaboon; she received the comforting assurance that there were but few, and these were not likely ever to be in her way.

"The most troublesome snakes we have," continued Mrs. Reading, "are those that get in our eyes."

"O mercy!" exclaimed Lulu with a shudder, "how can snakes get in your eyes?"

"There is a kind of Guinea worm," replied Mrs. Reading, "about two inches long, that has a flat head and looks just like a snake, that gets in our eyes sometimes and causes inflammation and pain. They remain in the eye for years, in fact until they are cut out. We do not all get them, but many of us do. Mr. Reading has one that troubles him very much, so that at times he is nearly blind for two or three days at once. He had one cut out when last in America, but he has another and I suppose must suffer from it until he goes to America again."

"Can no one here take them out?" inquired Lulu.

"Yes," was the reply, "there are here and there among the people those who say they can remove them with a thorn or bent pin; but the eye is a delicate organ and these country doctors are awkward surgeons, and we do not feel like running any risk."

"How do they get into the eye?" asked Lulu.

"Some think they get them by drinking unfiltered water," answered Mrs. Reading; "some, by eating meat or fish that is not well cooked; some say it is the sting of a fly, but the truth is, nobody knows; the first thing we know the eye is inflamed and painful, and there is the worm full grown and just under the skin of one of the lids."

Miss Lulu thought she had a sorry prospect before her of going home with her head full of snakes, but Mrs. Reading assured her the prospect was by no means certain to be realized. "For," said she, "I have been many years in this land and have never had one, and you can well afford to wait and not worry until the trouble comes."

Returning home, they went through Toko's town and so up to Baraka the back way, and a most enjoyable ride it was.

Early on Friday morning good old Uncle Adande came to Mr. Reading in a great state of excitement with the news that a large manatus was on the beach for sale, and that it had been lately killed, so that its meat was still sweet and good. Adande was at once sent back with the Kru-boys and the platform wagon, with instructions to bring the animal whatever it might cost, for these creatures are not numerous in the neighborhood of Gaboon, being closely hunted for the sake of their meat.

MPONGWE WOMEN, GABOON

The Band were eager to know what a manatus was, and Mr. Reading told them it was a warm-blooded animal belonging to the seal family, but, unlike the seal, it ate grass and not fish. In all the rivers and lakes of Central Africa there is a kind of grass that grows in the water upon which the manatus feeds. This grass has stems twenty or more feet in length; the top is always about two feet above the water, and to accommodate itself to the rise and fall of the water, the stem straightens out or curls up as may be necessary. The manatus swims about and crops the tender shoots of this grass, and when disturbed dives and swims away under water, sticking up his nose occasionally to get breath.

This is the animal which has given rise to the fable of the mermaid, and no wonder, for when swimming undisturbed upon the surface of the water, if its head is turned a little from you, it looks for all the world like a black woman; indeed strangers are often afraid to shoot it on that account. It is a perfectly harmless animal, very shy, and prefers the most secluded lake-shores and streams, far from the abode of men.

In about an hour the men were back, singing a wild song as they came, and with the dead manatus upon the wagon and a little crowd of sight-seers following. The animal was at least ten feet in length and weighed about six hundred pounds; it was of a dark dull color, smooth skin, short nose, and had flippers like a whale; its eyes looked like a person's, and its appearance about the neck and shoulders was too human to be agreeable.

The Judge and the Band examined it with great interest while Mr. Reading bargained with the owner. The price demanded was three hundred dollars in goods, but as this was too much, it was at length agreed that it should be cut up at once and Mr. Reading and his people buy all they wished, and then Adande and the Kru-boys would take the rest and sell it for all they could get, the owner going along. The body was then rolled to the ground and the skin taken off in long strips. This skin was a full inch in thickness and from it the cruel whips are made that are used to punish slaves and women with; the strips of skin are twisted and nailed to planks and dried in the sun until they become as hard as wood. The edges remain sharp, and having a twist they cut deep into the flesh, especially if the whip be drawn toward you when the blow is given. It is no unusual thing for persons to die from the effects of such a flogging; nor are the heathen the only ones who use it, for a few years ago it was not at all uncommon for white men to tie up their servants and flog them; now this practice is almost entirely abolished.

Beneath the skin was a layer of fat, and under that the flesh, which was white and attractive in appearance; a large fine piece was roasted for dinner and the Band thought it excellent, as well they might, for it is sweet and of good flavor.

Willie asked how the manatus had been killed, and the man replied through Adande that he had speared him, and pointed to a hole in the side showing where the spear had entered its body. He told Willie he had made a witch medicine of the powdered bark of a tree, and spread it upon the water; that the manatus came to eat the powder and he was hiding near and threw his spear into it. The composition of this powder, Mr. Reading added, was known only to a few families and was by them carefully kept secret, being handed down from father to son, and these families were the only ones who were permitted to hunt this animal.

In the afternoon Mrs. Reading and the girls attended the regular monthly meeting of the Ladies' Missionary Society of the Gaboon church. The girls were not a little surprised to learn that here in savage Africa was a band of Christian women praying and giving their money to send the gospel to the heathen. They had a regularly organized society, with president, secretary and treasurer, and did their work through committees the same as similar organizations in civilized lands.

After the devotional exercises and a short talk about South America, which was the subject for the month, the Society resolved itself into a sewing circle and sewed patchwork for quilts, which when finished were sold, and the money turned into the treasury. Conversation kept pace with the sewing, and the girls listened to many a story of African life, for most of these women had been educated in the mission and could speak English.

Saturday was a very busy day, but by two P. M. the multitude of business had been disposed of and the preparations going on in the house indicated that something unusual was to occur; all the chairs from the dining-room and bed-rooms were brought into the parlor and arranged in rows, the organ was opened, and it was evident a meeting of some sort was to take place. Out in the dining-room the table was covered with cups and saucers, there was a large bowl-full of sugar, a pitcher of condensed milk, and two dishes heaped full of sweet crackers. Mrs. Reading explained that the choir were to meet and practice, and it was the custom to offer some light refreshment when they were tired with singing. At three o'clock they began to come, and in half an hour there were sixteen young men and women present, and they sang with a hearty good-will that was comfortable to hear.

Services in Africa are long, and much of the time is taken up with devotional exercises, which necessitates a good deal of singing, and this requires a corresponding preparation. There were four hymns for the morning, and seven for the afternoon services, besides two voluntaries, and this took considerable practicing. No talking was allowed, and at the end of an hour of steady singing the vocal chords began to get tired; then at a signal from Mr. Reading the house-boys brought in coffee and the crackers, and the choir enjoyed a short recess. When this was over, two or three new pieces were tried, and then several of the Jubilee songs were sung and thoroughly enjoyed, especially "John Brown," "Mary and Martha," and "We Shall Walk Thro' the Valley," closing with "Good-bye, Brothers."

Contrary to the commonly-received idea, the Africans are not naturally good singers; the pathos which makes those Jubilee songs so popular in America, must have been born of centuries of enslavement—the wail of the shackled spirit for freedom—for here in Africa voices are rather harsh and wild, lacking in sweetness and feeling. Native songs are very monotonous and with little real music in them; those who have come into the church in mature years do not sing so well as those who have been brought up in the mission from childhood, and the children of educated persons, as a rule, do still better. Part of the hymns were in the native tongue, and a part were in English; one of the requirements for admission to the choir is ability to read English.

CATHOLIC MISSION, GABOON

CHURCH WORK AT GABOON

It is surprising to see what a hold the English language has taken along the entire western coast of Africa; the natives everywhere desire to learn it, and if it were not for the severe restrictions by the various Colonial governments, it would in time be spoken everywhere, and take the place of the native languages. It can no longer be taught in either French or German territory.

After the choir meeting was over, the bell rang, and the work of giving out "Saturday" was gone through with. The masons and carpenters receive each week, seven pounds of beef, seven pounds of hard bread, seven pounds of rice, seven heads of tobacco, two clay pipes, a bar of soap, a box of matches, a plate of salt, and some tea and sugar in lieu of rum which they get when they work for the factories. The Kru-men each get a bar of soap, a head of tobacco, and a box of matches, and all who have done especially well during the week get a little piece of salt beef for their Sunday dinner. This is the only time during the week when kerosene is sold at retail, and bottles may be seen coming from all directions for the precious light-giving oil.

Application is often made by people from town for breadfruit and cocoanuts, for food is never plentiful among them, and they are often hungry. By the time all these matters have been attended to it is dark and the missionary is thoroughly tired.

The Sabbath was a most delightful day to the Ogowe Band; excepting the part of a day they were ashore at Fernando Po, it was the first real Sabbath they had enjoyed for a long time. It was a perfect morning; the rain that had fallen during the night sparkled in tiny drops upon every leaf and blade of grass as the rising sun kissed the landscape, and the solemn hush that rested upon the world was suggestive of the eternal calm of Him whose day it was.

The house-boys went noiselessly about their work, and the working part of the force walked slowly about the yard with their cloths wrapped around them, enjoying the day of rest which God had given them. At half-past eight the bell rang, and again at nine, for service is early on account of the heat. O, how sweet was the sound of the Sabbath bell! Our young friends forgot they were far from home in a heathen land as they walked down the path to God's house, with its hallowed sound ringing in their ears.

The church was a bamboo one, and was filled with a well-dressed and attentive congregation. The visitors were surprised to see so large a part of the audience so nicely dressed; many of the women had on silk or worsted dresses of fashionable make, with the latest style of Parisian hats, kid gloves, shoes, and parasols. The men too were, many of them, as well dressed as city young men at home, even the Kru-men had on coats and pantaloons, and looked as intelligent as the colored citizen of America.

Mr. Reading and Mr. Owondo Lewis occupied the pulpit and divided the services between them. First there was the invocation, then a short psalm read in English and afterward in Mpongwe, an English hymn, and then a Scripture lesson, hymn, sermon, prayer, and voluntary by the choir—all in Mpongwe. After this there was the same in English, then notices, collection, closing hymn and benediction—the entire service lasting two hours. The choir sat in front, to the right of the pulpit, and was led by Mr. Reading. No organ was used as the people are so fond of hearing it they will not sing, or at least will only sing softly, preferring to listen to the organ.

After the services there were many introductions and hand-shakings, the people remaining for some time under the trees in front of the church to converse with one another before going home. Several of the older Mpongwe men and women followed Mr. and Mrs. Reading into the parlor where coffee was passed around, and after a pleasant chat they left.

Mr. Reading followed Mr. Luddington's plan of merging the afternoon Sunday-school, and the evening service, into one service at 4 P. M. and with satisfactory results. A congregation nearly as large as the morning one assembled promptly at four o'clock, and the exercises included seven hymns, two prayers, responsive reading of the Scripture lesson, catechism, exposition of the lesson lasting thirty minutes [in reality a sermon], and hearing of classes by the teachers. This service lasted an hour and three quarters; like the morning service it was in both languages.

The church at Gaboon has not grown as rapidly as could be wished, nor as rapidly as churches in other parts of the mission field. It has had a great deal to contend with, and many influences which may not be mentioned here have held it in check; still, the services are well attended and there are some who are the Lord's true children and who seek to grow in conformity with Him and in fitness for life in the beautiful home above. .

Chapter XIV.

NOMBA AND OVENDO POINT.

IT had been decided to make a trip up the Gaboon river, and so Monday was spent in making preparations for the journey. There are no hotels in this part of Africa except one at Banana at the mouth of the Congo river, nor houses of entertainment of any kind; when travelers wish to visit the country they must depend on private hospitality, or take their provisions with them.

Men who have been long on the coast and who have traveled much, have learned to exist for a time on native food, but new-comers cannot do so, and they must be well provided with canned provisions; moreover, it is not always easy to get even the few things the country does produce; often enough it happens that when, after a long, hard day in the hot sun, a town is reached, not a plantain or a cassava root is to be obtained at any price. Strange as it may seem, Africa with all its richness of vegetation, is as good a country to starve in as may be found anywhere in the world. It is not safe to depend upon getting supplies by the way, even for your men, and a

GABOON RIVER VILLAGE

wise traveler will always carry rice and meat with him as a reserve in case of need. In addition to food for himself and men, the traveler must take his bedding, if he wishes to use any, change of clothes, medicines, cooking utensils; and calico, soap, tobacco and other articles, to use as money for current expenses; and guns and ammunition if he feels afraid or wishes to do any hunting.

It is a disputed point whether fire-arms are needed in traveling in Africa; if there is a large quantity of goods in the traveler's possession, they are needed; or, if he feels afraid, they will be needed, not for use, but to bolster up his courage; for it will not do to go among these savages with a half-frightened look. A brave heart, and a knowledge of the language, and of the working of the native mind, with a fertility of resource under varying circumstances, is worth far more to help a stranger on his way, than all the weapons that can be carried; always provided there is not a great quantity of goods to excite cupidity.

In the present instance it was decided to do a little hunting if opportunity offered, as the Judge had brought out a beautiful little rifle which he was anxious to try; in addition to this Mr. Reading borrowed a double-barreled, breach-loading shot-gun from one of his friends on the beach.

The French authorities will permit any one to go out on the river for a ride if no goods are taken, provided the matter is first reported at the police station, but where goods, even in small quantities for current needs, are taken, regular clearance papers must be made out and duly signed at the custom-house and viséd at the police station—and the same must be done when the boat returns. This had been attended to on Monday, and on

NOMBA AND OVENDO POINT

Tuesday morning all was in readiness for the start. The girls were to remain with Mrs. Reading as some of them were not very well and they were not yet fully rested from the long ocean voyage.

There are two very nice boats belonging to the Gaboon station, the "Christine" and the "Minnesota," and it was thought best to take them both. The Kru-boys carried the luggage to the beach and put the boats in the water while Mr. Reading went to the police station to show his papers. Good old Uncle Adande went along in the capacity of navigator, for he is a famous boatman and always knows just what is best to be done in any emergency. The girls came down to the beach to see the party off, and after a little delay they started.

It was a cloudy morning, and very nice to be out upon the water; the tide had just turned to flood, and under the strong strokes of the Kru-boys the boats went ahead at a good speed. The rocks at low tide compel a boat to keep out pretty well, and this gave a wider view ashore than if they had skirted the beach; the view was lovely, with the broad river on one side and the town and hills on the other. By and by the town was left behind and the forest came down to the shore line.

Canoes were passed, some laden with plantains for sale in Gaboon, and others with palm-leaf mats for house-roofing. The land-breeze was blowing down the river and the canoes were coming under sail, and such old sails as they were too, made of all colors of calico sewed together, looking, as the boys said, "like Joseph's coat, only more ragged and dirty." It is only near the coast that the negro uses a sail, above the tide-water region canoes are propelled solely by paddles.

An hour's ride brought them to Nomba, a small village about three miles from Gaboon; here a creek comes in, but there was not water enough on the sand-bar at its mouth for the boats to cross yet, so Mr. Reading, the Judge, and Adande went up to the village to make arrangements for spending the night, leaving the boys to watch the boats and run about the beach after crabs. Nomba has no king, but Loembe Morris, a rich trader, is the most influential man.

Mr. Morris had been educated at the American Mission and was a really intelligent man; fortunately he was at home, and was delighted to learn that he was to have so many visitors in the evening; he at once placed his house at Mr. Reading's disposal and suggested that whatever in the boats was not needed for the day, had better be brought up to his house where they would be safe, and this was done. He thought the idea of going up the creek for a picnic in the woods was a good one, and offered to go along. By the time the bedding and extra provisions were in the house, the water had risen so that the boats could be dragged over the bar, and they came up to the town landing and the gentlemen got in. Mr. Reading, the Judge and Loembe went in the "Christine," and Adande with the boys in the "Minnesota"; Mr. Reading gave Adande the gun for the use of the boys, and the Judge had his rifle, so each party was armed. The boys were in a high state of excitement, expecting no end of strange adventures, and who can wonder that they did so, for there is a weirdness about African river travel that fascinates the mind and prepares it to believe that almost any unusual thing might occur.

The creek was about forty yards wide, and for the first two miles was bordered by mangroves; as the tide was yet scarcely half-full, many of the interlacing roots were exposed, and these had on them the small oysters which give rise to the oft-repeated story of oysters growing on trees. Oysters cannot grow unless they have some solid substance to which they can attach themselves; in the open ocean there are rocks and stones on the bottom, but here in these muddy creeks there is little else than the mangrove roots, and so they must take hold of these. The African oysters are very small, having rather dark-colored meat, and are thought to be unwholesome because of the dirty water in which they live.

An hour after leaving Nomba the character of the vegetation changed; pandanus, palms and other water-loving plants were mingled with the mangroves, and in another half-hour the latter entirely disappeared. Here they met a new plant, the papyrus, the flags or bulrushes spoken of in the Bible, among which Moses was hidden on the banks of the Nile. It is a beautiful and interesting plant, with a smooth, slender stem, six or eight feet high, surmounted with a tuft or head two feet in diameter, of very fine, dark green leaves. The main stem of the plant creeps along the river-bottom, rooting at every joint, and sending up these long, slender stems which rise above the water.

There is a small bird somewhat like a Baltimore oriole that builds its nest in these papyrus heads, and is rocked with its little ones to sleep by every passing breeze. Other birds were now seen, and the boys were on the lookout for some game. Upon the topmost branches of some of the larger trees great white fish-eagles were seen calmly surveying the watery jungle beneath them; they appeared to know the range of a gun, but presently the Judge tried his rifle on one and succeeded in bringing it down—his first game in Africa. The Christine turned its prow into the tangled growth, and a Kru-boy clambered ashore and got the bird.

A little further up the stream the banks became higher and the upland forest began to give the country a more inviting look; on rounding a turn Adande spied two monkeys in a palm-tree helping themselves to the rich, ripe nuts. The boys were all in a flutter to get one of them, but the monkeys heard the noise of the oars and jumped out of the palm-tree in a hurry; they did not descend to the ground, but leaped from one tree to the outermost branches of the next, ran along the limbs and jumped to another tree, and so away off in the forest out of harm's way.

Mr. Reading now gave the order for the oars to be taken in and paddles used instead; the Judge was stationed in the bow of the Christine, and Adande and Frank in the bow of the Minnesota, and one boat took one side of the creek, and the other boat the other side. The paddles made no noise, and they had not gone a quarter of a mile when another monkey was seen, a real hungry fellow who paid all attention to his eating, and as his back was toward the boats he did not see them and the Judge brought him down very neatly. He was a fine fellow, with a long tail and reddish grey fur.

Soon after this, a flock of parrots was seen on a tree a short distance ahead and a little way back from the water; Frank wanted to try his hand and so the Minnesota was run ashore and he got out and tried to make his way quietly to the tree where they were feeding. It was no easy matter to get through the undergrowth, but he was a plucky boy and presently he was near enough for a shot, and to his great delight brought down a fine fellow.

He picked up his bird and made his way back to the boat, proud and happy, but with hands and clothes somewhat torn by the briers. The parrot was greatly admired by the boys; it was of a grey color and had a bright red tail; Adande said it was good to eat, and it was decided to have it for dinner.

About a mile farther on, just as the Christine was rounding a turn in the creek, the Judge saw a beautiful little deer drinking at the water-side; he motioned with his hand for the paddlers to stop, and with a well-directed shot secured the prize.

Near where the deer was killed was a nice open place beneath a shady tree, suitable for a camping-ground, and it was agreed to land here and have dinner as all were hungry and the sun was getting hot; the boats were drawn up beside the bank and made fast to the bushes, and the cooking pots, plantains and other food were brought ashore.

Here a new difficulty presented itself—there was no good place to sit down. There is no grass or carpet of moss in the woods of Africa, and the ground is usually damp and unpleasant; the bedding had been left at Nomba, and all that could be done was to have the Kru-boys gather plenty of the broad leaves that grow abundantly, and make lounging places of them. When this was done, fires were built and the kettle put on to boil water for tea; plantains were given to the men for their dinner, and also the monkey and eagle; Frank held on to his parrot, and the deer was reserved for the white folks and Adande and Loembe. The game was taken off a little distance to be skinned and prepared, and while preparations were being made for cooking, the Judge and the boys lay down on the leaves to rest, after having first drunk a cup of tea. It takes longer to get dinner ready in the forest than one would think, and it was two hours before the Kru-boys announced the welcome fact that it was prepared. A part of the deer had been cut up in pieces and stewed in an iron pot, and two nice long joints had been cooked by running sticks through them and toasting them over the coals; plantains had been boiled, and there was bread and butter that Mrs. Reading had provided.

It was in many ways delightful to eat here in the wild woods, but after all it was not so handy to reach down to the ground for every mouthful of food, and the boys began to realize what handy things tables and chairs are: the greatest difficulty seemed to be to know where to put one's legs, they were always in the way and it was all the boys could do to keep from knocking something over with their feet. Mr. Reading told them he once had a nice table made with movable top and folding legs, but he found it was too much trouble to carry it with him, as food and other necessaries took up what little room there was in the canoe, so that he left it at home after one trip.

They had only begun eating when a shot was heard in the forest and Mr. Reading turned to Adande to inquire what it was, then it was discovered that Adande and Loembe were gone, their absence had not been noticed before; the shot-gun was gone too, and it was evident these two old men had gone off to see what they could do in the way of hunting. In a few minutes Adande's voice was heard calling the Kru-boys, and then it was certain some animal had been killed; the Kru-boys hurried into the bush in the direction of the voice and presently returned dragging a wild pig which Adande had shot.

This pig was different from any the Judge or the boys had ever seen; it was of a reddish color, like a breed of hogs in America called Jersey Reds, and had very long ears that lay back upon its shoulders and ended in tufts of long hair; upon the face were two large warts, and the body was not so fat and round as is usual with the domestic hog. The boys greeted the advent into the camp of the dead pig with a cheer, and were too excited to care much for dinner; as for Adande and Loembe, they looked happy and satisfied, and while they said nothing it was evident they had noted the fact that they had secured the biggest game.

After the men had eaten and enjoyed a good smoke, the dead pig and cooking utensils were put in the boats and the bows turned down stream; the tide had just begun to ebb and so was in their favor, and they went along at a lively pace, reaching Nomba at five o'clock. The people of Nomba were glad to see them back, and especially to see the pig, for in Africa, whenever a man has secured fish or game, he cannot keep it all to himself but must divide it with his neighbors, and so when the villagers saw the pig they knew they would have a piece of meat for supper.

Loembe made Mr. Reading and his friends at home in his house; it was a comfortable house, built of boards raised on posts five feet above the ground, like the mission houses at Baraka; Adande and the Kru-boys had a bamboo house set apart for them. In the evening Mr. Reading and Adande held a preaching service and when that was over the villagers got up a dance in honor of the distinguished visitors that had come to their town.

Men and women do not dance together as in civilized lands, but in parallel lines facing each other, the men on

one side and the women on the other. There are several kinds of dances, most of which have been interdicted by the Church because connected in one way or another with heathen practices; simple dancing does no harm, but the dancers, like those of Christian lands, too often resort to strong drink to increase the excitement and consequent enjoyment, and this of course can only be condemned.

After the people had danced an hour, the Judge thanked them for the compliment they had intended and Mr. Reading distributed some tobacco among them and sent them to their houses and told them to go to sleep. Loembe, the Judge and Mr. Reading had each a good bed, and the boys rolled themselves in their blankets and slept on the floor.

Wednesday morning every one was up bright and early; it was a little cool and a slight mist hung over the creek and the flooded land near it; the people of the town felt the cold, and moved about with their cloths wrapped tightly around them; and yet it was not really cold, for the thermometer registered 86° Fahr., but the early morning air always seems chilly until the sun has dispelled the night mists.

While our friends were drinking coffee the Kru-boys were putting the luggage in the boats and by a little after seven they had said "good-bye" to Loembe and the good people of Nomba and were on their way up the river. Several fishing canoes were passed and the boys were greatly interested in watching the men throw the nets.

These nets are circular at the bottom and cone-shaped, running up to a point at the top, to which a long cord is attached; around the bottom is a row of lead sinkers to make the net settle down in the water. Two men go out in a canoe together, one sitting in the stern to paddle, and

NOMBA AND OVENDO POINT

the other standing in the bow to throw the net. The fish are mostly of a kind that swim near the surface of the water; some are much like our herring, and others are like mullet, while a few are large ones like bass and sea-trout. The fisherman gathers the net on his left arm, holding the coil of heavy cord to which it is fastened, in his hand; the lower edge of the net is taken in his teeth, and a part of it in his right hand. There he stands in the bow of the canoe awaiting his opportunity while his companion noiselessly propels the canoe to the place where the unsuspecting fishes are playing about; when the proper moment has come, the net is thrown and falls all spread out flat upon the water with a loud splash.

One would naturally think, if the fish had a grain of sense, they would get out from under the net and make their escape, but for some unaccountable reason they do not, and the sinkers draw the net down in the water until the outer edge has come together in a bunch in the middle like a bag that is closed with a shirr-string, and the fish are enclosed in it. The fisherman now drags the net endways into the canoe, knocks the fish on the head with a short club carried for the purpose, shakes them out into the canoe, and gathers up his net for another throw. It was very fascinating to watch them and the boats remained near the canoes nearly an hour to give the boys a good opportunity to see this novel method of fishing.

A few miles above Nomba the grass fields came down to the water's edge, and several little clusters of houses were seen, showing there were plantations near by. The people of Gaboon, like the wealthier inhabitants of our cities, have their country places to which they retire in June, July, and August, which is the "season" here as well as in America. They spend their time hunting, fishing, gardening, and making mats for roofing their houses. When the rains begin they go back to town and leave their country places in charge of slaves, with usually one of their wives as overseer; these slaves tend the crop and if there is more food than they can eat they take it to the owner in town to help support his family.

A little after ten o'clock they landed at Ovendo Point, a bold grassy headland that stands at a break in the shore-line where it sweeps around to form a deep bay. There is a good-sized town on the flat at the foot of the hill, where Mr. Reading had stationed one of his Bible-readers, a young man named Igui [E-goo-wee]. The people came down to the landing to salute the strangers and after the luggage was taken from the boats they were anchored a short distance from the beach and then all went up to the village, the Kru-boys carrying the things. News had spread through the town that strangers had arrived, and they were gazed at as they passed along, after the usual village fashion. The chief of the village placed his house at the disposal of the white folks and Adande and the Kru-boys found places in a house near by. The little school Igui was teaching had its session quite broken up by the advent of the strangers, and the young man came promptly to pay his respects and hear the news.

When a traveling party enters an African village it is escorted to some public place, generally a house in the middle of the street built for a lounging-place and central news depot, and after the principal persons of the town have paid their respects, one of the strangers tells who they are, what are the objects of the journey and the incidents that have occurred by the way; a crowd gathers round to listen and express their approval or disapproval by various exclamations. When the story is finished houses are provided for their accommodation and they settle down as a part of the population for the time they are to stay.

When Mr. Reading and his friends were seated, Adande gave a short history of the journey, not forgetting to tell of the death of the pig, and also explained who the Judge and the boys were, and why they came to Africa; he ended by saying they had started early and the white folks were tired and hungry. This hint had a good effect, the people scattered to discuss the strangers, and the chief invited his guests to come in the house and lie down if they felt so inclined, which they were very glad to do. It takes but little exertion in the African climate to make one tired, and it is always best anyway to rest, not sleep, in the middle of the day.

Soon after the Judge and the boys had retired, Adande came in to report that the chief had brought as a present two chickens and two bunches of plantains, and Mr. Reading went out to receive them, and also to give out the rations to the men and to see about dinner. The food question in Africa is an important one for both the master and his people; if your men are well fed, and especially if they have enough meat to satisfy them, they will do almost anything for you, and it is always best for the master to give every man's daily rations into his own hand, as it is sure to save much quarreling.

After dinner Igui came in and gave a report of his work; his little school was prospering, having now twenty-two scholars, and the people fairly attentive upon the Sabbath services; they were all anxious to have a church built, and were ready to do all they were able to assist in its erection.

AN AFRICAN KING

About four o'clock Adande and the boys went out for a stroll over the hills; they took the gun with them thinking they might be able to shoot something. They climbed to the top of the Cape and were rewarded by a wide view of the river. It was so far to the opposite shore that all they could see was a low line of dark green. Up river were two large islands thickly covered with trees, and around to the left was a large bay into which the Ikoi river emptied; on the farther shores of the bay are the first cannibal villages, a people the boys had often heard of, but were just a little afraid to meet. When they had rested a little and enjoyed the view they walked back along the ridge and kept a good lookout for game, but they were too near the village and none was seen.

On their way back, Frank was tempted to try his skill on a flock of parrots that flew overhead, and to the surprise of Adande succeeded in bringing one down; it was not dead, but had a wing broken and was only captured after a lively skirmish. Parrots have such strong bills they can bite very hard, and a wild one, especially when wounded, is a savage bird. Frank wished to keep the parrot until its wing healed and then take it to America with him, and this he succeeded in doing, although it was a great deal of trouble and bother. The boys had serious trouble when they reached the village in tying on a bandage so as to hold the broken wing in place, but they succeeded after being severely bitten.

In the evening Mr. Reading and Adande held a preaching service, as they had done the night before at Nomba, and then Judge McGee had a long talk with the old men about their country, customs and superstitions; they insisted that the God who made the white man was not the God who made the black man, and that the white man's fashions were no doubt the best for him, but they did not suit the black man's condition and therefore it was unreasonable to expect him to adopt them. They thought there were a great multitude of spirits everywhere in the air about us, but all invisible to mortal eyes; and that these spirits were responsible for all natural phenomena such as clouds, storm and rain, and that they also were constantly interfering in the affairs of men. These spirits were much to be feared, for in addition to being powerful they could work unseen and so their efforts could not be counteracted. Besides these free spirits, there were the disembodied souls of men, who lingered about their former habitations, and were able to do much harm to those they disliked. The old chief thought the best way to deal with these was to drive them out of town, and this he said he always did whenever any one died, by firing off plenty of guns.

The Judge asked him if the souls would not come back again, and the chief answered that he prevented this by the powerful fetiches which he hung up on poles at the entrance of the village. Long and earnest was the conversation, and the Judge was surprised to see how well the old African held his own in the argument. On Thursday morning our friends left the kind people of Ovendo and after a pleasant ride reached Baraka, hot and tired, and glad to have a good place for resting.

Chapter XV.

PICNIC EXCURSION TO SANDY POINT.

MR. and Mrs. Reading made up their minds to give their guests a picnic, as the bright summer weather was quite suggestive of pleasant days spent in the woods and by the sea-shore in the home-land, and they wished to make the visit of their friends as agreeable as possible.

To be sure, it was some work to get ready, but in this world every desirable result requires effort, and plenty of it, and besides, there were many willing hands to help; so it was decided to start on Tuesday morning of the week following the trip to Ovendo. Mr. Reading's part was to secure the boats and crews and make all the business arrangements, while in the house the ladies baked and prepared all sorts of good things and got together bedding and other comforts; for the intention was to cross the river and remain away two nights. To be sure, the distance was not great, but the rate of locomotion was slow, for the improved methods of travel have not yet been engrafted upon the heathendom of this sunny land.

PICNIC EXCURSION TO SANDY POINT

On Monday morning Kamanandi was sent across the river to give notice that Mr. Reading and his friends were coming, so that accommodations might be provided; and all the necessary permits for the embarkation were secured from the government officials. Early Tuesday morning the household were astir, and after a cup of coffee and some bread and butter, the Kru-boys came in and carried all the food and luggage to the beach. Mr. Reading had already gone down some time before, and when Mrs. Reading and her guests arrived he had two boats in the water ready for them [one of these had been borrowed from a trader, for the Christine was too small], and the big surf-boat was at anchor just beyond the breakers, in which the luggage was to be sent direct to King William's town where the night was to be spent.

Several of the church people came down to the beach to bid them good-bye, and the police officer walked over to wish them "bon voyage." Embarkation through the surf at Gaboon is always somewhat trying, but at length they were off and the three boats made quite a little fleet; the land-breeze was blowing gently and the sails were hoisted, giving the boats a more easy motion than oars, and making it easier for the crews.

The Gaboon river is so wide that the first hour's sailing seemed to make no impression on the opposite shore; then presently it crept a little nearer, objects began to take some definite shape, and by the end of another hour they felt that they were across although they were still half a mile from shore. The surf-boat was a slow sailer and had fallen a long distance behind; it was heading for King William's town which is some distance up the river, and, leaving it to take care of itself, the two gigs ran

FRENCH TRADING FACTORY, GABOON

before the wind and headed for Sandy Point at the mouth of the river.

The south shore of the Gaboon river is flat and sandy and the deep water comes right up to the beach; the Point, too, keeps off the ocean swells and the water is more quiet than on the northern shore, but just where the river current meets the tide there is considerable commotion and it is not always safe for a boat or canoe. Mr. Reading thought best to land just inside the cape and walk down the beach to the woods, only a mile away, while the boats came round at their leisure.

It was now ten o'clock, but it was a little cloudy and the sun not so hot as usual, so that here on the ocean beach it was delightful to walk; shells of several varieties were abundant, and the boys had jolly times chasing the great sand-crabs that ran about in considerable numbers. As Lizzie could not keep up with the rest, Hattie and Gertrude, two members of the choir who had come along to assist Mrs. Reading, carried her by turns. There was abundant time and no occasion to hurry and the picnicers took it slow and easy, giving the young people ample opportunity to race around and enjoy themselves; and in truth it was delightful here, the great waves rolled in so grandly and broke in foam upon the sandy shore, while the duties of active life having been left behind, the mind was free to enjoy the beauties of nature.

A mile below the Point there is a rocky headland covered with a thick growth of palms and other trees, and here the party sat down in the cool shade and rested until the boats came up and landed the dinner baskets. A short reef of rocks extended out from the headland and made a little sheltered bay where the boats were anchored. The Kru-boys carried the baskets to a nice shady place among the rocks, where dinner was prepared under Mrs. Reading's directions by Hattie and Gertrude, assisted by the girls.

The Kru-boys cooked their plantains at a little distance and also boiled water to make tea. In hot weather at home we think we must drink ice-water to cool us, but there is no ice in Western Africa nor even cold water; drinking water is always warm, or at least tepid, and hot drinks are used instead. Not only are hot drinks in universal use, but those who have been long on the coast follow the native custom of eating quantities of chilli peppers. This to a northern mind would seem to be highly injurious, but the opposite is true, and not only are peppers wholesome as food, but they are an excellent remedy in fevers. The power of the sun which stimulates vegetable growth into unwonted activity, has a depressing effect upon animal life, and stimulants are demanded. Alcohol in every form, experience has proved to be injurious, and so also is quinine though in less degree, but peppers in any reasonable quantity do no harm and impart a a grateful glow to the system.

This headland by the sea was a better camping place than the gentlemen had found in the forest on the Nomba creek, for there were stones of various sizes for seats, and some little patches of grass here and there did very well as lounging places. Inland was a wide prairie with clumps of trees here and there giving it a park like appearance; this lovely prairie on the one side and the blue sea on the other, made a very attractive picture. In the trees over their heads little birds were flitting about, and in the centre of the grove parrots were whistling and talking to one another as they fed upon the ripe palm-nuts.

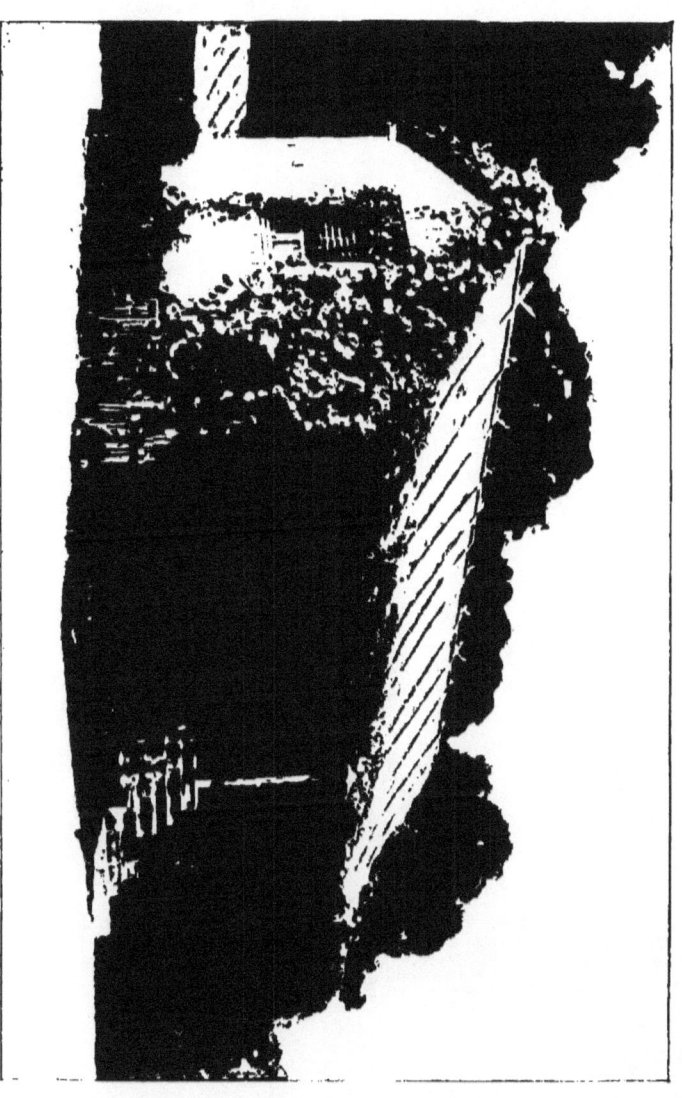
GARDENER'S HOUSE, GABOON

Dinner was over, and the picnicers were taking things as easy and comfortable as possible and engaged in quiet conversation, when a rustling was heard in the bushes, and, looking up, there stood a native African, pure and simple—a chimpanzee! He was a fine fellow, standing nearly three feet in height, and surveyed the pale-faced party with a puzzled look. To the frightened girls he appeared the size of a giant big enough to swallow them all, and they screamed in a manner befitting the occasion; the boys were quite as much frightened as the girls, and even little Lizzie, who ought to have known better, was panic-stricken as well as the rest.

The young folks lost no time in scrambling to their feet and running away, upsetting some of the dishes and breaking them as they did so, and the chimpanzee, equally alarmed at all this outcry, scampered into the woods, glad to be able to save his life. The Kru-boys took in the situation, and seizing a machete which they had used to cut fire-wood, hurried after the intruder; but they could not catch him and he got away, to their sorrow, for to them it meant the loss of just so much fresh meat.

This incident broke up the picnic and although it was still early in the afternoon there was nothing to do but pack up and go. The sea-breeze was now coming in, and with umbrellas to keep off the sun, the walk to the Point was enjoyable; here the boats met them, and they got in and sailed up the river to King William's town. The villagers saw the boat coming and were waiting at the landing to welcome the visitors; King William was there too; he usually resides at his plantation, but when Kamanandi brought the word that his friend, Mr. Reading, was coming, he had hurried into town.

Ntyndorema, the cook, had come with the surf-boat and he had gotten things ready to get supper whenever it might be needed; when he saw the boat coming so early he had prepared tea, and this was served as soon as the party had reached the King's house and taken seats. After the tea Adande gave an account of the day's occurrences and explained who the visitors were; when he told about the chimpanzee they all declared it was a witch or it would never have shown itself to the white man in such a manner.

King William II. is a man about fifty years of age, having had a good education, and is quiet and pleasant in his manner. His father, or Old King William, as he is called, was a wonderful man in his day; a man of strong character, shrewd, far-sighted and a thorough politician. He died a few years ago, full of years and honors. In his last years he was much troubled with tooth-ache and his people declared that he was so old he was cutting his fourth set of teeth. He possessed a hundred wives and a great many slaves; when dying he expressed the wish that none of these might be killed over his grave, but it is commonly believed that some were put to death secretly. His family would esteem it a deep disgrace for so great a man as he to enter the spirit-world without attendants. Gilt crowns, sceptres, gold chains and other valuable presents, were given him by some of the governments of Europe, and these are now in the possession of his son.

When the conference was over Mrs. Reading and the girls went to the house appointed for them, which was built of boards and elevated on posts in the usual style; there were three or four beds made by native carpenters, and for the rest beds had been made on the floor. Over all these were mosquito nets made of bright-colored calico, for on this side of the river there are a number of mosquitoes, while on the north side there are scarcely any.

All the natives of Central Africa, except the very poorest, sleep under these nets whether there are mosquitoes or not; when foreign cloth is not available they are made of the yellow grass-cloth mats manufactured in many parts of the interior; these mats are so closely woven as scarcely to admit any air passing through them, and how the people keep from smothering is somewhat hard to understand.

Most of the women of the town came in to have a chat and take a good look at the young ladies; the hair excited their wonder more than anything else, especially its length. The wool of the negro not infrequently attains the length of ten to twelve inches, but as it is usually matted up or tied close to the head, the length is not apparent, and a white lady's hair, especially if she let it hang down, seems to her black sisters very wonderful indeed. These African mothers told of some of the trials of their home-life, but as it was all through an interpreter the conversation was not as satisfactory as if they could have expressed themselves in English. Making allowance for the difference in country, race and national customs, it was wonderful to learn that the little things that trouble us and disturb our equanimity were the very trials of which these poor African mothers complained. With them as with us, a kind word and a little generous sympathy—things that cost us only a slight effort—are highly valued and do much to dispel the gloom from the mind, and brighten and cheer the spirit.

After supper the town's people were called together and Mr. Reading and Adande held a preaching service; then the ladies retired to their house, while the gentlemen and the boys arranged to go fishing. King William had a long seine or fishing net that some one had imported for him from England; this great net was put up in the stern of one canoe, and another took the fishing party to the scene of operations which was down toward Sandy Point.

When the fishing-ground was reached the second canoe was drawn ashore and the visitors landed; the rope attached to the land end of the net was taken by the shore party and the net was gradually payed out in a half circle, and then the crew pulled slowly for shore drawing their end of the net after them. The boys eagerly watched the sport and followed closely the land party who walked slowly along the beach as the net drifted with the tide; the Judge lingered somewhat behind, for to him the half naked fishermen on this wild coast presented a scene more attractive than the mere securing of fish.

The moon, obscured by broken cloud masses that drifted to the northeast, threw a fitful light over the men, and his mind went back eighteen hundred years to those midnight toilers on the Sea of Galilee, who saw by the first dawning light One who inquired of them, "Children, have ye any meat?" and he thought of the light that now was dawning on this dark land, a "light to lighten the Gentiles," brought from heaven by that divine One who in the early morning of the olden days trod the shores of Galilee closely watching his disciples as they fished, and he wondered if that same Almighty One might not be treading the shores of this far off land watching His toilers as they sought to catch its people in the gospel net.

As Peter and his companions toiled through the lengthening hours of the night, they knew not that Jesus was watching from the shore, noting all their efforts, their successes, their failures, and who can tell if He is watching His workers now as surely and as lovingly as He did through the night by Galilee?

The reverie was broken by the shouts of the boys over the fish as the "bag" of the net was drawn ashore, and the Judge hurried forward to see the game. The haul had been fairly successful, and the boys were in high glee, more especially as some of the fish were of strange forms, quite different from any they had before seen. King William and his men were in good spirits and made ready the net for another haul, and so continued until midnight, when the net was drawn in the canoe and all hands returned to town pretty well tired out; there was a goodly pile of fish as they all lay together but when divided it did not seem so much after all.

The next morning there were fresh fish for breakfast and they were good too; Ntyndorema cooked them by running a green stick lengthwise through them and then toasting them over the coals; if they fall in the ashes a few times before they are done, as they are quite likely to do, it makes no difference, the ashes are easily brushed off with the hand and fish taste better when they have the flavor of the wood through them.

The gentlemen concluded to walk out to the plantations, but the ladies thought best to remain in the village, as walking across country in Africa is not a very suitable occupation for them. After the gentlemen had gone, Mrs. Reading took the girls to see the operation of making eguma [e-goó-mah], which is the bread of the sea-coast tribes.

It is made from the roots of the cassava, of which there are two varieties, the sweet, and the bitter; the latter is more generally used as it will grow on poorer ground, and yield a larger and surer crop. It contains a poisonous juice which may be dispelled by heat, or by soaking it in water for several days as was done by the Kamerun women, and is the plan adopted in making eguma. Lying so long in water causes the roots to ferment, and they do not smell good by any means, as the girls soon discovered; these roots when taken from the water are peeled and grated and then boiled, which thickens the mass much as boiling thickens starch; it is then rolled in leaves and is ready to be eaten. In this condition it will save for a few days only and then a fresh supply must be made. It is pretty poor stuff and neither attractive in taste or smell; one of its advantages in the mind of an African is that it is indigestible and remains a long time upon the stomach, giving a sense of fullness; they always complain when they eat rice that they get hungry so soon again. On the contrary, the Kru-boys prefer rice, and it must be the more nourishing food of the two, for they are a better developed people than the cassava eating tribes.

Another product of this root is farina, much made by the Camma and other tribes south of Gaboon; in making farina the grated root is dried by heat, and the product is hard, dry grains that will keep longer than the eguma; but it requires an African taste to appreciate either of these foods, and strangers would soon lose their health if they attempted to live on them.

When missionaries first came to Africa they thought they ought to identify themselves the more closely with the country by eating its products and thus in a measure make Africans of themselves, but the plan did not succeed; nor will the idea of "self-supporting missions" at the present day be a success in the equatorial regions. Farther

PALM OIL READY FOR SHIPMENT

south, where the climate and natural products are more nearly those of the temperate zone, missionaries may live on the produce of the soil, but everywhere in the tropics foreigners will be compelled to import a good share of their food.

In one of the houses an old woman was seen weaving a mat, such as are used everywhere for bedding. The African does not use a mattress, or a tick filled with straw, husks, or feathers, for a bed, as we do; but he uses one or more thin mats according to how rich he may be, and these are spread on the bedstead, or on the ground, as may be convenient.

These mats are made from the leaves of the Pandanus, or screw-palm, and are five or six feet long by three wide. The leaves are gathered and made into strips half an inch wide and as long as the leaf will allow; these strips after being dried are dyed various colors and are then ready to be woven into the web. A frame is used, and the operation is one that resembles both weaving and plaiting; the result is a closely woven mat of pretty design and that will almost hold water. It is a great deal of work to make these mats and they are highly prized; foreigners too like them, using them as rugs on the floor.

The so-called "grass-cloth" used for mosquito-nets and by the poorer people for clothing, is made in the far interior from the cuticle of the unopened palm-leaf of the white palm. This cuticle is stripped off as we would take the skin from the rhubarb stalks, and is an eighth of an inch wide and three or four feet long; in drying it turns a straw color, and this deepens with age to old gold. These narrow strips are then woven in a regular loom such as is used for hand weaving in our own land, and the cloth thus made has a regular texture and much resembles, except in color, the linen woven by our grandmothers. It has such a close smooth surface that flowers and other figures may be painted on it the same as on canvas; if a little attention were paid to the matter, these mats might be made a desirable article of export.

The girls were here initiated into the art of eating African candy; this is neither more nor less than sugar cane. The African people do not know what sugar is, and of course do not use it, although when brought to their attention they are at once fond of it; but they raise sugar cane, and the juice of it is to an African maiden what caramels and "French mixtures" are to an American one.

To eat sugar cane aright is an art; the cane is cut in convenient lengths, and then with a piece of cane in the left hand, and a knife in her right, an Mpongwe girl, with a few deft strokes, will cut away the rind and shape the juicy interior into convenient mouthfuls, cutting, chewing, and enjoying herself in a way quite pleasing to see. The girls found the cane juice sweet, but on the whole preferred the more concentrated extract they had been accustomed to at home.

In the house where the old woman was weaving the mat, was a young mother and her baby, a queer looking little thing, with its body all rubbed over with red powder, and its eyes hardly open yet, like a young kitten. The girls were just delighted, for this was no doll baby, but a real true enough baby, and an African baby at that; they crowded about it and surveyed it with quite as much pleasurable interest as if they had discovered a gold mine. The next thing, of course, was to pick it up, and it was passed from one to another until each had taken a turn in holding it; before this operation was ended it cried, as all good babies should, and the girls noted with surprise that it cried just the same as white babies.

"Only to think," exclaimed Hattie, "that a black baby should cry just the same as a white one!"

"Yes," chimed in Mamie, "I thought they cried in some heathen fashion or other, I didn't know how."

"Say girls," inquired Lulu, "why is it that these babies cry just like ours do, and then talk such an outlandish gibberish when they grow up?"

This was a puzzle, for it seemed to the girls that if they started right, as they evidently did, they ought to speak the "Queen's English" when they were grown. It could not be in the color, for were there not any number of black babies in America, and did they not speak English? and then as to the color, this one was not black at all, but very much the same color as all young babies, only a little darker.

The girls were beyond their depth, and they turned to Mrs. Reading; she told them that words were nothing in themselves but mere sounds, and that the meaning given was purely arbitrary; that the English language that came so natural to us was not so soft, melodious or regularly constructed a language as the Mpongwe, and that to the ears of others it sounded harsh and discordant; that babies grow into their surroundings, and naturally express themselves in the same way as those about them. "There is my Lizzie," said she, "who spoke Mpongwe before she did English, and to this day she thinks in Mpongwe. As to the color of the skin, it is a pigment deposited there the same as it is in our hair, and this does not usually take place until after the child is born."

"What is this red stuff that is smeared all over it?" inquired Jessie.

"It is powdered redwood," replied Mrs. Reading; "they think it has a tonic effect, and they have it put on the baby to make it stronger; sometimes they rub the babies with chalk, and sometimes with ashes and other things. The poor little babies have a hard time of it, and a great many of them die when very young." While they were talking, the baby went to sleep, and as they did not wish to disturb it they went quietly out.

In the street, in the shade of one of the verandas, were two girls playing a game with a sort of back-gammon board; this board had two rows of open, cup like holes along the side, and a hole at each end; the players moved large beans from hole to hole by a rule the girls could not understand, and every now and then one took a trick which entitled her to all the beans in a certain hole. Mrs. Reading told the girls this game was a very intricate one and difficult for a white person to understand, and that it was common among all the tribes of Central Africa.

While they were watching the game Gertrude brought Lizzie some white, oily nuts, a little larger than peanuts, called coolah; these nuts grow in a husk the size of a walnut, and taste like chestnuts. They are great favorites with the people, and in the season are brought to town in basketfuls.

The girls this morning made a discovery, which was that it was hotter in a native house on the ground, than in a board house elevated five or six feet above the earth. In the Mission House at Baraka the temperature is seldom above 94° Fahr., but here in these bamboo houses opening upon the sandy street, it was over one hundred.

In the comfortable Mission House, so long as one does not need to go out doors in the middle of the day, it

NATIVE WOMEN, ACCRA, GOLD COAST

is very pleasant; but in native towns the middle of the day is very hot. But be the day ever so hot, the negro loves the fire; there is something in its cheerful warmth that comforts him, and be the temperature of the air what it may, he will sit down by a fire and enjoy it.

It was now eleven o'clock, and the girls thought they had enough of sight-seeing, so they went to their house and remained quietly resting until the sea-breeze in the afternoon made it pleasant to go out again.

The gentlemen returned in the early evening, having had an adventurous day, and the next morning they bade good-bye to King William and his people, and, promising to come again if it were possible, they sailed across the river and were home by noon.

Chapter XVI.

BENITA.

ON the return from King William's village it was decided that the Band should take a trip in the Mission cutter, Nassau, to the Benga portion of the mission-field. From Gaboon southward the Mpongwe language is spoken; from Corisco northward, the Benga, and these two languages are in many respects as unlike as English and German. The Nassau was given to the mission by the boys and girls of America, and is the main dependence for communication with all parts of the Benga portion of the field except Batanga, which is more easily reached by the regular German mail steamers which call there every month. Passengers and supplies for all these stations, except Batanga, are landed at Gaboon, and taken by the Nassau to their destinations.

The various foreign governments that have now seized on nearly every mile of the coast, have made the business part of the mission work much more arduous than it formerly was. These colonial settlements are simply money-making enterprises of the various governments

CHURCH AND SCHOOL-HOUSE, CORISCO

that have undertaken them, the idea being, that it will form an outlet for the manufactures of the home countries; in the meantime, to make the undertaking pay its way, duties on imports and exports are levied, and this requires a great deal of red tape in the way of declarations, bills of lading, manifests, passenger lists, permits, etc., etc., as well as makes missionary operations more expensive. The matter is still further complicated when a mission-field lies in the territory of two or more colonies, as is the case with the Gaboon Mission; under such circumstances the importation and distribution of supplies and trade goods, is a difficult and troublesome task.

The trip north having been decided upon, Mr. Reading set to work to get the cargo ready for the little vessel; this consisted of boxes of soap and canned goods, cases of kerosene, barrels of flour, bundles of fish, with calico, muslin, axes, charcoal irons, saws, planes, tobacco, books and many other things. All these had to be securely packed, weighed, measured, labeled, charged, billed, passed through the custom-house, and letters of explanation concerning them written, after which they were sent on board.

Sunday comes like a benediction after the distracting cares of the week, and none enjoy it more than the mission family at Baraka.

On Monday morning, November 21, all was bustle and excitement among the members of the Band with preparations for the trip in their "very own vessel," as they chose to call it; for were they not the representatives of the givers? To take a ride in their own ship along the bright green coast of sunny Africa, was a matter of surpassing interest indeed. The strong limbed Kru-boys were kept busy carrying to the beach wraps, portmanteaus, boxes of provisions, plantains, eguma, dried fish, cocoanuts, mangoes, bananas, and limes; wood and water, as well as the cargo, had already gone on board on Saturday. After breakfast they all took up their line of march for the beach, Mr. and Mrs. Reading and Lizzie going along to see them fairly started; the police officer came too, to bid them bon voyage and see if all was straight.

It was a lovely morning, the air was soft and delicious, and the Judge noted with pleasure that it came from a favorable direction. Out in the river, half a mile from shore, the good little ship was at anchor with her head to the current, patiently waiting for her young owners to come on board. The big surf-boat had now returned to the beach and the sturdy Kru-boys carried the passengers one by one through the breakers, and put them in it; then they pushed it off, and as the young folks waved their handkerchiefs and hats in a good-bye to the friends ashore, they paddled away to the cutter. It was not a great while before they were alongside and scrambing on board in their eagerness to see what the vessel was like.

The captain and crew were already on board, so there was no cause for delay; the surf-boat dropped astern, the captain shouted to his men, the sails crawled slowly up the masts, the anchor chain was drawn in link by link, the main sheet was hauled in, the helm put hard-a-port and the little vessel rounded up to the wind and bounded away over the waves, glad to be once more free. At the guard-ship she "rounded to" while the boat was sent with the pass; when the boat returned it was made fast astern and the voyage was resumed.

Now that they were fairly under way, the young folks took time to look around and see what the vessel

MBADE STATION, BENITA RIVER

was like. There was not much room on deck, and no guards to keep them from falling off; in the bow there was a winch to draw the anchor chain, and next to that a little stove to cook food on; the roof of the cabin occupied the middle of the deck, and there was a narrow passage on either side. This cabin roof was about two feet high and made a very fair place to sit on. Near the stern was the wheel with a sun-shade built over it; ropes, water barrels, firewood, plantains, wraps, and many other things were lying about, and there was no shade over the deck except the small one over the wheel.

The young folks thought it was all "just too jolly for anything," and after a look on deck they went down stairs to see what it was like there. They found a really nice cabin with four bunks, two on each side, and a small table; a comfortable enough place it was, but small. The Band were just delighted and declared it was no make-believe ship, but a real sure-enough vessel, not the largest and grandest in the world, but good enough; and, well, they just loved it.

Having come to this happy conclusion they went on deck; the sun was gaining in power and there was no shady place; the swell was coming in quite strong from the broad Atlantic, and the motion of the vessel was shorter and quicker than that of a large steamer, while the wind made her lean over, so it was not so easy to keep on one's feet. The Band had accounted themselves pretty good sailors, but it was now only too evident they were growing seasick; the Judge therefore suggested to the girls the desirability of going to the cabin and lying down, while he and the boys made themselves as comfortable on deck as circumstances permitted.

The day wore on, and as the sea-breeze increased in strength with the declining sun, the Band brightened some and began to forget their seasickness with the accelerated motion of the vessel; they were running, too, before the wind, and that made the cutter steadier. On the starboard bow was the small island called Banyan, a famous place for sea-shells, while Corisco loomed up in front not more than three miles away.

A chicken had been killed, and some soup made on the cooking stove; it had a couple of peppers in it, and although it tasted pretty strongly of the smoke, it helped to allay the nausea, and the young travelers pronounced it good. The soup loosened their tongues, and conversation, which had been interrupted during the day, was now resumed, and they were commenting at a lively rate upon their experiences, when two great whales spouted up near them. These great creatures did not seem in the least afraid of the cutter, perhaps mistaking it for one of their own kind, and swam up quite near, creating no little consternation on board. There was evident cause for alarm, for each of these huge animals was much longer than the Nassau, and they could no doubt have capsized the cutter if they had wished to; but they were peaceably inclined, and after playing about for a few minutes they dived down and were seen no more, to the intense relief of every one on board. The Captain, Mr. Menkel, told the Judge he quite frequently met whales, but that they seldom came so near; and that while he had never been harmed by them, he did not like them to come up too close.

At five P. M. the cutter anchored off the Mission Station of Alongo, which is on the northwestern corner of the island of Corisco, and the Captain went ashore to take the mail and a few small packages. This station is in

MR. DeHEER'S CHURCH, BOLONDO

charge of a native brother, and is not as prosperous as in former days; the people have been greatly debased by the rum traffic, and have steadily decreased in numbers until the population is now but a few hundreds.

Corisco is a bright little island four miles long and three miles wide, and presented a picturesque appearance as seen from the deck of the cutter. At the northern end the shores were rocky and steep, presenting a firm front to the waves which raged and dashed themselves to foam against it; while toward the southern end the shores were flat and sandy, forming beautiful white shell-strewn beaches, backed by lovely palms, among which the brown roofs of the little native villages could be seen clustered amid the broad leaves of the plantains. A great many beautiful shells are found on these beaches, and the girls thought they would love to look for them, and the boys, too, wanted to go ashore, for they had heard at Gaboon that turtles came ashore in the night, and they were anxious to "turn" them, as they had read about in books of travel; but there was no opportunity, for the vessel was going right on to Benita, and so they could only hope there might be a chance to do so on their way back. In a little over an hour Mr. Menkel was back and they resumed their voyage; they were fortunate in having no rain, and the night was much more agreeable than the day had been.

Soon after sunrise on Tuesday morning they crossed the bar at the mouth of the Benita river, and sailed slowly up to the station at Bolondo, two miles from the sea. The houses are situated in a grove of lovely palms, and as the little company looked eagerly ashore they thought they had never seen anything more inviting. Word was at once sent to Mr. DeHeer that the mission-band had come, and the whole family were soon at the landing to welcome their guests. Mr. DeHeer's boat was soon in the water, and this, with the Nassau's boat, was not long in transferring the passengers to the beach.

Mr. and Mrs. DeHeer and Mrs. Reutlinger welcomed their guests most heartily, and, leaving the luggage to be brought up later, they led them to the house, where a smoking hot breakfast was presently ready for them. The Band thought they had never eaten so good a meal, and no wonder, for Mrs. DeHeer is a famous cook, and they had scarcely eaten anything since they left Gaboon. After breakfast there was a good long talk, for white visitors are seldom seen at Bolondo, and then the Judge and his young companions retired to rest awhile, for they were pretty well used up.

Along in the afternoon Mr. DeHeer took his guests around to show them the premises; they found Bolondo was a clearing in the great forest growth that everywhere covered the country; trees and bushes were to be seen on every side, for, except in front of the house, there was a fringe of tall bushes left growing along the river bank. The house was built of boards and raised on posts like the houses at Gaboon, but it was two-storied, and so when you were inside it was more like a house at home. As the buildings were so shut in, there was no extensive view, and the profound stillness all about made it seem like Sunday. The good brother's whole heart and soul were wrapped up in his church; all his energies were bent upon the spiritual improvement of his people, and he has been successful in a remarkable degree. This anxiety for their welfare is highly appreciated by them, and they love their "Pa DeHeer" with a devotion that is indeed rarely seen. They worshipped in a bamboo structure a short distance from the house.

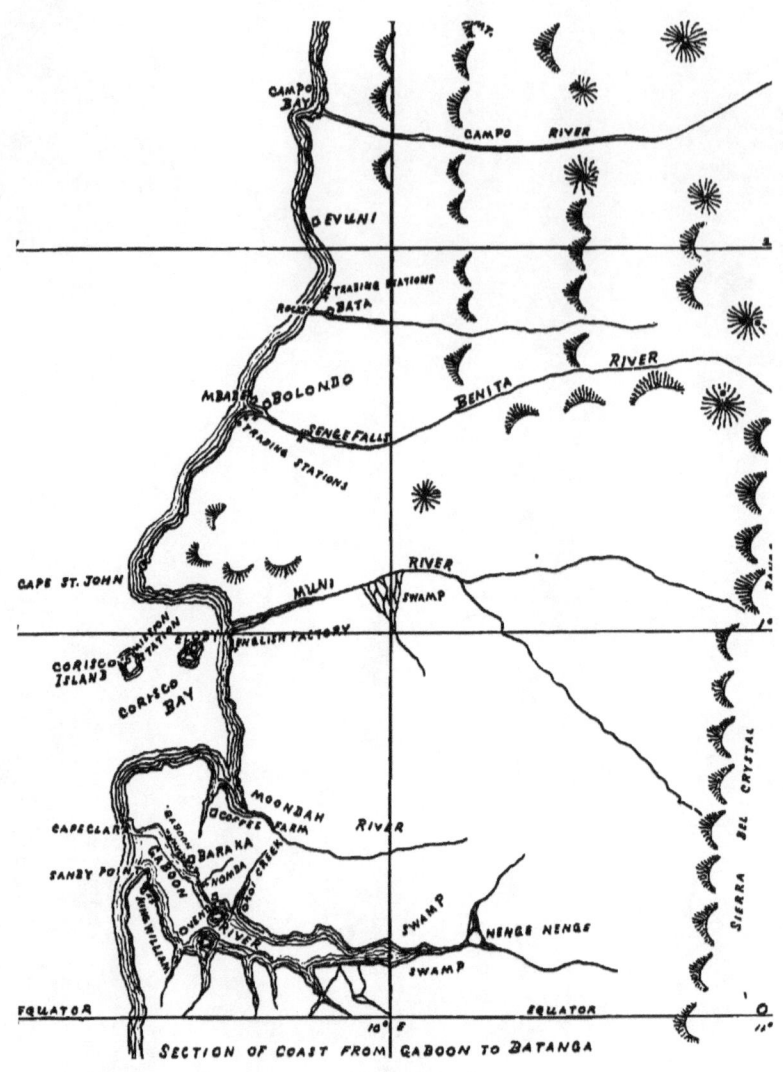

The Band soon discovered that Mr. DeHeer was one of the jolliest missionaries they had met, in fact, brim-full of fun, and he kept them laughing much of the time. Among his pets was a long-tailed monkey chained to a pole, a happy fellow, full of tricks. Mr. DeHeer had taught him to reach up and pull his handkerchief from his pocket and then look in the pocket for a lump of sugar; after the monkey had done this for Mr. DeHeer, Willie thought he would try, but there was no sugar in Willie's pocket, and when the monkey found that out he pulled at the coat hard enough to tear it, and then ran up the pole with his handkerchief. The Band had now found a playmate, and while they were having some fun with the monkey, Mr. DeHeer and the Judge sat down on the church steps and talked about the mission work.

The next morning Mr. DeHeer arranged a trip to Mbade [Em-bah-dah] a former mission station on the point of land at the entrance to the river a couple of miles from Bolondo. There is a path cut through the forest leading to Mbade, but it is a tiresome walk, and Mr. De-Heer took his guests by water in his two boats, and a jolly party they were. The beach is a rocky one, and not sandy as at Gaboon; and the reefs running out from the little points of land make it necessary for boats to keep well out. Mbade looks very pretty from the water, but the beauty diminishes on a closer inspection, for the ground on which it is built is sand, and the feet sink ankle deep in the yielding sand at every step.

When this station was built it was thought that as it was on a narrow point jutting into the sea, with a sandy soil, little vegetation, and freely exposed to the winds, it would prove to be healthy, but such has not been the case.

Malaria is a strange power; its origin and the laws that govern it are practically unknown.

The visiting party landed near a large mango tree that grew luxuriantly by the water-side, and climbed the bank to the level ground where the station was built. There was no missionary living here, and the place was in charge of a Bible-reader who kept the premises in order and taught a small school. When this station was begun there was a considerable population in the neighborhood, but now there are less than one hundred souls within a radius of a mile from the house.

It is a singular fact that all the seashore tribes are dying out, and unless other tribes move down from the interior to take their places, the country will be left without inhabitants. Although the Benita is quite a long river it is a poor one for trade; nothing is exported but a little rubber and barwood, and the principal stock in trade is rum. The factories are on the south side of the river, and as trade is so poor they have a pretty dull time of it.

The Benita is navigable for twenty miles to Senge, where there are rapids, and throughout the remainder of its course it consists of short, still reaches, separated by rapids and cascades; the country is one unbroken forest and is likely to remain a wilderness for a very long time to come.

Mr. DeHeer and his guests wandered around Mbade awhile and then returned to Bolondo, where the girls were initiated into the art of making palm-butter, for the manufacture of which Mrs. DeHeer has an enviable reputation. The bright scarlet nuts are boiled to soften them somewhat, pounded in a mortar to mash up the woody pulp, strained through a cloth, and the yellow liquid boiled to evaporate the excess of water, and then thickened with

SCENE ON THE BENITA RIVER

flour and seasoned with Chilli peppers. The palm-butter thus made is of a rich brown color, and has the consistency of apple-butter; it is used as a sauce or gravy on rice, bread-fruit, or any farinaceous food. It differs from the usual palm-chop in that it contains no oil or meat, and in being thickened with flour.

The remainder of the week was spent most pleasantly at this hospitable mission house, and in fact a more delightful family circle can not be found anywhere than the one that dwells amid the Bolondo palms.

The mission work is here carried on very differently from what it is at Gaboon; there is no government interference and no foreign influence to contend with, consequently the work is easier and more fruitful in good results. The school-house is built of bamboo, with a board floor; the Band peeped into it one morning and saw the dark-skinned little heathens sitting on benches and supposed to be studying their lessons, but mostly they were looking over the tops of their books and soon caught sight of the pale-faced strangers. One class was standing up in a row with their hands behind them and their toes to a crack in the floor, reciting in their wild, strange language, not one word of which our young friends could make out.

One feature of the Bolondo mission life was the coming of the town's women every morning to sell the produce of their gardens. This was the only market the women had for their products, and the mission family could consequently control the time of their coming; at Gaboon they come at all hours of the day, and it cannot be avoided. The women came early, and then attended morning prayers, after which the trading began; this interesting department of mission labor was conducted solely by the ladies.

At Bolondo the supply exceeds the demands of the market, and so only a stipulated quantity is taken from any one woman, in order that all may have an opportunity to procure at least a few of the goods the white ladies have to sell. One woman was bringing ten eguma every day until she should accumulate sufficient credit to purchase calico for a dress; another wanted a lamp, and was bringing plantains; another wished to exchange sweet potatoes for a plate; another, eggs for a head of tobacco, and so on. These native women could keep accounts fairly well in their heads, but to prevent mistakes where produce was not paid for at once, payment was made in tickets or cards somewhat like the tickets formerly given in Sabbath-schools as rewards of merit. These cards were both of different sizes and colors, so that those who could not read might easily distinguish them; they were payable to bearer so that they were current as money, and were the only money in circulation at Benita; at Gaboon there is French silver coin. All employees are paid at all the stations in this "paper cash," which may be exchanged for goods at stated times; this system is well liked by both the missionaries and the people.

There are excellent fish in the Benita river, but they are not so abundant as at Gaboon. The ocean current that flows northward along the coast comes from the South Atlantic, and as it proceeds gets increasingly warmer, and it would appear that the cooler the water the more numerous are the fish, for as we go northward their numbers constantly decrease. One evening the boys were on the beach near the little cape just below the boat landing, and an old man who was fishing with a long line

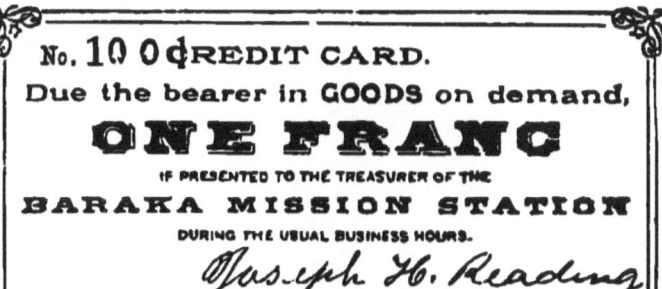

drew ashore a fine fish about two feet long and of a bright, pink color; as it came from the water, with its fins all bristling, it was a beautiful creature. The native fishermen have a custom that might well be adopted in more civilized lands; after catching a fish they do not allow it to die a lingering and torturing death, but kill it at once by a smart blow on the head.

A favorite dish in the Bolondo household is what is called an Ajomba [Ah-jom-bah] of fish. To prepare this dish the fish are cut into lengths of five or six inches and laid upon plantain leaves; these leaves are nearly two feet wide, and are cut into two feet lengths and laid together in several thicknesses. After the fish has been laid upon this pile of leaves, salt and red peppers are added and also odika, pau, palm-oil or some other native sauce; the edges of the leaves are then gathered up and tied and the "bundle" put in the hot ashes, and the cinders raked up near it, but not near enough to burn it. Both fish and meat cooked in this way are excellent; the leaves do not impart any unpleasant taste, and as every particle of steam is kept in the bundle the flavor is retained and the toughest meat becomes tender. The Band ate the ajombas with a relish, but they did not care much for the sauces that were cooked with them.

Here at this station, as at Gaboon, Sunday is the great day of the week; on Saturday the yard is cleaned, the church swept, and every preparation made for suitably celebrating the day of rest. The Sabbath the Band spent at Bolondo was one of unusual interest, for it was communion Sabbath and a goodly number were to come out on the Lord's side and unite with His people. All through the week there had been session meetings, so that the good Brother DeHeer had not been able to spend as much time with his guests as he would have liked. A great many candidates were examined and many pathetic scenes witnessed; one old woman had been a sorceress, but she brought the implements of her witchery and threw them on the floor of the session room, saying, "Now I belong to Christ, and have no use for these things." These people were all in great earnest, and they were able too to give a reason for the faith that was in them, for one of the qualifications for membership was a pretty comprehensive knowledge of the catechism.

Sabbath morning was calm and bright, as lovely a summer's day as ever dawned upon this earth; those from a distance who were to attend the services, had arrived on Saturday, for no traveling is permitted on the Sabbath. At the ringing of the first bell they began to assemble with serious faces, and every one dressed in his best.

The Judge and the Band were given seats on one side of the pulpit, and the other side was occupied by the children with Mrs. Reutlinger at the organ; the body of the house was filled with a sea of black faces, once wild sons of the forest, now humble worshippers of Jehovah. The candidates for baptism occupied the front seats, then came the church members, and what space was left was occupied by the heathen, many of whom could not gain admittance for lack of room. As soon as the second bell ceased ringing the doors were closed; they were opened again during the singing, after which they were closed and locked, so that there might be no distraction caused by late comers. The services were very impressive, although as they were wholly in the native tongue our friends could not understand a word. At the close of the sermon, thirty-two, old and young, arose from their seats, forming a semi-circle from wall to wall, and took the vows of God upon them.

The members of the Band were tired when they reached the house, for the services had lasted more than two hours. Throughout the day there were various prayer-meetings, as well as Sunday-school, and a preaching service in the evening; in fact the people just gave themselves up to meetings, and they made a full day of it.

On Monday morning the Judge and his companions took leave of the kind friends at Bolondo and embarked upon the cutter; their stay had been both instructive and very agreeable, and they saw the Bolondo palms fade into the distance behind them, with genuine regret.

After crossing the bar and making a good offing, they headed north, running parallel with the coast. The mountains of the Sierra del Crystal range were in sight far away to the eastward, and formed a beautiful background to the dark green forest that rested in an unbroken expanse upon the land; after a while the mists gathered about the mountains and hid them from sight. The wind was light and the sun scorching hot, but there was nothing to do but to bear it, and so they endured it with such grace as they could.

Toward sundown they anchored half a mile from the shore off the Bata [Bah-tah] river. It was a wild place; ashore was only the tangled forest, cleft in twain by the narrow river that forced an uncertain passage through the rocks, against which the surf beat, throwing up clouds of spray. The thought of going in a small boat through that surf into the river was not an inviting one, but there was no other way to get ashore, and so the Captain took the Judge and the girls, and then came back for the boys.

The cutter danced about so it was with extreme difficulty the girls were lowered into the boat, but after a few slight mishaps they were transferred to the boat and then the men pulled slowly toward the bar. The water boiled and foamed about them and some of the waves wet them, but they got over safely and all at once found themselves in a quiet river. Presently on rounding a point they saw a town and a long church among the trees, and in a few minutes were on the beach and cordially welcomed by Rev. Mr. Etianye [A-tee-an-ye], Mr. DeHeer's able and trusted lieutenant.

REV. B. B. BRIER

Chapter XVII.

BATA—EVUNI—BATANGA.

WEDNESDAY morning was damp and misty; a heavy rain had fallen during the night, everything outdoors was soaked and wet, and a fog hung over the river, but the sun soon dispelled the mists and dried the grass, and it proved to be a glorious day. After coffee the Band sallied forth to take a look at the town; they found it small and by no means well situated, for both banks of the little river were overgrown by mangroves and at low tides banks of noisome black mud were exposed to the sun.

It was evidently no fit place for a white man to live in, but Mr. Etianye appeared to enjoy it, and the river gave him an easy path to the hill country in the interior. This earnest brother had built a church in the midst of a grove of oil-palms, and he appeared to be thoroughly devoted to its interests and well loved by his congregation.

The people of the town did not seem to be in a flourishing condition; they looked thin, hungry, and poorly kept, and the Judge ascertained, upon inquiry, that their gardens were not very productive, and they seldom were able to obtain meat or fish.

From Benita northward, for some reason not well understood, the entire coast-line is a land of hunger, and the one great thought of the people is to get something to eat. It is true elephants are numerous and troublesome, but it would seem as if this evil might be turned to good account by killing the elephants, eating the flesh and selling the ivory; but to kill an elephant is a big undertaking, and is seldom done except by the cannibal tribes in the interior, and watching all night in the heavy rain is dreary business; so the people do little planting and are always looking about for something to put in their stomachs, nothing coming amiss if it can only be gotten; dogs, rats, snakes, monkeys, ants—all is game to their nets, and no doubt tastes as good to them as oysters and terrapin to us.

The Judge expressed a wish to take a ride up the river, so Mr. Etianye hired two canoes and crews, and at ten o'clock they started; this was the first time the Band had taken a journey in canoes, and they found them rather crazy affairs.

A fleet of canoes upon a tropic river, skimming along with ease and grace under the vigorous strokes of their dusky crews, is a pleasing and picturesque sight; but when the clumsy white man gets in, he finds to his dismay that they will capsize with the greatest ease, and require as much skill in balancing as a bicycle. Mr. Etianye seated his guests upon low stools, and after going a mile or two they began to breathe more easily, but the cramped position was far from comfortable.

The river was fifty yards wide and bordered by mangroves; a mile or so above the town, on the left bank of the river, was a prairie which is said to extend all the way to Benita, running parallel with the beach. This level prairie, with the tall woods on either side of it and single trees growing upon it here and there, was beautiful, and was evidently appreciated by the animal creation, for parrots and other bright-feathered birds were flying about, and on the more secluded portions wild buffalo and deer delight to graze. Elephants also frequent the edge of the prairie, but not to eat the grass, for the elephant is not a grass-eating animal, but prefers the leaves and fruits of trees, so it must be that he haunts the edge of the woods merely to enjoy the beauties of the scene. This at least was Mr. Etianye's opinion, and he was reckoned among his people to be a great elephant hunter because he had killed two or three of these huge beasts.

As they proceeded it was easy to see that the river ran in a trough or deep valley with hills covered with heavy forest on either side. By and by the water became sweet and the mangroves were succeeded by the pandanus, papyrus, and palms on the flooded lands, and large forest trees where the ground was higher.

At one o'clock they came to a village and halted for rest and lunch; the village was a little way back from the river on rising ground, and as the trees had been cut away to allow the plantains to grow it was hot there, so a temporary camp was made beneath some tall trees near the landing where it was shady.

The villagers were somewhat annoyed by the presence of so large a party of white folks and kept at a respectful distance, but they sold Mr. Etianye some plantains for tobacco and soap, and by and by a few of the men, armed with guns and spears, ventured to come and make a closer inspection. The men boiled the plantains which were green and hard, while a few riper ones were roasted in the ashes like potatoes, and these, with some canned corn-beef, made a frugal dinner for the Judge and his young friends.

This was the first time the girls had actually camped out in the wild woods and they enjoyed it very much; especially were they pleased with some small monkeys they saw in the trees called Kalinga [Kah-leen-gah], by the Mpongwes. These monkeys were no larger than kittens and had tails twice the length of their bodies; they were playful little fellows and appeared to lead a jolly life in their leafy home. Mamie wondered what they did in the night when it rained so hard, and the general opinion was that as they had no houses to shelter them they must get very wet and miserable.

After a good rest they again took their seats in the canoes and with the aid of the ebb tide sped swiftly homewards. They had not gone a mile when on rounding a turn they saw in the quiet river ahead of them a column of water like the "spout" of a whale, and a moment after a great ugly head was shoved up into view. The Band viewed the apparition with consternation and the crew shouted out "En-goo-voo," and began to back vigorously with their paddles. Now en-goo-voo means hippopotamus, and this great river horse was splashing around there in the water as if he thought the river was his home and he could do as he pleased in it. Neither crew nor passengers were disposed to dispute with him, and so the canoes quietly waited until he chose to get out of the way, which he did in a few minutes.

The hippopotamus furnished a subject for conversation all the way home, and the Band were agreed there was nothing awkward or clumsy in his movements when

MRS. B. B. BRIER

splashing freely about in his native river. Mr. Etianye informed them the flesh was excellent eating and the boys wished they might have some for supper.

This was the night for the regular Wednesday evening prayer-meeting; it was held in the church, and as the news had spread of the arrival of the strangers, there was a large audience in attendance. The church was of bamboo, and copied after Mr. DeHeer's at Bolondo, but it was more narrow. Kerosene lamps along the wall shed a rather dull light upon the congregation in various stages of dress and undress, but all with earnest, eager faces, although not all were Christians. Hymns were sung in the native tongue, and after reading and prayer by the pastor, the Judge addressed them, using an interpreter. Speaking through an interpreter is not easy; the sentences must be short, and while they are being repeated the speaker's mind is apt to wander, making it difficult to keep up the connection; however, the Judge did very well, and the people were greatly pleased.

Thursday morning the visitors found they were quite sore and stiff from the cramped position in the canoes, and so they determined to remain a day and rest. It was a good resolution, for on Friday they were bright and fresh, and were on board the cutter in good season in the morning, having enjoyed their visit at Mr. Etianye's town. As they rounded the first point along the coast on their way north they saw the trading post of Bata, a mile or more from the river; here there are three factories, a French police-station, and a French Catholic mission station.

At four P. M. the cutter anchored off Evuni [A-voonee], about twenty miles north of Bata. There was a surf about five feet high caused by the brisk sea-breeze, and in going through this they all got wet—a far from comfortable experience, but our young tourists were now getting somewhat accustomed to the discomforts of travel, and had learned to notice them as little as possible. They found a large community with a rambling town or collection of villages, and no white man, either missionary or trader, so that they must look wholly to the native people for entertainment.

The cutter had been recognized before she anchored, and Mbeyi [Em-ba-ye], the Bible-reader in charge of the church, was on the beach to welcome the Judge and his companions, and took them to the house of one of the elders, which was built on posts, and was comfortable. They were all so tired and seasick that they did little that evening but rest, and the people who came to pay their respects were told to come again in the morning.

Saturday morning they held a grand levee, when nearly the entire population came to see the strangers and shake hands; this latter ceremony being almost the only civilized custom that had as yet reached this remote region. It was indeed a heathen community, rough and rude, but kindly disposed toward the strangers, and they had nothing to fear.

The Judge was surprised to learn that here there was a church with more than a hundred members, and that among the by no means attractive crowd was many a true disciple of the meek and lowly Jesus; it seemed scarcely credible that this wild tribe was pressing into the kingdom; and yet such was the case.

When a white person goes into an African village he is regarded as a great natural curiosity, and all of his movements being a matter of wonder, are closely watched, so that there is little privacy, and this our friends found to

WATERFALL AT BATANGA

be true in their case; go where they would there were always followers, respectful, to be sure, but the sense of being always gazed at is not always pleasant.

Evuni is built on a level, sandy plain, and owing to the great number of oil and cocoanut-palm trees, plantains and cassava bushes, there is little breeze, and it is very hot indeed. The young folks were covered with prickly heat, so that the skin was as rough as nutmeg graters.

Sabbath morning was bright and clear, and throughout the town work was generally suspended, and toward nine o'clock the people began to assemble in the church. This building was entirely the product of native skill, no white man having in any way assisted in its construction; it is low, built of bark, with two doors at either end, but with no windows or openings of any kind on the sides. The floor is mother earth, trampled hard and smooth. Down each side were two long, parallel poles supported on crotched sticks. Across this space, from pole to pole, were slabs cut from trees, and part of the congregation rested uneasily on these; the remainder brought in with them empty kerosene and gin boxes, pieces of broken canoe and chunks of fire-wood, and setting these wherever they could find room, they sat upon them as well as they were able, being often obliged to share a portion of the space with a friend.

The pulpit platform was three cord-wood sticks covered with boards from old boxes; these boards were of different lengths and thicknesses, and withal somewhat twisted, nor were they nailed to the cord-wood, so that the preacher needed to be supple to keep from getting his feet tangled. The pulpit itself was made from the same kind of boards, and covered with a trade blanket. Although the house was not large, three hundred persons crowded themselves in it, and another hundred stood about the doors; the sun shone down with great power and the heat presently became almost insupportable.

After the devotional exercises Judge McGee was invited to preach, which he did, using an interpreter as at Bata. The sea of wild faces that were turned toward the speaker was a wondrous sight to behold, and as their unattractive features lighted up with the glow of heavenly love, it seemed as if already the kingdoms of this world had become the kingdoms of our Lord, when such wild tribes as these obeyed His word.

After the sermon a collection was taken, and as there is no money here the people gave such things as they had. Four men worked their way through the mass and took the offerings of the people, which consisted of plates, mugs, handkerchiefs, leaves of tobacco, brass and copper rods, bowls, glasses, knives, beads and baskets; and one man gave his shirt. The Judge was an old Presbyterian elder, but he had never seen such a "collection" as that. When the services were ended the white visitors were "nearly melted," but they could not go home until they had shaken hands all around, and this took almost an hour; it was very trying, but it was all they could do for these poor people, and so they did it willingly.

On Monday morning the Band were on the beach by eight o'clock; the surf was about four feet high, the rolling billows combing over finely and breaking in masses of foam upon the sandy shore. The young folks remembered their wetting on Friday and they expected the same again, but were agreeably disappointed for the Kru-boys managed the boat with great skill and a few drops only sprinkled them. When all were on board the cutter, the

Nassau spread her white wings to the morning breeze and sailed away to the northward, keeping the coast-line always in sight.

Toward sundown she passed the mouth of the Campo river which is the dividing line between the French and German possessions; when the boys heard that this river had never been explored they were seized with a desire to ascend it at once, but their ardor was somewhat cooled when they were told that if they did so the natives would almost surely murder them.

The boys asked the Judge why it was that the Africans did not like to have white men travel in their country.

The Judge replied there were two reasons: first, the negro loves his country and he very naturally wants to keep it for himself; the white man belongs to a superior race and if he visits the country, who knows but he may like it so well he will want to return and take it for his own? The second reason is, that the profits of trade depend upon keeping the white man near the sea, otherwise he will deal directly with the interior tribes and their percentage as middlemen will be gone.

The boys admitted the negro's head was a level one, viewed in the light of Anglo-Saxon wisdom, but still they felt they would like to see the river and when they got to be men they would come out to Africa and see what could be done.

At sunrise the next morning the Nassau anchored off Batanga and the Band gazed eagerly to see what the place looked like. As the sun rose over the tree-tops and lighted up the eastern hills, it shone on as fair a landscape as is seen in the tropics. Away to the southeast was Elephant Mountain covered to its summit with a thick forest growth; in the far distance were the peaks of the coast range, while in the foreground was a rolling country thickly dotted with villages, and with rocky headlands at intervals jutting into the sea.

The friends at the American mission had already noticed the cutter and had hung a flag out over the end of the piazza, and several of the native people had come down to the beach and were waving their handkerchiefs; evidently a warm welcome was awaiting them ashore and they lost no time in getting the boat ready. As at Bata, only half the Band could be accommodated in the boat at once, so the boys were left to come on the second trip.

Good Brother Brier was watching them through his glass, and when he saw how many passengers were coming, he and Mrs. Brier went down to the landing to meet them. There are a great many rocks along this part of the coast and it is not always easy to land; Mr. Brier pointed out the way to steer and so they passed safely among the great black stones and reached the beach without mishap. Mrs. Brier was particularly delighted to see the girls, for she was the only white lady at Batanga and it was like home again to see so many bright faced girls.

The Mission House is near the sea, and indeed the premises include a part of the beach; this struck the Judge as a good idea, for as the sea is the only highway of travel, why the mission premises should be half a mile away as at Gaboon, he could not understand.

This station has been occupied by a white missionary but a very short time and the buildings are therefore new. The Judge noted with interest the progress that had been made in the art of building; the posts were of brick laid in cement, instead of wooden piles; the framework was stronger; the roof of galvanized iron instead of palm-leaf mats, and the paint a pretty tinted shade instead of the glaring white, which in the brilliant sunlight is painful to the eyes. The steps leading to the piazzas were solid brick-work, the kitchen had a brick floor and there were excellent cisterns for holding the water that came from the iron roofs. The house, although but of one story, had high ceilings, and Mrs. Brier had decorated it with many nice little keepsakes—memories of her girlhood days—so that it had a wonderfully home-like appearance. Near by was a factory belonging to a Bristol firm, and across the small creek that flowed by the mission premises, were two German factories. Just beyond the English factory was the house of Madula, the chief of this district, and a humble consistent Christian.

After the boys came ashore and a good hot breakfast had dispelled the last feeling of seasickness, the Judge and Mr. Brier adjourned to the piazza for a good talk, while Mrs. Brier took the girls with her, and the boys went down to the beach with Rev. Mr. Etongolo to see the fishermen go out in their small canoes.

The Batanga fishermen use a small canoe not found elsewhere on the coast; it is made of soft wood, pointed at both ends, and is so light that it may easily be carried in one hand. It is not more than ten or twelve inches wide in the middle and is so frail in appearance that it seems incredible that it can support a man upon a rough sea. But these Batanga fishermen do not fear, and to them the little canoes are all-sufficient, for under their skillful handling they ride the seas like a duck. Mr. Etongolo explained to the boys that when paddling, the men put their feet in the canoes, but when they wished to anchor they hung their feet over the sides and worked them back and forth in the water, thus steadying the craft and leaving their arms free for handling the lines. Nets are not used here as at Gaboon, but all the fishing is done with hook and line. There are few fish and these keep near the bottom in three to four fathoms of water, so that ordinary nets would not reach them.

Fishing is not a paying business, and yet as there is no other way of getting flesh it is a necessary occupation, and every family sends at least one representative to the sea every morning. The men go out from eight to nine o'clock in the morning and return at noon; the boys looked in several of their canoes and found they averaged about four fish each; these were like our catfish and one kind was like a large sunfish, but of a pink color. Mr. Brier sent his cook down to get some fish, but he could only buy them with cans of compressed corn-beef, and even then he had to pay large prices.

All other kinds of native food are as scarce at Batanga as fish, and it is a constant struggle with the poorest to get enough to eat, and then they do not always succeed. The reason for this is that the men are wholly given to the ivory trade, and like our merchant princes at home, they do not care to dig in the ground; there is no back country here able and willing to supply the provision market, and so the successful traders buy rice, codfish and other food from the factories, large quantities of which are imported for the purpose.

The country back of Batanga consists of one unbroken jungle or forest through which extends a range of mountains of moderate height at a distance of forty or fifty miles from the coast, with here and there a detached hill nearer the sea, of which the Elephant Mountain is an example. So far as known, this forest continues in an easterly direction all the way to the Congo river; but in

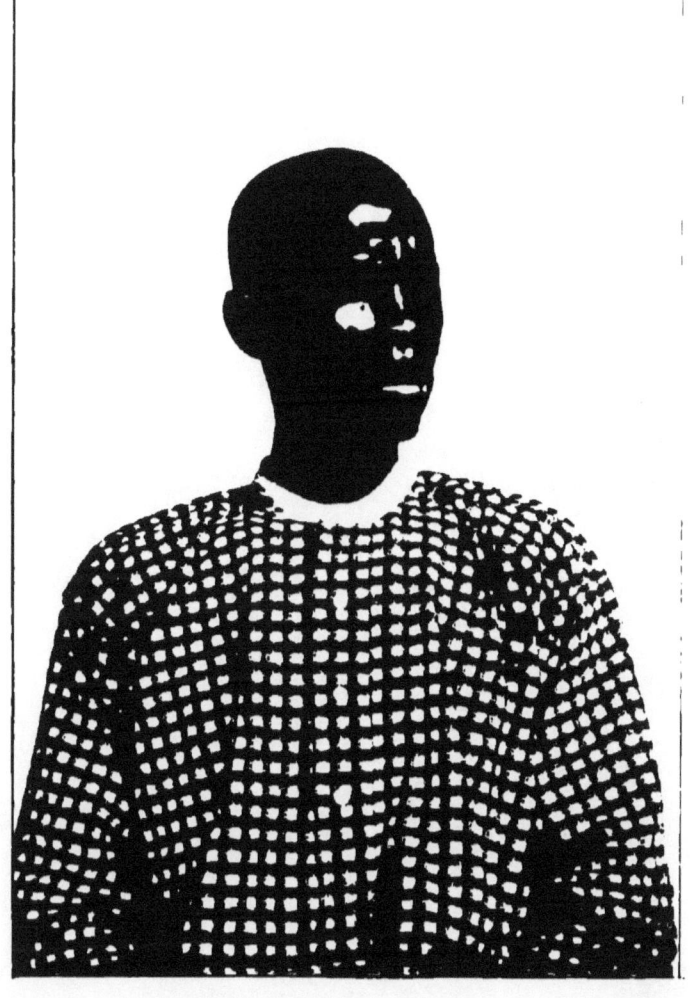

NATIVE TRADER, OLD CALABAR

a northeasterly direction, at a distance of two hundred and fifty miles, there is an open, grassy country, with a large population, and beyond these, say some two hundred miles more, the people build houses of a circular form and use horses. A narrow strip of this forest land next to the sea, say perhaps twenty miles in width, is inhabited; after which the forest is a wilderness until the open, grassy country is reached.

Throughout this forest the rubber vine is abundant, and there is some ivory in the country beyond the forest, and the price is very low, owing to the difficulty of transporting it to the sea. The article that bears the highest price is salt; a small handful is the price of a slave, and a basinful will purchase a tusk of ivory. The people of this inland country are industrious and carefully cultivate the soil, and if a railroad were built to their country and rum kept out, they might be induced to raise many valuable articles for export. The cost of building such a road would not be great, and if a subsidy in land were given, in a few years it would pay well.

Toward evening Mr. Brier and the Judge walked up the beach a couple of miles to inspect a tract of ground Mr. Reading had purchased a few months before, upon which it was proposed to build a new central station for the work to be carried on in the German possessions. In the year 1888, Mr. Reading made an arrangement with the German governor, Baron Soden, by which the Society he represented should be permitted to extend its work and acquire property in the Batanga district, and as far interiorward as it was able to go; preaching and religious teaching was to be unrestricted, and schools might be formed and taught wholly in the native tongue, but if a foreign language were taught, it should be the German.

These terms are more liberal than those given by the French colonial government, and it was thought best to extend the work in the German territory as soon as men and means might be obtained.

The land purchased for the new central station rises abruptly from the sea to a height of forty feet and then extends away in an almost level plateau to the eastward. There is a rocky headland jutting out into the sea, and this shelters a little bay from the southwest sea-breeze, which makes a comfortable landing place. The soil is rich, and there is a small stream of never failing water. From the bluff a fine view was obtained of the sea, and also up and down the coast; the Judge was much pleased with the situation, and thought it would be a comfortable place in which to live, as it was open on all sides to the breeze.

On Wednesday an excursion was made to the waterfall, which is a little more than a mile beyond the new mission premises, visited by the Judge the evening before. Chief Madula loaned his big canoe and men to paddle it, and this, with Mr. Brier's boat, comfortably accommodaed all the party.

They got away early, and the ride along the shore in the fresh morning air was delightful, and the young folks were in the best of spirits. These falls are within three hundred yards of the ocean, and it is a novel sight to be able to see a fine waterfall from the deck of an ocean steamer. They crossed the bar, entered the river, and made a careful inspection of the falls; these are in two sections as at Niagara, only one section of which is seen in the engraving, the other being away to the right. The fall is about forty feet, and the water is nearly ten degrees colder than the sea water. It is safe to go up to the very edge of the falling water, and thus an excellent view may be obtained, although in going so near the spray soon thoroughly wets one's clothing.

After rowing about and enjoying the falls from every point of view, the party landed, and after a call at the English factory on the point, they went up into the native town to pay a visit to Bevinia [Ba-vee-nea] the chief of this district. This young man had in former years been one of Mr. Reading's pupils in Gaboon; now he was the head of his tribe, a man of influence, and a most consistent Christian. He lived in a good house and had a nice family, and it was pleasant to see such a real Christian home in this wild country.

Mr. Hervey, the gentleman at the factory, had invited them all to lunch, and about noon they went to his house and the Band had a good time looking at his pictures, for he is an amateur artist and takes photographs for amusement. About the middle of the afternoon they went home, and that night their dreams were full of all kinds of impossible cascades and waterfalls.

Chapter XVIII.

RETURN TO GABOON.

SABBATH morning, December 4th, was another of those beautiful days so common in Western Africa. The rains had passed to the southward and the delightful dry-season had begun; the heavens were not covered with dull gray clouds as is often the case in the dry-season farther southward on the coast, but great masses of white cumuli, like immense snow-banks in the air, reflected the brilliant sunlight. A solemn hush had fallen upon the landscape; the factories were closed, and no fishing canoes were to be seen upon the water.

About nine o'clock the people from a distance began to stream by with their best clothes under their arms; they had come from a distance to attend the church services and were going to their friends in the town, where they would dress and come forth in a manner befitting the occasion. As men's ready-made clothing is more easily obtained than women's, the men appeared to better advantage than did their wives and daughters;

CHURCH BUILT BY MR. READING, GABOON

nearly all the dresses were made by the wearers and did not fit well, and there is no doubt that experienced dressmakers could find abundant employment if they should go to Batanga.

The church in this place is over sixty feet long, but on special occasions it can hold but little more than half the people who come to the services. The floor is elevated on posts about five feet above the ground, and the space underneath is occupied by a good-sized audience seated on chairs, stools, empty boxes and pieces of firewood. On this particular Sabbath morning, along the shady side of the church, cord-wood sticks had been laid down in rows and boards laid on them, thus increasing the seating capacity.

In order that this outside congregation might hear the better, when the church was built, not only were many windows made in the sides, but large openings were also made near the floor, so that sound might find its way down underneath as much as possible. By the time the second bell had ceased ringing, the building was packed, and a sea of dark faces gathered about every door and window.

As the services progressed the Judge noticed another use made of these openings near the floor. At Batanga there are a great many babies, which is in marked contrast with Gaboon, where babies are a rarity unless it be mulattoes. These babies are brought to church and as the services are long, the babies by and by get tired and cry; the crowded condition of the house makes it difficult for the mother to get out, so she slips her little one down through one of these openings to a friend outside who takes it away to town. This handy contrivance excited the admiration of the Judge, and proved to his mind that the African is capable of invention.

The Sabbath-school in the afternoon numbered over four hundred scholars, and the church work at this station is very successful in all its branches.

On Tuesday morning the outward-bound German steamer Ella Woermann, commanded by Captain Dittmer, anchored off Batanga, and the Judge determined to return to Gaboon in her. The prevailing wind on this part of the coast is from the southwest, and this, with the strong northerly current, makes it easy to sail north, and correspondingly difficult to sail in a southerly direction. It takes a week for the Nassau to go from Batanga to Gaboon, and sometimes longer, and even though it were the young folks' "very own vessel," a week on board such a small craft would be not only tedious, but very exhausting.

Then too Mr. and Mrs. Brier wanted to go to Gaboon, and so it was arranged that all should go on the Ella Woermann together and let the cutter follow at its leisure. By five o'clock that afternoon they were all on board, and at sundown the steamer weighed anchor and started for Gaboon, which port it reached on Friday morning, having spent one day at Bata, and one day at Eloby.

Mr. and Mrs. Reading gave their guests a warm welcome, and the Band found it very nice to be once more back at Gaboon, which was so home-like, that notwithstanding its tropical appearance, they could almost forget they were in the Dark Continent. It took them a day or two to get rested, and then they spent some time exploring Gaboon and getting better acquainted with its people.

They visited among others the Rev. Toko Truman, an old blind preacher, who told them a great many stories and always had something new with which to amuse them. Toko had lived for many years among the cannibals and the Band never tired of hearing stories of these strange people. "One time," said Toko, "a man asked me, 'Toko when I die will I go to heaven?' and I told him, no, God has made a law that a man can have but one wife, and you have four wives, and so you cannot go to Heaven.

"'Well, Toko,' said this cannibal, 'when God calls me I will say, all right Father, I will come, but you have all the power, so don't be in a hurry, let us sit down and talk a while. Then, Toko, I will say to Him, you knew when I lived in the earth that if you gave me plenty of trade goods I would go and buy women with them, and so you ought not to have given me these goods; therefore the palaver [or fault], is yours!'"

"Another time," continued Toko, "I was preaching about the resurrection and after the service some of the chiefs came to my house and asked me, 'Toko, these things that you told us to-day, are they true?' and I told them, 'Yes, those things I told you, they are true;' and then they said to me, 'Toko, we want you to write to God and tell Him when He goes to make this war He must send and give us notice, and then, Toko, we will go in the bush and call more than fifty thousand Pangwes [Pangwees], and we will have a big fight.'"

"Another time a man said to me, 'Toko, I want you tell me, are there any egumas in Heaven, and are there any plantains there?' and I said to him, 'Heaven is a world of spirits, and I do not read that there are any egumas or plantains there.'

"'Well, Toko,' said this man, 'I don't see what God wants with so many people when He has no egumas or plantains to feed them; now if you will tell me there are egumas in Heaven, I will go there, but if not, then, Toko, I don't want to go there.'"

"Another time I think they must have gotten hungry for in the night a big canoeful of men came to kill me, but just as they were coming around the bend in the river one of the men stood up in the canoe and said, 'What are we going to do this for? we cannot kill Toko because he settles all our quarrels for us.' Then another answered and said, 'When we go to war, we go to war, and we cannot stop because a man settles our quarrels for us.' So then they soon began to quarrel among themselves and while they were quarreling the canoe drifted back, and presently they went home and I knew nothing of it until several days afterward."

The young folks were also interested in watching the singular actions of a very curious little bird which had, in great numbers, built their nests in a large palm tree near Mr. Reading's house. The habits of these gay little workers are most remarkable, and the Band never wearied in watching their movements. They are not much larger than a sparrow, with black and yellow plumage, and their eggs are light pink with dark spots.

These sociable little birds always prefer to live in the neighborhood of a village, as they seem fond of the society of man, something as our own swallows are. When they have settled upon a tree on which to plant a colony, they labor from daylight to dark, day after day, with the utmost joy, and fun, and perseverance, in building their singular pendant nests. These nests are nearly round, with a tight roof overhead, and an opening underneath to go in and out, and are securely fastened to the end of a palm-frond, so as to be out of reach of monkeys and serpents.

INTERIOR OF NEW CHURCH, GABOON

To build these fine nests the birds strip the tough outside fiber of the palm or plantain leaf, and tear this fiber into long fine threads; they then weave their nests with these threads, using both beak and feet, working most industriously and chattering all the while, no doubt to encourage one another; anyhow that is what the Band thought. These nests are real little houses in which the birds live all the year; when the young birds are large enough the older ones help them to build a nest, and so, as it were, begin housekeeping for themselves.

The second Sabbath after the return of the Band from Batanga was a great day for the congregation of the Gaboon church. The old church building had stood for some thirty years, and had been often repaired, but it was now nearly past repair, and for more than a year Mr. Reading had been directing his men in the building of a new house of worship. The labor was all done by native workmen, and the mechanical execution was superior to that found in many pretentious buildings in America. The house is of frame with galvanized iron roof, and is supported upon brick piers covered with cement. The steps are made of brick and stone and united by mortar and cement into one solid structure, and does not quite touch the church so that the rain will not rot the sills by reason of their being in contact with the bricks. It is beautifully finished inside, the pews being in old oak and the walls and ceiling pearl color, with darker trimmings about the doors and windows. The pulpit furniture was given by the Ladies' Aid Society connected with the church, and a part of the cost was defrayed by the congregation.

Long before the second bell rang the people began to gather and soon the house was filled to overflowing. The choir were out in full force and sat on the right of the pulpit [the left hand side of the illustration], while the Band occupied the opposite corner near the door.

After the invocation and the reading of CXXII Psalm, the congregation sang "Holy, holy, holy, Lord God Almighty!" and Mr. Brier read the eighth chapter of the First Book of Kings, and then the choir sang "I will tell the wondrous story," to the tune of "My Redeemer." Mr. Owondo then read the same lesson in Mpongwe and the congregation sang an Mpongwe hymn.

Mr. Brier read the order of dedication and offered the dedicatory prayer, and Mr. Reading preached the sermon from the text "I have surely built thee a house to dwell in; a settled place for thee to abide in forever." There were several more hymns and an exhortation from Mr. Brier, closing with the benediction by the old blind minister, Rev. Toko Truman.

It was a glad day for every one, and all the people rejoiced and congratulated each other upon the completion of God's house.

Saturday, the twenty-fourth, was celebrated for Christmas; this festival is well observed in Gaboon, although, of course, little is known of it in the country districts; indeed one should remember that while Gaboon is a civilized city, it is only necessary to go ten miles in the country to find the grossest heathenism, accompanied by human sacrifices and cannibalism.

In Gaboon, Christmas is a day of sight-seeing and pleasure; in the morning the towns-people, dressed in their best, call upon the traders and other foreign residents and wish them "Kismas," of course expecting some substantial return.

CHURCH AT OLD CALABAR

After this ceremony they repair to the cathedral to see the sights and hear the music, and then give themselves up to all kinds of pleasure for the remainder of the day and evening, ending with a big dance in the public garden.

At the American mission, work went on as usual until noon, and then every one received a good piece of salt beef for his dinner. The mission family had their dinner at one o'clock, and it may be interesting to know of what an African Christmas dinner consists.

The dining-room was beautifully decorated with ferns and flowers by Hattie, assisted by the girls of the Band, and both Africa and America contributed to the table; the roast ducks, sweet potatoes, spinach, plantains and peppers, were native, while the oysters, Irish potatoes, baked beans, sweet corn, bread, butter, coffee, mince-pie and cheese were imported. The weather was as warm as in July at home and the doors were wide open to admit the breeze, while through the open windows came the rustling of palm leaves and the twittering of birds.

It was a Christmas such as the Band had never experienced before, and the thoughts of the young people turned from the bright scene about them to the land of ice and snow across the stormy ocean, where dear ones were gathering by home firesides, while the chill winds moaned through the bare tree tops and the air was filled with falling snow. What a contrast!

In the afternoon there was a special service in the new church, in which the choir took a leading part, and the evening was spent in pleasant conversation on the veranda.

And now with the closing year we must close our story, and leave for another volume the record of our friends' journey toward the interior upon the great Ogowe river, and their wonderful adventures among the cannibals and the pigmies of that unknown land.

Chapter XIX.

POLITICAL DIVISIONS ON THE WEST COAST.

To give some idea of the extent to which Africa is being divided among the nations the following "political section" of Western Africa is given:

Spain, . . .	Morocco
France, . . .	Morocco
Spain, . . .	Opposite the Canaries
France, . . .	French Senegambia
England, . . .	British Senegambia
France, . . .	French Senegambia
England, . . .	British Senegambia
Portugal, . . .	Portuguese Senegambia
England, . . .	Sierra Leone
Independent, . .	Republic of Liberia
France, . . .	Gold Coast
England, . . .	Gold Coast
France, . . .	Dahomey
England, . . .	Niger Delta and Old Calabar
Germany, . .	Kamerun

POLITICAL DIVISIONS ON THE WEST COAST

France,	Bata
In dispute,	Benita
Spain,	Eloby
France,	Gaboon
Portugal,	Kebenda
Congo Free State,	Congo
Portugal,	Angola
Germany,	Angra Pequena
England,	Walvisch Bay
Germany,	Orange River
England,	Cape of Good Hope

www.ingramcontent.com/pod-product-compliance
Lightning Source LLC
Chambersburg PA
CBHW030542300426
44111CB00009B/831